Partitioning and Scheduling
Parallel Programs
for Multiprocessors

Dev Chen

TITLES IN THIS SERIES

Optimizing Supercompilers for Supercomputers, Michael Wolfe, 1989

Reconfigurable Processor-Array: A Bit-Sliced Parallel Computer,
Andrew Rushton, 1989

Partitioning and Scheduling Parallel Programs for Execution on Multiprocessors,
Vivek Sarkar, 1989

Functional Programming for Loosely-Coupled Multiprocessors, Paul H. J. Kelly,
1989

RESEARCH MONOGRAPHS IN PARALLEL AND DISTRIBUTED COMPUTING

Vivek Sarkar
IBM Thomas J. Watson Research Center

Partitioning and Scheduling Parallel Programs for Multiprocessors

Pitman, London

The MIT Press, Cambridge, Massachusetts

PITMAN PUBLISHING
128 Long Acre, London WC2E 9AN

© Vivek Sarkar 1989

First published 1989

Available in the Western Hemisphere and Israel from
The MIT Press
Cambridge, Massachusetts (and London, England)

ISSN 0953-7767

British Library Cataloguing in Publication Data
Sarkar, Vivek
  Partitioning and scheduling parallel programs for
  multiprocessors.
  1. Computer systems. Parallel-processor systems.
  Programming
  I. Title
  005.1
  ISBN 0-273-08802-5

Library of Congress Cataloging-in-Publication Data
Sarkar, Vivek.
  Partitioning and scheduling parallel programs for execution
on multiprocessors / Vivek Sarkar.
      p. cm.—(Research monographs in parallel and distributed
processing)
  Includes index.
  ISBN 0-262-69130-2 (pbk.)
  1. Parallel processing (Electronic computers) 2. Multiprocessors.
I. Title. II. Series.
QA76.5.S2178 1989
004'.35—dc19

Reproduced and printed by photolithography
in Great Britain by Biddles Ltd, Guildford

Preface

There are three fundamental problems to be solved in the execution of a parallel program on a multiprocessor – identifying the parallelism in the program, partitioning the program into tasks and scheduling the tasks on processors. Whereas the problem of identifying parallelism is a programming language issue, the partitioning and scheduling problems are intimately related to parameters of the target multiprocessor, like the number of processors and synchronisation[1] and communication overhead. It is desirable for the partitioning and scheduling to be performed automatically, so that the same parallel program can execute efficiently on different multiprocessors. This dissertation presents two solutions to the partitioning and scheduling problems. The first approach is based on a *macro-dataflow* model, where the program is partitioned into tasks at compile-time and the tasks are scheduled on processors at run-time. The second approach is based on a *compile-time scheduling* model, where the partitioning of the program and the scheduling of tasks on processors are both performed at compile-time.

Both approaches have been implemented to partition programs written in the single-assignment language, SISAL. The inputs to the partitioning and scheduling algorithms are a graphical representation of the program, and a list of parameters describing the target multiprocessor. Execution profile information is used to derive compile-time estimates of execution times and data sizes in the program. Both the macro-dataflow and compile-time scheduling problems are expressed as optimisation problems, which are proved to be NP-complete in the strong sense. This dissertation presents efficient approximation algorithms for these problems. The effectiveness of the partitioning and scheduling algorithms is studied by multiprocessor simulations of various SISAL benchmark programs for different target multiprocessor parameters.

---

[1]British spelling is used throughout this dissertation.

Contents

1. Introduction   **1**

   1.1. Multiprocessors   2
   1.2. Programming Languages for Multiprocessors   8
   1.3. Partitioning and Scheduling   13
   1.4. Dissertation Outline   16

2. The Problem   **19**

   2.1. Compile-time and Run-time approaches   19
   2.2. Problem Representation   22
   2.3. Previous Work   23
   2.4. Contributions of this dissertation   27

3. Program Representation and Multiprocessor Model   **29**

   3.1. Graphical Representation – Background   29
   3.2. The Graphical Representation GR   31
   3.3. Execution Profile Information   37
   3.4. Cost Assignment   39
   3.5. Multiprocessor Model   50

4. Macro-Dataflow   **55**

   4.1. The Model   55
   4.2. The Partitioning Problem   69
   4.3. Partitioning Algorithm   76
   4.4. Performance Results   89

5. Compile-time Scheduling   **101**

   5.1. The Model   102
   5.2. Node Expansion – Selection of Primitive Nodes   114
   5.3. Internalisation Pre-pass   123
   5.4. Processor Assignment   132
   5.5. Performance Results   138

6. Conclusions   **147**

   6.1. Macro-Dataflow vs. Compile-time Scheduling   147
   6.2. Future Work   152

Appendix A. Benchmark Programs   **161**

Appendix B. Raw Simulation Data   **183**

List of Figures

Figure 1-1: Shared-bus multiprocessor   3

Figure 1-2: Shared-memory Multiprocessor with an Interconnection Network   5

Figure 1-3: Message-passing Multiprocessor with an Interconnection Network   6

Figure 1-4: Classification of programming languages for multiprocessors   9

Figure 1-5: The Parallelism-Overhead Trade-off   14

Figure 1-6: General strategy for using a partitioning and scheduling system   17

Figure 3-1: SISAL program for Quicksort   33

Figure 3-2: GR graphs for function QuickSort()   34

Figure 3-3: Procedure AssignCosts   41

Figure 3-4: Algorithm to compute F_T for an entire GR program   46

Figure 3-5: Procedure InitCalls   47

Figure 3-6: Procedure AssignInternalCalls   47

Figure 3-7: Inter-processor communication model   50

Figure 3-8: Behaviour of average waiting time, T_w 53

Figure 4-1: Possible classifications of GR nodes for macro-dataflow   58

Figure 4-2: A simple GR graph   65

Figure 4-3: Sample partition cost values   66

Figure 4-4: Variation in partition cost, $F(\Pi)$ 77

Figure 4-5: Procedure PartitionFunctions   79

Figure 4-6: Procedure PartitionGraph   81

Figure 4-7: Procedures SetupMerge and MergeTasks   83

Figure 4-8: Procedure SetTaskCosts   84

Figure 4-9: Procedures SetGraphCP and SetENCP   86

Figure 4-10: Procedure InitPrimitiveNodes   88

Figure 4-11: Overview of Partitioning and Simulation system   90

Figure 4-12: Software line count of prototype implementation   93

Figure 4-13: Macro-Dataflow: Speed-up vs. Number of Processors   94

Figure 4-14: Macro-Dataflow: Speed-up vs. Scheduling Overhead   95

Figure 4-15: Macro-Dataflow: Speed-up vs. Communication Overhead   96

Figure 4-16: Macro-Dataflow: Speed-up for different Multiprocessor Inputs   98

Figure 4-17: Macro-Dataflow: Speed-up for different Profile Inputs   99

Figure 5-1: Possible classifications of GR nodes for compile-time scheduling   103

Figure 5-2: Procedure ExecuteGraph   105

Figure 5-3: Procedure DetermineTimes   111

Figure 5-4: Procedure ScheduleProgram   113

Figure 5-5: Procedure DeterminePrimitiveNodes   114

Figure 5-6: Procedure ExpandNodes   115

Figure 5-7: Procedure PreprocessFunctionCall   118

Figure 5-8: Procedure ExpandFunctionCall   120

Figure 5-9: Procedure ExpandParallelNode   122

Figure 5-10: Counter-example for single-pass scheduling   124

Figure 5-11: The constructed instance of INTERNALISATION   127

Figure 5-12: Procedure PartitionGraph 129
Figure 5-13: Procedure BuildPrimitiveGraph 132
Figure 5-14: Procedure ProcessGraph 133
Figure 5-15: Procedure ScheduleGraph 135
Figure 5-16: Counter-example for simple list scheduling 136
Figure 5-17: Compile-time Scheduling: Speed-up vs. Number of Processors 140
Figure 5-18: Compile-time Scheduling: Speed-up vs. Communication 142
Overhead
Figure 5-19: Compile-time Scheduling: Speed-up for different 143
Multiprocessor Inputs
Figure 5-20: Compile-time Scheduling: Speed-up for different Profile 144
Inputs
Figure 6-1: Comparison of Speed-ups 148
Figure 6-2: Comparison of Speed-ups (Predicted and Actual values) 150
Figure 6-3: Comparison of Execution Times 151
Figure A-1: Hypothetical execution times for simple operations 162
Figure A-2: MM – ideal parallelism profile for $P = \infty$ 165
Figure A-3: MM – ideal parallelism profile for $P = 20$ 166
Figure A-4: CYK – ideal parallelism profile for $P = \infty$ 168
Figure A-5: CYK – ideal parallelism profile for $P = 20$ 169
Figure A-6: MESORT – ideal parallelism profile for $P = \infty$ 171
Figure A-7: MESORT – ideal parallelism profile for $P = 20$ 172
Figure A-8: FFT – ideal parallelism profile for $P = \infty$ 174
Figure A-9: FFT – ideal parallelism profile for $P = 20$ 175
Figure A-10: SIMPLE – ideal parallelism profile for $P = \infty$ 177
Figure A-11: SIMPLE – ideal parallelism profile for $P = 20$ 178
Figure A-12: SLAB – ideal parallelism profile for $P = \infty$ 180
Figure A-13: SLAB – ideal parallelism profile for $P = 20$ 181

Acknowledgements

It was a great pleasure to have John Hennessy as my adviser at Stanford. He has been an unfailing source of knowledge, encouragement and support. His guidance was crucial for the development of my initial ideas to their final form in this dissertation. His research interests and methodology perfectly capture the spirit of the Computer Systems discipline as an exciting confluence of different areas of Computer Science – Foundations, Algorithms, Programming Languages, Compilers, Architecture and VLSI. This inter-disciplinary outlook has had a profound influence on my thesis work and research interests.

Ernst Mayr introduced me to Parallel Processing. He started a seminar at Stanford which sparked my interest and introduced me to many new and exciting theoretical developments. He guided me through my study of the literature and always made time to discuss my questions. In his course on Parallel Computation, he encouraged me to investigate the idea of using single-assignment languages to program multiprocessors. I concluded in the project report that single-assignment languages could indeed achieve high performance on multiprocessors, provided the compiler was "smart enough". And so I discovered my thesis problem!

Mike Flynn and Steve Lundstrom have been very supportive of my work. Steve Lundstrom drove me across to Livermore one morning, and introduced me to Jim McGraw and Steve Skedzielewski from the SISAL group. This led to a collaboration which proved to be essential for my prototype implementation. I am grateful for all the help I received from the members of the SISAL group at Livermore. At the same time, I would like to thank the members of the SAL and Compiler groups in the Stanford MIPS-X-MP project for all their comments, criticisms and discussions. My research was supported by an NSF grant (DCR 8351269), which I gratefully acknowledge.

I would also like to acknowledge the help I received in preparing this revised version of my dissertation. The comments and suggestions from an anonymous reviewer were invaluable in identifying the general trouble spots in the original dissertation. I also received several comments from Kourosh Gharachorloo, a fellow student at Stanford, though extensive discussions via electronic mail. I joined IBM

Research in August 1987, and am fortunate to be working with an excellent and stimulating group of people in the PTRAN group – Fran Allen, Michael Burke, Ron Cytron, Jeanne Ferrante and Dave Shields. My managers gave me as much time as I needed to revise my dissertation, which I gratefully acknowledge.

Finally, during my student years in India and the U.S., I have received a lot of support, friendship, and encouragement from several people in matters unrelated to my dissertation. I am grateful to all of them for their kindness and love. It is not possible for me to mention those acknowledgements in this space, so I end with the following dedication.

To my mother, Anita

To my father, Ashit

To my wife, and best friend, Ratna

Notation

Symbol	Description
$\approx$	Approximately equal
$\leftarrow$	Assignment
$\perp$	Bottom node of a GR graph (page 33)
$\lceil \ \rceil$	Ceiling function
$\varnothing$	Empty set
$:=$	Equality by definition
$\lfloor \ \rfloor$	Floor function
$\rightarrow$	Function mapping, Limit
∞	Infinity
$\cdot$	List concatenation
$\Leftrightarrow$	Logical equivalence
$\Rightarrow$	Logical implication
$\neg$	Logical negation
$>>$	Much greater than
$<<$	Much less than
$\leq$	Node sequence in a schedule (page 103)
$\leq^*$	Partial order on nodes in a GR graph (page 33)
$|S|$	Set cardinality
$\in$	Set membership
$\mathbf{Z}_0^+$	Set of non-negative integers
$\mathbf{Q}_0^+$	Set of non-negative rational numbers
$\mathbf{Z}^+$	Set of positive integers
s.t.	Such that
$\top$	Top node of a GR graph (page 33)
$\|g\|$	Total size of GR graph g, including all graphs contained within g
$\in^*$	Transitive containment of GR nodes and graphs (page 36)

1 Introduction

The phenomenal increase in the speed of computers since the first electronic digital computer (ENIAC) was built in 1945, can be attributed primarily to logic technology. Switching speeds fell from one-tenth of a second to nanoseconds as the logic technology moved from electromechanical relays to vacuum tubes to transistors to small, medium and large scale integrated circuits. In the last few years, it has become more difficult to achieve order of magnitude speed-ups in computers by solely upgrading the logic technology. There has been a move to parallel processing in order to build faster computers. MIMD multiprocessors with multiple instruction-streams and multiple data-streams promise to be the general-purpose computers of the future. In fact, the first generation of multiprocessors has already arrived in the marketplace e.g. consider the multiprocessors manufactured by Alliant, BBN, Cray, Digital, ELXSI, Encore, IBM, Intel, NCUBE and Sequent.

Unfortunately, there is as yet only a small number of parallel programs executing on these new multiprocessors. The major obstacle to the widespread parallel programming of multiprocessors is the lack of convenient parallel programming language systems. The languages currently available on multiprocessors are basically existing sequential languages (C, Fortran, Pascal) with a few *ad hoc* extensions for parallelism, leading to highly obscure and unportable code.

Parallel languages based on a task model (e.g. Ada) appear to be the next generation of languages for multiprocessors. Compared to their predecessors, these languages offer portability but still force the programmer to explicitly decompose the program into tasks and control their synchronisation and communication. This approach places a tremendous burden on the programmer – both for correctness and performance. For correctness, the programmer now has to worry about problems like deadlock and race conditions, which do not arise in sequential programs. Performance is a very important issue for multiprocessors because the primary motivation behind parallel processing is the potential speed-up in program execution times. The problem with explicit partitions in task-based languages is that the performance of a given partitioned program may vary dramatically over different multiprocessors, thus rendering the program unportable in practise.

The parallel programming language situation appears bleak. We have grown used to sequential languages like Fortran and Pascal which execute efficiently on several uniprocessors, with little or no interference from the programmer. It is desirable to do the same for parallel languages on multiprocessors. This dissertation on partitioning and scheduling parallel programs is a step in that direction.

1.1. Multiprocessors

Multiprocessors are general-purpose, asynchronous parallel machines with multiple instruction-streams and multiple data-streams [Flynn 72], [Hwang 84]. They can be classified as being *tightly coupled* or *loosely coupled*. Processors in a tightly coupled multiprocessor communicate through a shared memory (e.g. Alliant FX8, BBN Butterfly, Denelcor HEP [Kowalik 85], ELXSI 6400, Encore Multimax [Encore 86], IBM RP3 [Pfister 85], Sequent Balance [Sequent 86]). Processors in a loosely coupled multiprocessor communicate by exchanging messages (e.g. Caltech Cosmic Cube [Seitz 85], Intel iPSC, NCUBE-10 and workstation-based distributed systems). The partitioning and scheduling techniques presented in this dissertation are designed to be tractable over this wide range of tightly coupled and loosely coupled multiprocessor architectures.

An important issue in multiprocessor performance is the granularity of program execution. The *granularity of a parallel program* can be defined as the average size of a sequential unit of computation in the program, with no inter-processor synchronisations or communications (e.g. the average task size). For a given multiprocessor, there is a minimum program granularity value below which performance degrades significantly. This threshold value can be called the *granularity of the multiprocessor*. It is desirable for a multiprocessor to have a small granularity, so that it can efficiently support a wide range of programs. It is also desirable for a parallel program to have a large granularity, so that it can execute efficiently on a wide range of multiprocessors.

Scalability is another important property of multiprocessors. Scalability is the ability of a multiprocessor to provide a linear increase in speed-up with an increase in the number of processors, assuming that the program being executed has sufficient parallelism and a large enough granularity. A multiprocessor architecture is usually designed to be scalable up to some specified number of processors.

There is a trade-off between granularity and scalability in a multiprocessor. Increased scalability is typically achieved at the cost of large granularity. Tightly coupled systems generally have a smaller granularity and scalability than loosely coupled systems.

1.1.1. Tightly coupled multiprocessors

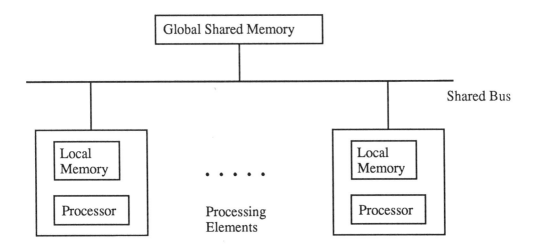

Figure 1-1: Shared-bus multiprocessor

Perhaps the simplest form of a tightly coupled multiprocessor is the *shared-bus* multiprocessor, shown in Figure 1-1. A shared bus connects processing elements to a global shared memory. Each processing element contains a processor and some local memory. Processors communicate by read and write accesses to the shared memory. Most designs use the local memory as a private cache, giving rise to the *cache coherence problem* [Archibald 86]. A mechanism must exist to ensure that all private cache copies of a shared memory location are consistent. The cache coherence problem can be solved in software or hardware. The common solution (e.g. Xerox Dragon, DEC

Firefly) is to use a hardware *snooping cache controller* for each cache, which monitors the bus transactions to maintain cache consistency. For efficiency, snooping cache controllers can also often satisfy a cache miss by accessing another cache instead of main memory. Bus bandwidth is the primary limitation to the scalability of a shared-bus multiprocessor. Current designs contain less than 30 processors.

It is necessary to provide more communication bandwidth to support more processors than can be supported by a single bus. One approach is to allow the processors to share multiple buses (e.g. Pluribus [Heart 73]). Unfortunately, this approach increases system complexity significantly (due to bus arbitration and active devices) giving a much higher price-to-performance ratio than a single shared bus. Another approach is to use a hierarchical structure with *clusters* connected by an inter-cluster bus (e.g. Cm* [Jones 80]). Each cluster is like a single shared-bus multiprocessor with processors connected to a local bus. Communication between two processors in the same cluster is significantly cheaper than between two processors in different clusters. This design is effective for divide-and-conquer style programs which exhibit a corresponding locality in inter-processor interactions. However, if the inter-processor interactions are uniform over all processors, then the performance will be limited by the bandwidth of the inter-cluster bus, just as in a single level shared-bus multiprocessor.

The common way to avoid the bus bottleneck problem is to use an *interconnection network* instead of a bus. Figure 1-2 shows the general structure of a shared-memory multiprocessor with an interconnection network. The interconnection network connects P processing elements to M shared-memory modules. As the number of processors increases, the interconnection network becomes the dominant component of the multiprocessor, both in cost and performance. The *crossbar* network (e.g. as used in the S-1 multiprocessor [Widdoes 79]) offers full P×M connectivity, but its quadratic size makes it too expensive to be practical for a range of processors larger than that of a shared-bus multiprocessor. Instead, multistage networks built out of k×k switches (for small k, say k = 4) are the most common kind of interconnection networks used for a large number (say 1024) of processors and memory modules, in multiprocessors like BBN Butterfly, Denelcor HEP, IBM RP3, NYU Ultracomputer.

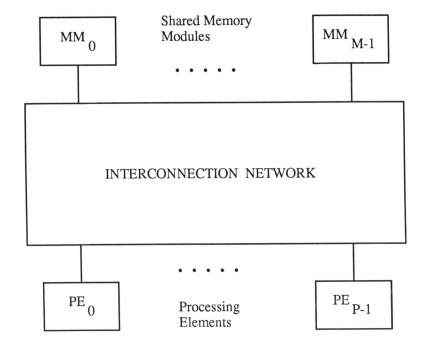

Figure 1-2: Shared-memory Multiprocessor with an Interconnection Network

1.1.2. Loosely coupled multiprocessors

Figure 1-3 shows the general structure of a loosely coupled multiprocessor. Loosely coupled multiprocessors have no global shared memory. Instead, processors communicate by sending and receiving messages. Again, the performance and scalability of the multiprocessor is primarily determined by the interconnection network. The simplest interconnection network for loosely coupled multiprocessors is a bus capable of handling inter-processor messages (i.e. a local area network!). Distributed systems have this structure and can indeed be used as multiprocessors for programs with sufficiently large granularity [Cheriton 87], with a scalability up to 30 processors or so. Loosely-coupled systems typically use interconnection networks with direct, point-to-point connections between processors, rather than multiple stages containing switches. These interconnection networks have already been studied in detail for SIMD machines [Siegel 79], and include the star, tree, mesh,

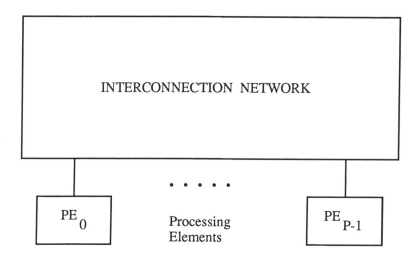

Figure 1-3: Message-passing Multiprocessor with an Interconnection Network

shuffle-exchange and hypercube. The hypercube interconnection network has been used in at least three multiprocessor designs – the Caltech Cosmic Cube, Intel iPSC and NCUBE-10.

1.1.3. Theoretical model

As a final note on multiprocessors, let us compare the real multiprocessor architectures discussed earlier with the theoretical model used in the design and analysis of parallel algorithms. The standard theoretical model of parallel computation is the P-RAM (Parallel Random Access Machine) model [Fortune 78]. A P-RAM consists of n processors, P_1, ..., P_n and m shared global memory cells, M_1, ..., M_m. Each processor is a RAM (*Random Access Machine* [Aho 74]) with its own local memory. Processors communicate by reading from or writing to global memory cells. A P-RAM has a single program which is executed by all processors. However, each processor can have a different instruction stream based on its processor number. The instructions are assumed to be executed synchronously by all processors, as if there was a global clock.

The major discrepancies between the P-RAM model and real multiprocessors have to do with the cost of inter-processor synchronisation and communication. The "global clock" assumption is unrealistic for real multiprocessors, which are asynchronous machines requiring explicit synchronisation. Assuming a bounded degree synchronisation network, the average cost of inter-processor synchronisation must be $\Omega(\log n)$ for n processors. A more serious issue for synchronisation is granularity. Inter-processor synchronisation will cost much more due to waiting times, if the synchronisation granularity in the program is too fine for the target multiprocessor. Most multiprocessors cannot efficiently support more than 1 synchronisation in 100 instructions (per processor). The P-RAM model of instruction-level synchronisation would be much too inefficient to implement on real multiprocessors.

The P-RAM assumption that a read or write access to a shared memory cell takes constant time is also unrealistic. First, a bounded degree interconnection network for n processors and m memory cells must incur an average access time of $\Omega(\log n + \log m)$. Second, granularity is also an issue for inter-processor communication. If the shared memory access rate exceeds the available memory bandwidth, then the access time will be much larger due to waiting times. Finally, real multiprocessors partition the shared memory cells into *modules* to make the number of processors and modules approximately equal. Accesses to different memory modules can be performed in parallel, but accesses to the same module must be serialised. Thus, the time to access shared memory also depends on the memory module access pattern.

Despite these discrepancies, the P-RAM model can still be useful in evaluating parallel algorithms for execution on multiprocessors. For example, consider Dekel and Sahni's parallel algorithm for computing partial sums [Dekel 83]. It takes $O(\log n)$ time for *n* elements on $\lceil n/\log n \rceil$ processors. Assuming a $\log P$ memory access time on a real multiprocessor with P processors gives a parallel execution time of $O(n \log P / P)$, or a nearly linear speed-up. Synchronisation and communication overhead will be negligible for this algorithm when $n \gg P$ (i.e. when the granularity of parallelism is large enough to dominate the overhead).

It is common practise to ignore constant, and sometimes logarithmic, factors in parallel execution times on a P-RAM model. However, these factors must be considered in a real multiprocessor implementation, because they could easily exceed the potential speed-up factor of P (≤ 1024, say).

1.2. Programming Languages for Multiprocessors

Comparison of programming languages is always a difficult task because of the wide variety of programming paradigms and features available in different languages. For the purpose of this discussion, we only consider those language characteristics which are relevant to a multiprocessor implementation, while ignoring other issues which are orthogonal to parallelism. Thus, Figure 1-4 classifies programming languages for multiprocessors according to 4 attributes:

1. **Implicit or explicit parallelism?**
   Does the language have explicit constructs for concurrency (e.g. cobegin-coend, doall, tasks) or is the parallelism implicit (e.g. dependence analysis of "dusty decks")?

2. **Implicit or explicit partition?**
   If the language has explicit parallelism, then is the partition implicit (e.g. doall) or explicit (e.g. tasks)? The partition of a parallel program specifies the sequential units of computation in the program and hence the granularity of execution.

3. **Implicit or explicit schedule?**
   If the language has explicit parallelism and an explicit partition, then is the schedule implicit or explicit (e.g. explicit use of processor numbers)? The schedule of a parallel program specifies the mapping of computations onto processors.

4. **Shared-memory?**
   Is the communication model in the programming language based on a shared global memory? Of course, any non-shared-memory model can be easily implemented on a shared-memory multiprocessor, but this attribute is relevant because the converse is not true. In general, it is very difficult to efficiently implement a language with a shared memory model on a message-passing multiprocessor.

The first three attributes are not independent, since implicit parallelism implies that the partition must also be implicit, and an implicit partition implies that the schedule must also be implicit. Therefore, Figure 1-4 lists 7 possible combinations of the 4 attributes[2]. Let us briefly discuss each category in Figure 1-4 with examples. This discussion is not an attempt to classify different languages into "pigeon holes"; instead, it is an attempt to understand how languages differ in issues related to parallel processing.

---

[2]Actually there are 8 possible combinations. We just combined *Yes* and *No* into *Either*, for the *Shared-memory?* attribute in the first entry.

	Parallelism	Partition	Schedule	Shared-memory?	Examples
1.	*Implicit*	*Implicit*	*Implicit*	*Either*	Fortran, Lisp
2.	*Explicit*	*Implicit*	*Implicit*	*Yes*	IBM Parallel Fortran
3.	*Explicit*	*Implicit*	*Implicit*	*No*	SISAL, ALFL, Concurrent Prolog
4.	*Explicit*	*Explicit*	*Implicit*	*Yes*	Ada, Multilisp
5.	*Explicit*	*Explicit*	*Implicit*	*No*	CSP
6.	*Explicit*	*Explicit*	*Explicit*	*Yes*	
7.	*Explicit*	*Explicit*	*Explicit*	*No*	Occam, Hypercube model

Figure 1-4: Classification of programming languages for multiprocessors

In the first category, the parallelism, the partition and the schedule are all implicit. This approach is applicable to "dusty deck" programs. The main problem in implementing these languages on multiprocessors is the automatic dependence analysis necessary to identify parallelism. Computations in imperative languages are based on complex, sequential state transitions [Backus 78]. A careful dependence analysis is required to reveal any possible parallelism. This is a difficult problem in the presence of aliasing and procedure calls with side effects. Whether the parallel program produced by automatic dependence analysis has a shared-memory model or not depends entirely on the techniques used for automatic parallelisation. The current state-of-the-art in automatic parallelisation of Fortran programs (e.g. PTRAN [Allen 87]) is targetted to shared-memory multiprocessors, and would have to be significantly enhanced to be effective on a non-shared-memory multiprocessor.

A language in the second category should have explicit parallelism and a shared-memory model, while leaving the partition and schedule unspecified. However, most extensions to sequential languages (e.g. Concurrent Pascal [Brinch Hansen 75], Concurrent C [Cmelik 86]) use *processes* or *tasks* to specify parallelism, thus making the partition explicit as well. It is relatively easy to design a new language without explicit partitions, by incorporating well-known structured parallel programming constructs (e.g. cobegin-coend, doall) and synchronisation primitives (e.g. semaphores, monitors) in a sequential language like Fortran, Pascal or C. IBM's Parallel Fortran [IBM 88] is placed in Figure 1-4 as an example of the second category because it contains features like Parallel Loops (doall), Parallel Cases (cobegin-coend), parallel locks, and private variables, which make it possible to write a structured parallel program without using processes explicitly.

The third category mainly contains value-oriented, applicative languages. Though applicative languages do not have explicit parallelism in the form of constructs like doall, cobegin-coend, tasks, etc., their freedom from side effects makes it trivial to identify parallelism. Therefore, these languages were not placed in the first category, so that they could be distinguished from languages like sequential Fortran and Lisp, which need more extensive and sophisticated dependence analysis to identify parallelism. The other property of the third category is that the language not require a shared-memory model for concurrent execution. In principle, all applicative languages are *referentially transparent*, and have a value-oriented execution model which allows for data communication based on message-passing. However, in practise, many applicative languages need a shared-memory model for efficient execution, using pointers to avoid copying large data structures. We will only include in the third category those applicative languages for which an implementation on a message-passing multiprocessor has been attempted e.g. SISAL [McGraw 85] [Gaudiot 86], ALFL [Goldberg 88], Concurrent Prolog [Shapiro 83]. Other applicative languages should be considered to belong to the second category by default, until it is demonstrated that they can be feasibly executed on a message-passing multiprocessor.

Next, the partition is also made explicit in the fourth and fifth categories. Several languages fall in this class, with Ada [Mundie 86] and Multilisp [Halstead 86] as representatives of the shared-memory model and CSP [Hoare 78] as a representative of the message-passing model. These languages are significantly easier to implement than the previous categories. Apart from enforcing the inter-task or inter-process synchronisation and communication specified by the programmer, the language system only needs to implement automatic scheduling of tasks on processors. The parallel program should generally run efficiently, if the granularity of its programmer-specified partition is large enough for the target multiprocessor. The disadvantages of these languages is the increased scope for programmer errors in task management, and the general lack of portability in terms of granularity and performance.

The last two categories in Figure 1-4 give total control to the programmer, allowing the schedule to be explicit as well. A programming language in this category allows the programmer to directly refer to processor numbers for efficiency, at the expense of portability. In the seventh category, this model is used in programming languages for message-passing multiprocessors, like Occam on the Transputer [Inmos 87] and C processes on the Caltech Cosmic Cube [Su 85]. The reason why Occam is placed in the seventh category, and CSP in the fifth, is that the current Occam implementation forces the programmer to explicitly perform the mapping of processes to processors, and communication channels to hardware links [Inmos 87]. The Occam language contains *configuration* statements to perform these mappings, whereas the CSP language does not contain any such information to control execution on the target multiprocessor. If some future implementation of Occam were to provide automatic process scheduling without requiring explicit processor assignment from the programmer, then Occam would be placed in the fifth category along with CSP. Conversely, if CSP were to be extended with Occam-like configuration statements for a real multiprocessor implementation, then CSP would join Occam in the seventh category.

There are no obvious or well-known examples of languages with explicit schedules and a shared-memory model, for the sixth category. Most shared-memory multiprocessors are *symmetric*, in that all processors communicate through the shared memory and are equidistant from each other. In such a situation, there is little motivation to require that the programmer control the processor assignment.

Though many of the multiprocessors discussed in the previous section have already been built, few of the languages described in this section have been implemented on them. This is clearly a case of "compilers playing second fiddle to hardware". As mentioned earlier, currently available parallel languages are basically sequential languages with *ad hoc* extensions. The trend appears to be towards languages with explicit partitions, i.e. the fourth and fifth categories. However, these languages are easier to implement only at a large cost to the programmer. The programmer now has to worry about errors in inter-task synchronisation and communication, which may have race conditions and could also lead to deadlock. Errors based on race conditions are notoriously difficult to debug, or even reproduce. In fact, tasks are the GOTO's of parallel programming. The use of structured, parallel programming constructs like doall, cobegin-coend, monitors, data parallelism, etc. is far superior to just using tasks or processes. It took over a decade for sequential languages to respond to the ideas of the structured programming revolution. Why not cut short this delay in parallel languages, and use a structured programming paradigm to start with?

Another problem with languages in the fourth and fifth categories is that granularity considerations can clutter up the code and become an extra burden to the programmer. Though the same partition may be reasonably efficient for different multiprocessors built in today's technology, the next generation of multiprocessors could have vastly different granularities, depending on overhead values and instruction execution times. Thus, programs written with an explicit partition may not be portable (in performance) to multiprocessors of the future. There are other benefits of leaving the partitioning to the compiler. The programmer can use a uniform programming model to express parallelism at all granularity levels. The compiler may then choose to use the fine grain parallelism for vector or VLIW execution within a processor, and coarser grain parallelism for multiprocessing across processors.

There is also a large interest in industry towards implementing existing sequential programs (''dusty decks'') on multiprocessors, as described by our first category. This is an ambitious approach with potentially great rewards. However, it is well known that an efficient parallel algorithm for a problem is often substantially different from an efficient sequential algorithm for the same problem [Anderson 84]. It remains to be seen what fraction of existing sequential programs can be effectively executed on multiprocessors by using this approach of automatic parallelisation.

Though the current emphasis in multiprocessor systems is on languages in the first, fourth, fifth and seventh categories, the focus of this dissertation is on languages with explicit parallelism, but implicit partitions and schedules (i.e. the second and third categories). These languages promise to be successful as general-purpose parallel programming languages of the future because they do not have the problems of explicit partitioning or the problems of automatic parallelisation. In fact, they are a good balance between the automatic and the programmer-controlled approaches. The main obstacle to the widespread use of these languages is the problem of partitioning and scheduling. Since the partition and schedule are implicit in these languages, can a compiler automatically determine reasonably efficient partitions and schedules? The answer provided in this dissertation is ''YES''!

1.3. Partitioning and Scheduling

In the previous section we saw that programming languages for multiprocessors can have implicit or explicit partitions and schedules. Partitioning and scheduling are multiprocessor-dependent issues. Partitioning is necessary to ensure that the granularity of the parallel program is coarse enough for the target multiprocessor, without losing too much parallelism. Scheduling is necessary to achieve a good processor utilisation and to optimise inter-processor communication in the target multiprocessor.

Let us first consider the partitioning problem. The partition of a parallel program specifies the sequential units of computation in the program. For convenience, we call such a sequential unit of computation a *task*, though it does not necessarily have the characteristics of an operating system task or an Ada task. The properties of a task which interest us are:

1. The task's sequential execution time (also called the task's size).

2. The task's total overhead, which includes scheduling overhead and communication overhead for the task's inputs and outputs.

3. The task's precedence constraints, which specify the parallelism in the partitioned program.

The execution time of a parallel program depends on its partition and its schedule. Figure 1-5 illustrates the general way in which the parallel execution time depends on the partition. The abscissa gives the average task size of the partitioned program. The ordinate gives the parallel execution time, normalised with respect to the parallel execution time necessary for ideal speed-up. This normalised parallel execution time is also the same as the ratio, (Number of processors)/(Actual speed-up). The curves in Figure 1-5 were plotted assuming 10 processors, a sequential program execution time of 10^5 cycles and an overhead of 10^3 cycles per task. These curves do not correspond to a particular program, but just indicate the general trend. Later in Chapter 4 (Figure 4-4), we will see a similar curve plotted for the partition cost function, $F(\Pi)$, for function Conduct in the benchmark program SIMPLE.

The stipple curve with o points represents the *ideal parallel execution time* of the partitioned program, in the absence of overhead. As the task size increases from 10 cycles to 10^5 cycles, the normalised ideal parallel execution time rises from 1 to 10 due to loss of parallelism.

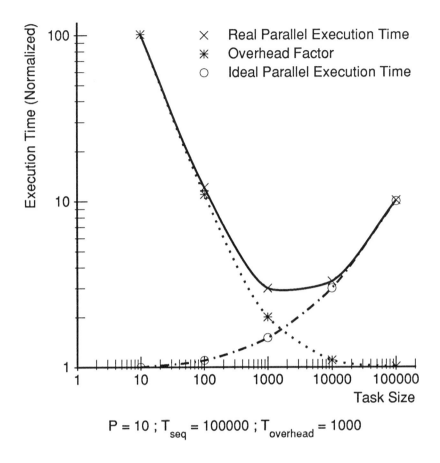

Figure 1-5: The Parallelism-Overhead Trade-off

The dotted curve with * points gives the *overhead factor*, which is the ratio (Task Size + Task Overhead)/(Task Size). The overhead factor falls from 101.0 to 1.01 as the task size increases from 10 to 10^5.

Finally, the solid curve with × points gives the *real parallel execution time*, obtained by multiplying the ideal parallel execution time by the overhead factor[3]. This curve illustrates two important points:

---

[3]Note that the product curve actually looks like the sum of the two curves in Figure 1-5, because the axes are plotted on a logarithmic scale.

1. The presence of overhead in a multiprocessor can make it impossible to achieve ideal speed-up.

2. The real parallel execution time is minimised at an optimal intermediate granularity. The partitioning problem is to find the corresponding optimal intermediate partition.

Figure 1-5 illustrates the general trade-off between parallelism and overhead. However, the continuous variation in task size is a very simplistic view of partitioned programs. Real programs are discrete structures. It may not be possible to partition a real parallel program into tasks of equal size. Further, the overhead incurred by a task depends on the partition itself (e.g. communication overhead is determined by the *cut-set* of communication edges in the partition). Thus finding the optimal partition of a real program is a much harder problem than finding the minimum of the solid curve in Figure 1-5. In fact, we show in Chapter 4 that the problem is NP-complete in the strong sense.

The scheduling problem is to assign tasks in the partitioned program to processors, so as to minimise the parallel execution time. The parallel execution time depends on processor utilisation and on the overhead of inter-processor communication.

The problem of multiprocessor scheduling without communication overhead has been studied in great depth [Graham 79]. The general problem with arbitrary execution times and precedence constraints is NP-complete in the strong sense, along with many apparently simple special cases, e.g. 2-processor scheduling with execution times equal to 1 or 2, but arbitrary precedence constraints. Despite this pessimistic result, the good news is that a simple, linear time *list scheduling* algorithm has a constant performance bound of 2 [Graham 69], i.e. the schedule generated by the list scheduling algorithm will have a parallel execution time which is at most twice the optimal parallel execution time. Thus, the multiprocessor scheduling problem is not an obstacle to achieving linear speed-up.

Unfortunately, the scheduling problem becomes more difficult when considering communication overhead with arbitrary data sizes. Section 3.5 formally describes the model used for communication overhead. Its fundamental property is that communication overhead is only incurred if the sender and receiver are on different processors. Like the partitioning problem, the scheduling problem also involves a trade-off between parallelism and overhead. Parallelism dictates that tasks should be assigned to different processors as much as possible. But communication overhead is reduced when tasks are assigned to the same processor. This trade-off makes multiprocessor scheduling harder than before. List scheduling (or any other single-pass scheduling algorithm) does not have a constant performance bound for multiprocessor scheduling with communication overhead. In Chapter 5, we show that the scheduling problem with communication overhead is NP-complete in the strong sense, even if there are an infinite number of processors available.

An effective solution to the partitioning and scheduling problems is the key to implementing languages with explicit parallelism and implicit partitions and schedules (second and third categories in Figure 1-4). This dissertation presents two approaches to automatic partitioning and scheduling, which are introduced in Chapter 2.

Figure 1-6 shows the general strategy for using an automatic partitioning and scheduling system, in the implementation of a parallel language on a multiprocessor. A program in a parallel language is translated to a graphical representation (similar to a *dependence graph*). This program graph is an input to the compile-time analysis phase of the partitioning and scheduling system. It is also an input to the execution profile generation system which produces frequency parameters for use during compile-time analysis. The third input for compile-time analysis is a list of parameters describing the target multiprocessor. The output produced by compile-time analysis is a partition of the program graph into subgraphs which represent tasks. Each subgraph is then translated to a sequential intermediate language, using the benefit of standard sequential code optimisations. Finally, the code generation phase produces machine code for the target multiprocessor, which is linked together with any run-time support routines necessary for partitioning and scheduling.

1.4. Dissertation Outline

The rest of the dissertation is organised as follows.

Sections 2.1 and 2.2 in chapter 2 present an overview of the partitioning and scheduling problems addressed in this dissertation, and the approaches taken in solving these problems. Section 2.3 briefly describes previous work in related areas and section 2.4 contains a summary of the major contributions made by this dissertation.

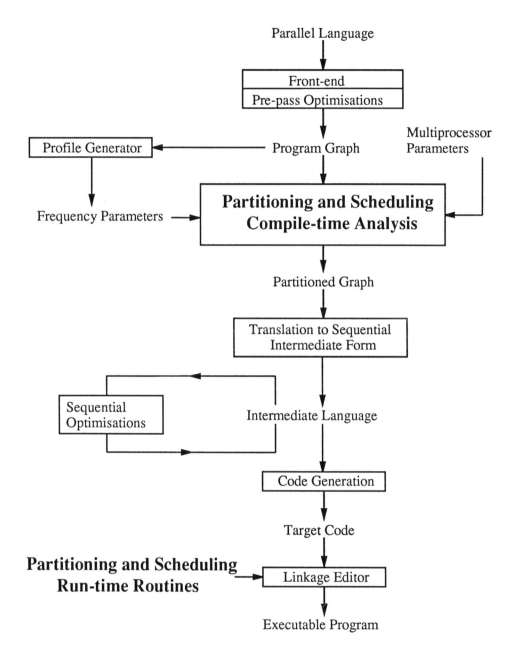

Figure 1-6: General strategy for using a partitioning and scheduling system

Chapter 3 describes in detail the *graphical representation*, GR, used for parallel programs. It also presents a *cost assignment* algorithm which uses execution profile frequency information to derive costs for execution times and communication sizes in the program. Finally, a *multiprocessor model* is defined to specify the number of processors, sequential performance, scheduling and communication overhead in the target multiprocessor.

Chapter 4 describes the *macro-dataflow* approach based on compile-time partitioning and run-time scheduling. Section 4.1 formally defines the macro-dataflow model and develops an objective function, $F(\Pi)$, which gives the cost of partition Π. Section 4.2 shows that the problem of determining the optimal partition, with the smallest $F(\Pi)$, is NP-complete in the strong sense. Section 4.3 describes the approximation algorithm used to solve this problem. Finally, section 4.4 presents simulation results to demonstrate the effectiveness of the partitioning algorithm on benchmark programs written in the single-assignment language SISAL [McGraw 85].

Chapter 5 describes the *compile-time scheduling* approach, where both partitioning and scheduling are performed at compile-time. Section 5.1 formally defines the compile-time scheduling model. Sections 5.2, 5.3 and 5.4 are devoted to the three major phases of the scheduling algorithm. Section 5.3 also shows that the problem of determining the optimal schedule is NP-complete in the strong sense, even on an unbounded number of processors. Section 5.5 presents simulation results to demonstrate the effectiveness of the scheduling algorithm on the SISAL benchmark programs.

Chapter 6 wraps up with some concluding remarks. Section 6.1 compares the macro-dataflow and compile-time scheduling approaches, and section 6.2 presents possible future directions in this area.

Appendix A contains data on the SISAL benchmark programs used in the simulations. This data includes *parallelism profiles* of the programs.

Appendix B contains the raw simulation data produced by the simulation experiments, which was used to generate the speed-up plots shown in sections 4.4 and 5.5.

2 The Problem

There are three fundamental problems to be solved when compiling a program for parallel execution on a multiprocessor:

1. *Identifying parallelism* in the program.

2. *Partitioning* the program into sequential tasks.

3. *Scheduling* the tasks on processors.

In general, the parallelism in the program (1 above) depends on the parallel algorithm designed by the programmer. So, the problem of identifying or expressing parallelism belongs to the domain of programming languages. The partition and schedule (2, 3 above) should be designed to minimise the parallel execution time on the target multiprocessor, and depend on various parameters e.g. number of processors, sequential execution times, communication overhead and scheduling overhead. This dissertation addresses the problem of automatically determining an efficient partition and schedule for a given parallel program and target multiprocessor.

2.1. Compile-time and Run-time approaches

There are three possibilities for automatic partitioning and scheduling:

1. Run-time partitioning and run-time scheduling.

2. Compile-time partitioning and run-time scheduling.

3. Compile-time partitioning and compile-time scheduling.

Note that run-time partitioning and compile-time scheduling is not a meaningful combination, since the scheduling must follow the partitioning and cannot be done at compile-time, if the partitioning is postponed till run-time.

In the first approach, both the partitioning and the scheduling decisions are postponed till run-time. This approach was taken in the Stardust system [Hornig 84]. The major disadvantage in doing everything at run-time is the extra overhead incurred during program execution. The advantage is the availability of run-time information which may lead to a better partition and schedule. However, the large overhead of run-time analysis necessitates very simple partitioning and scheduling algorithms. In Stardust, automatic partitioning was simply based on an upper bound on the task size, without considering communication overhead. A maximum task size restricts the sequentialisation which could occur at too coarse a granularity, but cannot prevent a large overhead due to fine granularity execution. We did not pursue the run-time partitioning and scheduling approach because of the problems with excessive run-time overhead, and the corresponding limitations on the partitioning and scheduling algorithms.

This dissertation investigates the second and third approaches to automatic partitioning and scheduling. The second approach of compile-time partitioning and run-time scheduling is the most common model of program execution in current multiprocessor systems. In current systems, the scheduling of tasks on processors is performed automatically at run-time, but the programmer must explicitly partition the program into tasks and control their synchronisation and communication. We address the problem of automatically determining an efficient partition. The problem is to determine a partition at compile-time which yields the smallest parallel execution time at run-time, for a given parallel program and target multiprocessor. As discussed later in this section, we restrict the task partition so that the inter-task dependences are *acyclic*. With this restriction, the model of compile-time partitioning and run-time scheduling is like the *dataflow* model at the granularity of tasks, rather than machine instructions. So, we refer to this problem of compile-time partitioning and run-time scheduling as the *macro-dataflow* problem.

In the third approach, both partitioning and scheduling are performed automatically at compile-time. Compile-time scheduling is attractive because it eliminates scheduling overhead entirely at run-time. The disadvantage is that the compile-time estimates of execution times and overhead may be inaccurate for some program inputs, leading to inefficient schedules. We address the problem of automatically determining an efficient partition and schedule at compile-time. The considerations are now very different from the macro-dataflow problem. There is no scheduling overhead, since the processor assignment is performed at compile-time. Further, there is a greater opportunity to optimise inter-processor communication when the processor assignment is known at compile-time. The problem is to determine a partition and schedule with the smallest parallel execution time. We refer to this problem as the *compile-time scheduling* problem.

The remainder of this section is devoted to the issue of run-time scheduling for macro-dataflow. If there is run-time scheduling, the task scheduling mechanism used can have a severe impact on multiprocessor performance. So far, the approach in parallel language systems has been to schedule tasks for multiprocessing on a multiprocessor in the same way as processes have traditionally been scheduled for multiprogramming on a uniprocessor. Whereas multiprogramming on a uniprocessor has been eminently successful in timesharing systems, the scheduling problem becomes more difficult on multiple processors due to frequent context switching, necessary for synchronisation, and frequent task migration, necessary for load balancing. If context switches and task migrations occur too frequently, the overhead incurred in task scheduling may well undo the potential speed-up obtained by multiprocessing. The task scheduling problem is different for multiprocessing and multiprogramming. For tasks within the same parallel program, scheduling for multiprocessing must address the new problems of task synchronisation and load balancing, while ignoring some classical considerations from scheduling for multiprogramming, like fairness and response time.

The task scheduling problem for multiprocessing is greatly simplified if the inter-task dependences are acyclic. In this case, we can schedule a task when all its predecessors have completed execution. Once scheduled, the task can run to completion without interacting with other tasks. The advantage of this approach is that context switching and task migration are no longer necessary for synchronisation and load balancing respectively. Scheduling overhead is only incurred when the task starts execution. We ensure that the task partition created by the macro-dataflow partitioner is acyclic, so that the total scheduling overhead will be smaller and more predictable than the general case. This restriction to an acyclic task partition is later called the *convexity constraint*. With the convexity constraint, the worst case scheduling overhead is comparable to the best case, since each task incurs a one-time scheduling overhead. A general partition may contain larger tasks, compared to an acyclic partition with the same amount of parallelism, and could perform better in the best-case scenario when there are no context switches or task migrations. But the performance of a general partition can degenerate unboundedly if context switches and task migrations occur too frequently. We have to wait till both schemes have been implemented on real multiprocessors before we can decide if the "average program" performs well under acyclic partitions or general partitions or both!

2.2. Problem Representation

How should the partitioning and scheduling problems be represented? Perhaps the obvious approach is to choose a particular parallel language (or even just a single parallel program) and a particular multiprocessor, and then attempt to develop partitioning and scheduling techniques which yield the best performance for them. This has been done before for a few language-multiprocessor combinations (e.g. [Gilbert 80], [Hornig 84]). Though such exercises are interesting, they fall short of our goal because the results will, in general, not be applicable to other languages and multiprocessors. It is desirable to isolate the general issues of partitioning and scheduling in the representation of the partitioning and scheduling problems. A similar approach has long been advocated and practised in the use of language-independent machine-independent code optimisers in compilers for sequential languages. Code optimisation problems, like the elimination of common subexpressions and induction variables, can all be represented in a language-independent and machine-independent way. Our goal is to represent the partitioning and scheduling problems in a language-independent and multiprocessor-independent way as well.

In this dissertation, the partitioning and scheduling problems are represented by a graphical representation for parallel programs and a cost model for multiprocessors.

A *dependence graph* [Kuck 81] is a natural representation of parallelism in a program. We have designed a graphical representation (GR) for parallel programs. GR is a hierarchical dependence graph structure with several attributes (e.g. frequencies, execution times, communication sizes). GR can be used to represent parallel programs from different languages. The languages which can be represented in GR either have explicit parallelism (e.g. SISAL [McGraw 85], IBM's Parallel Fortran [IBM 88]), or have implicit parallelism which can be determined automatically (e.g. Fortran, Lisp). We assume the existence of parallelising transformations to determine the parallelism in the latter case, and do not address the problem of automatically determining parallelism.

The target multiprocessor is represented by a cost model. The performance characteristics of interest in the target multiprocessor are execution times, and communication and scheduling overhead. The multiprocessor model contains an execution time function which gives the sequential execution times of all simple nodes in GR. The model also specifies the overhead for scheduling a task, and the overhead functions for communicating a given data size. The multiprocessor model can be used to estimate the parallel execution time of a partitioned GR program, for both run-time and compile-time scheduling.

The primary goal in addressing the partitioning and scheduling problems is to obtain the smallest parallel execution time, for a given GR program and multiprocessor model.

2.3. Previous Work

As discussed in Chapter 1, the problem of implementing parallel languages on multiprocessors has been largely ignored in parallel processing research. Automatic parallelisation of dusty decks is the most attractive approach from the viewpoint of industry. In fact, the Illinois Parafrase system [Kuck 81], [Padua 80] and the Rice PFC system [Allen 82] have been reasonably successful in extracting parallelism from Fortran programs, for execution on vector machines like the Cray-X/MP. This parallelism is typically at the innermost level because global parallelism (between subroutines say) is difficult to extract from a sequential language and because vector machines can only use parallelism in innermost DO loops. The PTRAN project [Allen 87] is an effort to recognise parallelism in Fortran at all levels – for vector machines and for multiprocessors. Whether these approaches will be effective for multiprocessors depends on their ability to recognise significant amounts of large grain parallelism.

We pointed out in Section 2.1 that we did not pursue the option of run-time partitioning and run-time scheduling in this dissertation. Such an approach was in fact implemented in the Stardust system [Hornig 84] on a network of personal computers. Stardust is an applicative language based on Lisp and APL. It has higher-order functions and data structures requiring lazy evaluation, making it more powerful but less efficient than single-assignment languages. A Stardust program is evaluated (interpreted) on a virtual reduction machine, rather than being compiled to machine code. Parallel execution is achieved by using a distributed evaluator. Functions are annotated by the programmer with integer valued expressions which compute execution time estimates at run-time (e.g. N^3 for matrix multiplication). Partitioning is based on a maximum task size criterion, causing expressions with larger execution time values to be decomposed at run-time. The advantage of run-time partitioning is that it uses more accurate estimates of execution times. The disadvantage is that partitioning is a significant performance overhead at run-time, especially since the total contribution of partitioning overhead is proportional to the program's dynamic execution time, rather than its static code size. It is mandatory for a run-time partitioning algorithm to be very simple. Stardust's approach of a maximum size avoids sequentialisation at a coarse granularity, but can incur a large overhead due to a fine granularity decomposition. This is especially significant for its target system, which is a loosely coupled network of personal computers. It would be interesting to see how the compile-time partitioning techniques presented in Chapter 4 compare in performance with run-time partitioning in Stardust.

The trade-off between parallelism and overhead, and the implied motivation for macro-dataflow, has often been mentioned in the literature. Gaudiot and Ercegovac [Gaudiot 84] present a simple, mean-value, analytical model of *variable resolution dataflow*. They illustrate the phenomenon of an optimal resolution which minimises parallel execution time. Since it is a mean-value analysis, it does not apply to a particular program with a given assignment of execution times and communication sizes. Instead it describes the average performance of all programs, for a given macro-actor size. Also, they do not address the compiler issue of actually partitioning the program to achieve a desired resolution.

The *serial combinators* approach for graph reduction systems [Hudak 85] is based on compile-time partitioning and run-time scheduling, like the macro-dataflow approach presented in this dissertation. An important difference from our approach is that serial combinators require a context-switching facility, whereas macro-actors are guaranteed to run to completion without interruption. However, our macro-dataflow partitioning algorithm can be used just as well to identify *acyclic* serial combinators which do not need context-switching for run-time scheduling. It would be interesting to compare the effectiveness of our partitioning algorithm with the algorithm presented in [Hudak 85]. The partitioning algorithm in [Hudak 85] is based on heuristics to address the trade-off between parallelism and overhead:

- Given a choice of parallel subexpressions, include the most complex subexpression in the main sequential thread, while making the other subexpressions available for execution as separate serial combinators.

• Use a threshold value below which expressions are not decomposed for parallelism.

Instead, we develop a single partition cost function to express the trade-off between parallelism and overhead. Though the partitioning problem is similar for macro-dataflow and serial combinators, there are several implementation issues which make graph reduction languages significantly more difficult to implement on multiprocessors than single-assignment languages. These issues (e.g. copy avoidance, lazy evaluation) are essentially uniprocessor performance issues which carry over to multiprocessors as well.

The Bulldog compiler [Fisher 84] [Ellis 85] is an example of compile-time scheduling for VLIW (Very Large Instruction Word) architectures. VLIW architectures provide a fine-grained, synchronous parallelism at the instruction level. A single VLIW instruction contains P fields (typically 8 or 16) for P *clusters*. The compiler extracts local parallelism and packs operations into wide instruction words. Partitioning is not an issue for VLIW machines since the granularity of operations is fixed at the instruction level. Since basic blocks have very limited parallelism (usually less than a factor of 3) [Tjaden 70], the Bulldog compiler uses techniques like loop unrolling and trace selection to extract more parallelism for VLIW machines. Thus, a VLIW compiler starts with parallelism at the innermost level and moves outwards by unrolling loops and building traces of basic blocks to extract sufficient parallelism for the given number of clusters. The synchronous nature of VLIW instructions constrains the VLIW compiler to extract parallelism from only within traces of basic blocks; it is not possible for the VLIW compiler to cross control structure boundaries like loops and procedure calls while extracting parallelism. On the other hand, our approach to compile-time scheduling for multiprocessors starts at the outermost level and moves inwards across arbitrary control structures (including recursive function calls) to expose sufficient parallelism for the given number of processors.

In the Hughes Data Flow Machine compiler [Campbell 85] [Finn 85], dataflow nodes (actors) are allocated to processing elements at compile-time. The allocation is based on separate heuristic functions to minimise inter-processor communication and maximise parallelism. The communication cost function is based on inter-processor distance, but does not consider data size. The parallelism cost function is based on a count of parallel actors, but does not consider execution frequencies. Static allocation of an actor causes all its invocations to be sequential, since they are executed on the same processing element. This is a general problem with static dataflow which cannot exploit (for example) parallelism between iterations of a Forall or parallelism between independent calls to the same function. Our compile-time scheduling approach is also faced with these problems, which are solved by *node expansion* (Section 5.2). Node expansion performs in-line expansion of function calls and splitting of Forall nodes, so that the parallelism is made visible in the static program graph.

Another interesting comparison between our compile-time scheduling approach and the Hughes Data Flow Machine compiler has to do with the graph algorithms used. Any approach to compile-time scheduling must somehow compute the transitive closure of the program graph to determine parallel nodes. Warshall's algorithm [Warshall 62] takes $O(N^3)$ time for an N×N relation. If the graph is sparse with $O(N)$ edges, then an algorithm based on depth-first search just takes $O(N^2)$ time [Hunt 77]. The Hughes Data Flow Machine compiler appears to take $O(N^2)$ time in practise, since their ''local allocator'' took 10 VAX CPU minutes for 96 actors and 3 VAX CPU hours for 415 actors [Campbell 85]. Because of this prohibitive cost, their compiler first uses a ''global allocator'' as an approximation to decompose the graph into smaller subgraphs, and then uses the more accurate local allocator on the subgraphs. Parallel nodes are determined in our compile-time scheduling approach by computing the term, PARWORK, in procedure ExpandNodes (Figure 5-6). This computation uses the $O(N^2)$ sparse relation algorithm, with one important optimisation. GR's hierarchical structure is exploited so that the $O(N^2)$ algorithm is only used at each level, with an $O(N)$ traversal to combine results from different levels. This makes the entire algorithm $O(N)$ in practise if the graph structure contains several subgraphs of constant size. This graph structure trick has been used before in computing the path relation of an arbitrary graph (e.g. path-preserving homomorphic graph structures in [Pfaltz 77]). Thus, transitive closure is not an issue in our compile-time scheduling approach, e.g. the entire node expansion algorithm (Procedure ExpandNodes, Figure 5-6), which includes transitive closure and in-line expansion of function calls, just takes 2 VAX CPU minutes for 1600 nodes in SIMPLE.

2.4. Contributions of this dissertation

In addressing the general problem of automatic partitioning and scheduling of parallel programs, this dissertation makes the following specific contributions:

1. The definition of a language-independent *graphical representation* (GR) for parallel programs. GR can be used to represent a wide range of parallel programming languages – from applicative languages like SISAL to imperative languages like Parallel Fortran.

2. The definition of a *cost model* for multiprocessors. The model is general enough to represent a wide range of multiprocessors from tightly-coupled shared-memory systems to loosely-coupled message-passing systems.

3. A scheme for *compile-time cost assignment* of execution times and communication sizes in a program, based on frequency information obtained from execution profiles. With compile-time cost assignment, the same profile information can be used to derive execution times for different target multiprocessors.

4. A *macro-dataflow* model for program execution based on automatic compile-time partitioning and run-time scheduling. An objective function, $F(\Pi)$, is derived to provide the cost of a task partition, Π. $F(\Pi)$ provides tight lower and upper bounds on the parallel execution time of the partitioned program. The problem of finding a partition with the smallest $F(\Pi)$ is shown to be NP-complete in the strong sense. An efficient partitioning algorithm is presented, which is close to optimal in practise.

5. An automatic *compile-time scheduling* model for program execution. The cost function to be minimised in this case is the estimated parallel execution time. Again, the problem of finding a schedule with the smallest parallel execution time is shown to be NP-complete in the strong sense. An efficient scheduling algorithm is presented, which is close to optimal in practise.

6. A *prototype implementation* to demonstrate the suitability of single-assignment languages, in particular SISAL [McGraw 85], for execution on multiprocessors.

3 Program Representation and Multiprocessor Model

This chapter describes the graphical representation (GR) for parallel programs and the performance model for multiprocessors, which together form a framework for partitioning and scheduling parallel programs.

The partitioning and scheduling techniques described later are based on estimates of the program's performance characteristics, such as parallelism and costs for execution time, communication and synchronisation. GR expresses these performance characteristics and leaves the remaining aspects (e.g. semantics) of the program unspecified. This facilitates the use of GR for parallel programs written in different languages. Other phases in program compilation may find it convenient to use GR as an intermediate form by adding appropriate attributes or annotations. In this chapter, we describe only those features necessary to support partitioning and scheduling.

Our performance model for multiprocessor execution represents general-purpose Multiple Instruction-stream Multiple Data-stream (MIMD) computer organisations. A multiprocessor is a collection of communicating processing elements. The performance characteristics which concern us are processor execution times and scheduling and communication overhead.

3.1. Graphical Representation – Background

Graphs are a popular data structure in program representation. Dags, flow graphs and dataflow graphs are commonly used to represent programs. We review these graph data structures in this section.

Expression *dags* (directed acyclic graphs) [Aho 86] are used to represent expressions which contain common subexpressions. An internal node represents an operator and its children represent its operands. Thus, an edge in an expression dag expresses a *data dependence*. A basic block dag [Aho 86] is similar to an expression dag, but represents an entire basic block. It requires extra precedence edges to represent operators with side effects correctly (e.g. array and pointer assignments, function calls). A dag's edges express dependences and induce a partial order $\leq^*$ on the execution of its nodes. $n_a \leq^* n_b$ means that node n_a must precede node n_b. This partial order indicates the parallelism in the dag; nodes n_a and n_b can be executed in parallel if and only if $\neg(n_a \leq^* n_b) \wedge \neg(n_b \leq^* n_a)$.

The *flow graph* [Aho 86] of a program is another kind of graph used in program representation. Its nodes represent computations and edges represent flow of control. A path in the flow graph represents a possible execution sequence in the program. A flow graph expresses sequential control dependences. Branching in the graph represents alternative computation paths rather than parallel computations.

The dataflow model of computation is also based on a graphical representation of programs. A *dataflow graph* is the executable machine code for a dataflow machine [Gurd 85]. As in a dag, nodes represent operators and edges represent operands. All data is represented by tokens which flow along the edges of the dataflow graph. A node which has tokens on all of its input edges is ready to fire. It executes by consuming all its input tokens and producing a token on each of its output edges. Dataflow's parallelism lies in the nodes' ability to fire concurrently, and in the pipelining due to token streams. Special control nodes direct the flow of tokens to implement conditionals and iterations. These nodes have *non-strict* transfer functions, as they do not necessarily consume tokens from all input edges or produce tokens on all output edges. Dataflow graphs are in fact networks which implement programs rather than just program representations.

Shaw [Shaw 74] introduced a *process flow graph* representation to describe a system of processes with precedence constraints. The process flow graph is a dual of the dag representation in the sense that it inverts the use of nodes and edges. Edges in a process flow graph represent processes and nodes enforce precedence constraints by serving as synchronisation points. No process represented by an output edge of a synchronisation node can start execution till all processes represented by the node's input edges have completed execution.

Process flow graphs are a form of Activity On Edge (AOE) networks, where the activity occurs on edges and the vertices define the precedence constraints. AOE networks are used in performance evaluation techniques like PERT, CPM and RAMPS [Horowitz 76]. Dags are a form of Activity On Vertex (AOV) networks, where the activity occurs in the vertices and the edges define the precedence constraints. An AOE network can be automatically transformed into an equivalent AOV network, and vice versa. In both cases, dummy nodes and edges need to be introduced to avoid a worst-case quadratic increase in the size of the graph.

3.2. The Graphical Representation GR

This section defines the graphical representation, GR, designed to support automatic partitioning and scheduling of parallel programs. A parallel program is represented by a GR graph for each procedure or function in the program. For convenience, we shall use the word "function" from now on to mean a procedure or a function.

> **Definition 3-1:** A GR *program* is a set of function definitions, PROG = $\{(g_1,f_1), (g_2,f_2), ..., (g_{NF},f_{NF})\}$, where NF is the number of functions in the program. A function definition (g_i,f_i) consists of:
>
> - A GR graph g_i (see Definition 3-2) representing function i's computation.
>
> - $f_i \in Q_0^+$ is a frequency count which gives the average number of calls to function i in a single execution of program PROG.

> **Definition 3-2:** A GR *graph* is a 6-tuple G = $(N, T, \perp, E_C, F_C, F_T)$, where
> - N is a set of objects called *nodes*. GR graphs can have four kinds of nodes:
>   1. A *simple* node $n_s \in N$ represents an indivisible sequential computation (which may be arbitrarily complex).
>   2. A *function call* node $n_u \in N$ contains a function number $n_u.u$, $1 \leq n_u.u \leq NF$, and represents a call to that GR function.
>   3. A *parallel* node $n_p \in N$ contains a GR graph $n_p.g$ and a frequency value $n_p.f \in Q_0^+$. n_p expresses the <u>concurrent</u> execution of $n_p.g$, for zero or more iterations. $n_p.f$ gives the average number of iterations of $n_p.g$ in n_p. Parallel nodes are used to represent parallel iterative constructs like the Forall expression in SISAL, or the DOALL loop in parallel versions of Fortran.

4. A *compound* node $n_c \in N$ contains a set of graph-frequency pairs, $n_c.s = \{(n_c.g_1, n_c.f_1), (n_c.g_2, n_c.f_2), \ldots, (n_c.g_k, n_c.f_k)\}$, where $n_c.g_i$ is a *subgraph* of n_c, and $n_c.f_i \in Q_0^+$ is $n_c.g_i$'s average execution frequency in n_c, $\forall \ 1 \le i \le k$. Each execution of n_c is an arbitrary <u>sequential</u> execution of its subgraphs, i.e. a sequence from the set $(n_c.g_1 \mid n_c.g_2 \mid \ldots \mid n_c.g_k)^*$, so that subgraphs may be executed any number of times in any order. If we consider the subgraphs to be like basic blocks, this general definition corresponds to a sequential flow graph which is complete (contains all possible edges) and thus includes all other flow graphs.

Define $id:N \rightarrow Z^+$ so that $id(n)$ gives a unique identifier for node n, over all GR graphs in the program.

- $\top$ (*top*) and $\bot$ (*bottom*) are distinguished simple nodes in N. They are used to identify the import and export edges of GR graph G.

- $E_C \subseteq N \times Z^+ \times N \times Z^+$ is a set of *communication edges*. $(n_a, p_a, n_b, p_b) \in E_C$ represents a communication from output port p_a on node n_a to input port p_b on node n_b. Two edges with the same producer node and port represent a fan-out of identical data values. An input port on a node can have at most one edge connected to it – fan-in is not permitted on input ports. The communication is assumed to occur after node n_a completes execution and before node n_b starts. Therefore, communication edges also enforce precedence constraints among nodes. In fact, node synchronisation is just represented in GR by a communication edge with zero data size. The communication edges in E_C must be acyclic. E_C imposes a partial order on N, $\le^* := (E_C|_{N \times N})^*$, the transitive closure of the node adjacency relation. We require that $(\top \le^* n) \wedge (n \le^* \bot) \ \forall \ n \in N$, so that $\top$(top) precedes all other nodes and $\bot$(bottom) follows all other nodes.

  $IMP_C := \{(n_a, p_a, n_b, p_b) \in E_C | n_a = \top\}$ is the set of G's *import* edges, and $EXP_C := \{(n_a, p_a, n_b, p_b) \in E_C | n_b = \bot\}$ is the set of G's *export* edges. There is a correspondence between the input and output edges of a function call node, n_u, and the import and export edges of the callee's graph $g_{n.u}$:

  - n_u's input edge (n_a, p_a, n_u, p) corresponds to the value on import edges $\{(\top, p, n_b, p_b)\}$ in $g_{n.u}$.

  - n_u's output edges $\{(n_u, p, n_a, p_a)\}$ correspond to the export edge $(n_b, p_b, \bot, p)$ in $g_{n.u}$.

- $F_C:N \times Z^+ \rightarrow Q_0^+$ is the *communication size cost function*. $F_C(n_a, p_a)$ gives the average data size produced on output port p_a of node n_a, and transferred along any communication edge $(n_a, p_a, n_b, p_b) \in E_C$, in a single execution of G. Data size is measured in some pre-determined unit like bits, bytes or words. A communication edge may have no data, if used solely to enforce a precedence constraint. The data size of such an edge is assumed to be zero.

- $F_T : N \cup \{G\} \rightarrow Q_0^+$ is the *execution time cost function*. $F_T(n_a)$ gives the average sequential execution time of node n_a, in some pre-determined unit like machine cycles or nanoseconds. $F_T(G) := \sum_{n_a \in G} F_T(n_a)$ is the average sequential execution time of the entire GR graph, G. We require that $F_T(\top) = F_T(\bot) = 0$ since $\top$ and $\bot$ are special nodes, provided only to define G's import and export edges. They do not represent any computation.

```
define QuickSort

function Split(data:array[integer]
              returns array[integer], array[integer], array[integer])
    for i in array_liml(data), array_limh(data)
    returns
          array of data[i] when data[i] < data[1]
          array of data[i] when data[i] = data[1]
          array of data[i] when data[i] > data[1]
    end for
end function

function QuickSort(data:array[integer] returns array[integer])
    if array_size(data) < 2 then data
    else
    let
        l, middle, r := Split(data)
    in
        QuickSort(l) || middle || QuickSort(r)
    end let
    end if
end function
```

Figure 3-1: SISAL program for Quicksort

As an example, Figure 3-1 contains the SISAL program for *quicksort*, taken from the SISAL language manual [McGraw 85]. Function QuickSort() checks that the array has at least two elements, before calling function Split() to break up the array in three parts, and recursively calling QuickSort() on the left and right sub-arrays. The ‖ operator stands for *array concatenation*, and is used to combine the results of the recursive calls. Like most SISAL programs, QuickSort() makes extensive use of the *dynamic array* facilities in SISAL, where an array value may have arbitrary size at run-time (including being empty).

The GR graph for function QuickSort() is shown at the left of Figure 3-2. It consists

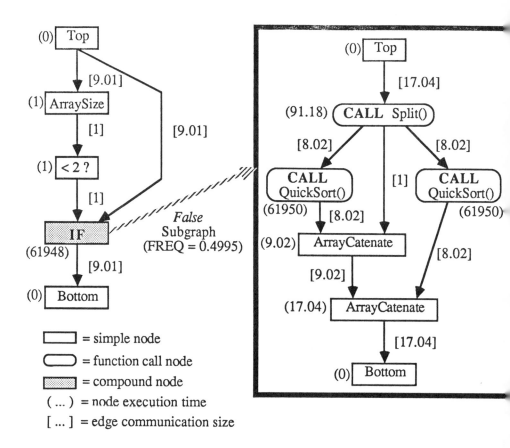

Figure 3-2: GR graphs for function QuickSort()

of four simple nodes (including ⊤ and ⊥) and one compound node for the *if* expression. The GR graph for the *false* subgraph of the *if* expression is shown at the right of Figure 3-2. It consists of three function call nodes and four other simple nodes. The main parallelism is between the two recursive calls to QuickSort(), as is clearly visible in the GR graph. For simplicity, we did not show input and output port numbers on the nodes in Figure 3-2, but they can be easily determined by a simple left-to-right numbering scheme. The numbers in parentheses next to the nodes and edges are the average execution times (F_T) and communication sizes (F_C) respectively. We discuss how these average values can be computed in Sections 3.3 and 3.4.

Since GR is designed for automatic partitioning and scheduling, its parallelism primitives are more restrictive than in languages where the partition or schedule are specified explicitly by the programmer. The main restriction is that GR can only express parallelism visible at compile-time; of course, this restriction applies to any form of compile-time analysis or optimisation. Therefore, GR cannot express parallelism due to arbitrary producer-consumer relationships, e.g. I-structures in Id Nouveau, arbitrary rendezvous within an array of tasks in Ada.

Another restriction is that GR only contains one kind of parallel loop, namely DOALL. A DOALL loop has no cross-iteration dependences. However, it is also possible to execute loops with cross-iteration dependences concurrently. The DOACROSS loop [Cytron 86] covers the full spectrum from DOALL to DOSEQ. It would be interesting to extend GR as well as the partitioning and scheduling algorithms presented later to handle general DOACROSS loops, instead of only DOALL loops. The extension would involve the use of cross-iteration dependences to estimate the amount of overlap between successive iterations of the DOACROSS loop. The corresponding critical path length can then be computed wherever required in the partitioning and scheduling algorithms. This DOACROSS extension will be useful for programs with limited amounts of parallelism. For programs with large amounts of parallelism, the real problem is to identify the parallelism subset which can be exploited usefully on a given parallel architecture[4].

The first step in partitioning and scheduling is to build GR graphs for the parallel program. A GR graph contains information on program structure, parallelism, execution frequencies and costs for communication and execution time. These pieces of information come from different sources in the compiler.

The hierarchical structure in GR due to parallel and compound nodes is derived from the nesting of compound expressions or statements in the parallel program. Algorithms which process GR graphs usually follow the hierarchical structure in a depth-first traversal. For convenience in the description of hierarchical structure in later algorithms, we define a PARENT function and a containment relation, $\in^*$. Define PARENT(x) := y if and only if one of the following conditions is true:

---

[4]Programs which can trivially achieve linear speed-up on multiprocessors are often referred to as being "embarrassingly parallel", e.g. displaying Mandelbrot curves where each pixel can be computed independently. However, it is not the amount of parallelism in these programs which is "embarrassing"; it is the lack of synchronisation and communication accompanying the parallelism.

1. y is a GR graph, $(N, \top, \bot, E_C, F_C, F_T)$, and $x \in N$ is a GR node in y.

2. y is a parallel node, and $x = y.g$ is y's GR graph.

3. y is a compound node, and $x = y.g_i$ is a GR graph in y.

Therefore, PARENT(x) = y if and only if x is directly contained in y. This definition guarantees that for a given x, there is at most one y which satisfies one of the above conditions. PARENT(x) is undefined if there is no such y. PARENT can also be viewed as a binary relation, PARENT = $\{(x,y) \mid \text{PARENT}(x)=y\}$. Consider PARENT^*, the transitive closure of PARENT. Define the containment relation, $x \in^* y$, to be true if and only if (x,y) belongs to PARENT^*.

GR communication edges are easily determined in value-oriented, functional languages, which make explicit the communication of arguments and result data. For procedural languages, communication edges are easier to establish in programs based on message passing or communication channels. Programs based on arbitrary accesses to shared memory pose the biggest problem. Dependence analysis is needed to establish the precedence constraints. Further analysis (e.g. as in [Gallivan 88]) is necessary to identify the set of data values which need to be communicated. Both analyses will have to be conservative. Improvements in either analysis will result in more parallelism or reduced communication overhead respectively.

The execution frequencies for functions and subgraphs of parallel and compound nodes are usually unavailable from the programming system. Our approach is to obtain these values from an execution profile of the program. The communication cost function, F_C, can often be computed by examining the type information for the data being communicated. This method breaks down for dynamically sized types like union types and dynamic arrays, and is not applicable to typeless languages. So we rely on the execution profile to provide average data sizes as well. The disadvantage in using profile information for data sizes is that the execution profile has to be regenerated when partitioning and scheduling the same program for a new target multiprocessor with different data sizes, even though the graph frequencies remain the same. The execution time cost function F_T is heavily dependent on the target architecture, and is best computed by using the frequency parameters and a target description which provides the cost of all simple nodes.

3.3. Execution Profile Information

As described in the previous section, execution profile information plays an important role in building a GR program. It provides average frequency values for functions and subgraphs of parallel and compound nodes, as well as average data sizes for all communication edges. For efficiency and convenience, execution time costs are not generated in the profile, but are computed by using frequency values. The profile information needed consists only of counts and sizes which, unlike execution time, can be measured exactly. Also, this information can be generated by any (possibly sequential) execution of the program on any machine (possibly different from the target multiprocessor).

Execution profiles have traditionally been used to help a programmer identify the most frequently executed and time consuming parts of a program. Optimisation of these statements yields the greatest improvement in the program's execution time. In recent years, profile information has been gaining more importance for automatic compiler optimisations. Register allocation [Wall 86], procedure merging [Scheifler 77], trace scheduling [Fisher 84] and optimisation of delayed branches [McFarling 86] all benefit from profile information.

An important issue in the use of execution profiles is the sensitivity of the optimisation to changes in profile information due to different program inputs. A large sensitivity is undesirable because it tailors the optimisation to the program inputs used to generate the profile. Most optimisations just use profile information to identify the most frequently executed instructions. For many programs, this use is reasonably insensitive to program inputs. We use profile generated frequency counts and data sizes to estimate execution time and communication costs. Partitioning decisions are based on *comparisons* of costs rather than their actual magnitudes. Different cost assignments with identical comparison results will still yield identical partitions and schedules. Therefore, the partitioning and scheduling algorithms will be generally insensitive to different profile inputs for programs which are reasonably "predictable". This claim is validated in the simulation results presented in Sections 4.5 and 5.5. As discussed later, the "predictability" of execution profile information can be improved by averaging over different inputs. In the worst case, the most frequently executed region in the program could vary widely with each distinct input. The general solution for programs with unpredictable run-time behaviour is to use on-line optimisations performed at run-time. Our partitioning and scheduling techniques are intended to be performed off-line at compile-time and are less effective for such programs.

The execution profile information needed for partitioning and scheduling consists of:

1. Average number of calls to each function in the program.

2. Average execution frequencies for all GR graphs in parallel or compound nodes.

3. Average data sizes at all output ports of all nodes.

These values can be measured by executing special code to increment counters at appropriate positions in the program. Traditional profilers have used this approach to measure statement counts [Knuth 71]. This approach was used in our prototype implementation for partitioning SISAL programs.

Definition 3-3: Let $F(g)$ be the total frequency count of GR graph g, over a single execution of the program. Then

- The average frequency count of the ith function in program PROG $= \{(g_1, f_1), (g_2, f_2), \ldots, (g_{NF}, f_{NF})\}$, is given by $f_i = F(g_i)$, $\forall$ $1 \le i \le NF$.

- For any parallel node n_p in GR graph G, the average frequency count of its subgraph is given by
  1. $n_p.f = 0$, if $F(G) = 0$,
  2. $n_p.f = F(n_p.g) / F(G)$, otherwise.

- For any compound node n_c in GR graph G, the average frequency of its ith subgraph is given by
  1. $n_c.f_i = 0$, if $F(G) = 0$,
  2. $n_c.f_i = F(n_c.g_i) / F(G)$, otherwise.

Average data sizes can also be accumulated by using counters. Special code is required to evaluate the size of a datum at run-time. The complexity of this code depends on the data types available in the language and their machine representation. The size can be efficiently determined for types built out of scalars, records, unions and (possibly dynamic) arrays. It is more complicated and time-consuming to determine the size of pointer structures, like generalised lists or S-expressions. Accumulated data size counts at all output ports are used to derive average data sizes of communication edges.

Definition 3-4: Let $S(n_a, p_a)$ be the total size of all data produced at output port p_a on node n_a in GR graph G, over a single execution of the program. Then the average data size for a single execution of G is given by

1. $F_C(n_a, p_a) = 0$, if $F(G) = 0$,

2. $F_C(n_a, p_a) = S(n_a, p_a) / F(G)$, otherwise.

Since fan-out edges connected to the same output port carry the same data, we avoid redundant effort in the profiler by accumulating data sizes for all output ports rather than for all communication edges. This is a significant saving for a GR graph with $O(n^2)$ communication edges and $O(n)$ nodes and output ports.

Execution profile information can be improved by averaging over several program inputs. In that case, Definitions 3-3 and 3-4 would use values of $F(g)$ and $S(n_a, p_a)$ averaged for a single program execution. This is important for programs which break up into a small number of cases according to the input. The profile should then cover executions for all cases. Given its growing importance, execution profile information ought to become an indispensable component of future programming environments and systems. For example, the PTRAN system [Allen 87] maintains a *program database*, which could easily store frequency information as well. Similarly, the IF1 intermediate language [Skedzielewski 85a] for SISAL has *pragmas*, which can be used to annotate the nodes and edges with frequency information (or any other information). In the future, these environments could automatically maintain the profile information and incrementally update average values with each run of the program.

3.4. Cost Assignment

In the last section, we saw how execution profile information is used to determine average execution frequencies and average communication sizes. The only remaining information in the construction of GR graphs is the estimation of average execution times, F_T. As mentioned earlier, we have intentionally avoided measuring F_T values in an execution profile of the program. The main reasons for not doing so are:

- Execution time measurements are only valid for the machine on which the profile was generated. Frequency counts do not have this restriction.

- By computing, rather than measuring, average execution times, the same frequency profile information can be used to derive average execution times for different target architectures, or even different code generators for the same target architecture.

- Measurement of execution times in an execution profiler is usually an approximation, unlike frequency counts which are exact.

- Further timing inaccuracies occur when the execution time of profiling code itself contributes to the execution times being measured.

The average execution times of simple nodes are the starting values from which all other F_T values are derived. They depend on the target architecture and must be initialised appropriately. We will not discuss the possible techniques for estimating F_T for simple nodes, as they vary widely for different architectures. A simple approach is to just add the execution times of the target instructions which implement the simple node. A more careful estimation is required when resource conflicts have to be taken into account in overlapped or pipelined architectures. Also, some approximation of cache effects will also have to be taken into account. Throughout this dissertation, we assume that a cost function, F_S, is available in the multiprocessor model to provide F_T values for all simple nodes in the program's GR graphs.

The main complication in estimating F_T values is due to function calls. While function definitions are essential for structured and modular programming, it may appear that the function calls can be eliminated in the compiled code by in-line expansion. In fact, in-line expansion is an important optimisation which can improve sequential execution times by 10-30% [Chow 83] [Scheifler 77]. In-line expansion also offers greater flexibility in partitioning and scheduling by exposing the computation of a function call in the context of its call site.

The two cases in which it is not possible to expand all function calls in-line are:
1. When the expanded code size becomes too large. This restriction has become less serious in recent times due to the availability of larger main memories as well as virtual memory systems. But, in the worst case, the expanded code size can grow exponentially with the number of functions expanded and can always overflow the limit on code size.

2. When the program has recursive function calls (which are not just tail-recursive). Even without the code size restriction, function definitions are necessary to implement recursion. Though recursive functions can be mimicked by non-recursive functions with goto's and local stack data structures, this only complicates the control structure in the function without reducing the overhead of storing arguments and results.

Therefore, in general, all function calls cannot be expanded in-line, and our partitioning and scheduling techniques must take function calls into account.

Figure 3-3 outlines the algorithm used to compute average execution times, when F_T is defined for all simple nodes and function call nodes. The algorithm is based on three simple rules[5]:

1. $F_T(g) = \sum_{n \in N} F_T(n)$, the average execution time of a GR graph is the sum of the average execution times of all its nodes.

2. $F_T(n_p) = n_p.f \times F_T(n_p.g)$, the average execution time of a parallel node is the product of its average number of iterations and its subgraph's average execution time.

3. $F_T(n_c) = \sum_i n_c.f_i \times F_T(n_c.g_i)$, the average execution time of a compound node is the sum of the products of each subgraph's average frequency and execution time.

Procedure AssignCosts in Figure 3-3 assigns F_T values by a recursive depth-first traversal of the GR graph structure. Its execution time is linearly proportional to the total number of nodes contained within the GR graph.

```
Inputs:
    1. A GR graph, g=(N, T, ⊥, Ec, Fc, FT), with FT defined for all
       simple nodes and function call nodes contained within g.

Outputs:
    1. FT is defined for all nodes and GR graphs contained within g.

Algorithm:

procedure AssignCosts(g)

begin
    1. for each node n ∈ N do
            a. if n is a parallel node then
                    i. call AssignCosts(n.g)
                   ii. FT(n) ← n.f × FT(n.g)
            b. else if n is a compound node then
                    /* let n.s = {(g1,f1), (g2,f2), ..., (gk,fk)} */
                    i. for each GR graph gi in n do call AssignCosts(gi)
                   ii. FT(n) ← Σ1≤i≤k fi × FT(gi)
    2. FT(g) ← Σn ∈ N FT(n)
end
```

Figure 3-3: Procedure AssignCosts

Procedure AssignCosts assumes that F_T values for all simple nodes and function call

---

[5]Recall that F_T represents average *sequential* execution times

nodes are available as input. F_T values for all simple nodes are considered to be parameters of the target architecture. The F_T values of all recursive and non-recursive function calls are computed as described below.

The problem of computing average execution times in the presence of function calls is straightforward if no function calls are recursive. The major assumption is that the execution time of a function call is independent of the call site, so that the average execution time at a particular call site is the same as the average execution time of the function over all call sites. This assumption is commonly made in execution profilers, e.g. the UNIX profiler *gprof* [Graham 82]. The problem gets more complicated for recursive function calls. Mutually recursive functions are grouped together by determining the *strongly connected components* (SCC's) [Aho 74] of the function call graph. We distinguish between an *external* call (between functions in different SCC's) and an *internal* call (between functions in the same SCC). Clearly, the execution time of a function call depends on whether it is external or internal. An external call includes the total recursive computation in the SCC. The execution time of an internal call depends on the recursion depth at the time of the call. We derive average execution times for external calls to functions in the same SCC and then determine costs for internal calls which are consistent with our costs for external calls.

The first step in determining average execution times in a GR program is to build a function call graph from the function definitions. The call graph $CG = (V,E)$ is a directed graph in which

- $V = \{1, 2, ..., NF\}$ is the vertex set representing the NF functions.
- $E \subseteq V \times V$ is the edge set; $(i,j) \in E$ if and only if there is at least one call in function i to function j.

CG can be built in linear time by a depth-first traversal similar to procedure AssignCosts, in which function call nodes add pairs to the edge set, E.

Next we have to determine the SCC's in CG to identify mutually recursive functions. Tarjan [Tarjan 72] gave an optimal linear time algorithm to determine the strongly connected components of a directed graph. The output of the algorithm can be represented as a reduced call graph (also known as the *condensation graph*) $RCG = (V^*, E^*)$, where

- $V^* \subseteq 2^V$ is a partition of V into its SCC's. $v_i^* \in V^*$ is the set of all functions belonging to the ith SCC.

- $E^* \subseteq V^* \times V^*$ is the edge set for RCG; $(v_i^*, v_j^*) \in E^*$ if and only if $v_i^* \neq v_j^* \wedge \exists\, k \in v_i^*, l \in v_j^*$ such that $(k,l) \in E$.

RCG is a directed acyclic graph. For convenience, we assume that the vertices in V^* are in reverse order of a topological sort on E^*, so that $\forall\ i < j$ there is no path in E^* from v_i^* to v_j^*.

Consider SCC $v_i^* = \{u_1, \dots, u_k\}$. Each function $u_j \in v_i^*$ has a GR graph g_{u_j} and an execution frequency f_{u_j}. Define

- $t_j := f_{u_j}$, the total number of calls to function u_j in the entire program.

- $c_{ij} :=$ the total "coefficient" of all function calls in u_i to u_j. The coefficient of any GR node is the product of the frequencies of all its enclosing GR graphs, up to but not including the function graph. c_{ij} is the sum of the coefficients of all function call nodes in u_i with $n_u.u = u_j$. All the c_{ij} values can be computed by a linear time, depth-first traversal of the function graphs $g_{u_1}, \dots, g_{u_k}$, as presented later in procedure InitCalls (Figure 3-5).

- The total number of internal calls to function u_j is given by

$$i_j := \textstyle\sum_{1 \leq i \leq k} t_i\, c_{ij} \tag{3.1}$$

- The total number of external calls to function u_j is given by

$$e_j := t_j - i_j \tag{3.2}$$

- $B(j) :=$ base cost of function u_j, assuming all internal calls in u_j have zero cost. The cost of external calls in u_j is obtained from the F_T values assigned to the callees' GR graphs.

- $E(j) :=$ our approximation to the cost of an external call to function u_j.

- $I(j) :=$ our approximation to the cost of an internal call to function u_j.

Of the values defined above, t_j, c_{ij}, i_j, e_j and $B(j)$ can be easily computed by using their definitions. That leaves $E(j)$ and $I(j)$. Since $\sum_{1 \leq j \leq k} t_j\, B(j)$ is the total computation performed in SCC v_i^* due to all external calls, we must have

$$\textstyle\sum_{1 \leq j \leq k} e_j\, E(j) = \sum_{1 \leq j \leq k} t_j\, B(j) \tag{3.3}$$

The difference $E(j) - B(j)$ in function u_j is due to (recursive) internal calls. Using the coefficients, c_{ij}, we have

$$E(j) - B(j) = \textstyle\sum_{1 \leq h \leq k} c_{jh}\, I(h) \tag{3.4}$$

Just as we assumed that the execution time of a function call was independent of the call site, the natural approximation to be made now is that the execution times $E(j)$ and $I(j)$ are independent of j. But assuming $E(j) = E'$ and $I(j) = I'$ for all functions u_j in the same SCC v_i^* can be inconsistent with equations (3.3) and (3.4), when $k > 1$. e.g. if $k = 2$, equations (3.3) and (3.4) become

$$(e_1 + e_2)\, E' = t_1\, B(1) + t_2\, B(2)$$
$$E' - B(1) = (c_{11} + c_{12})\, I'$$
$$E' - B(2) = (c_{21} + c_{22})\, I'$$

which has no solution for E' and I', if (say) $B(1) = B(2)$ and $(c_{11}+c_{12}) \neq (c_{21}+c_{22})$.

Our approach is to assume that only all internal calls have the same cost, $I(j) = I'$. I' can be derived by using equation (3.4) to substitute for $E(j)$ in equation (3.3), and by using $i_j = t_j - e_j$ from equation (3.2). Therefore

- $I' = 0$, if $\sum_{1 \leq j \leq k} \sum_{1 \leq h \leq k} c_{jh} = 0$
- $I' = \sum_{1 \leq j \leq k} i_j\, B(j) / \sum_{1 \leq j \leq k} \sum_{1 \leq h \leq k} c_{jh}$, otherwise

The above expression for I' also used $i_j = t_j - e_j$ from equation (3.2). The $E(j)$ values can be obtained by using $I(j) = I'$ in equation (3.3), so that

$$E(j) = B(j) + I' \sum_{1 \leq h \leq k} c_{jh}$$

Note that these definitions also guarantee that $I' \geq 0$ and $E(j) \geq 0$. The assumption that all internal calls have the same cost is only necessary for programs with recursive function calls. If there are no recursive calls, then $E(j) = B(j)$ and $I(j) = 0$.

Figure 3-4 outlines the algorithm used to assign average execution times to all nodes and GR graphs in a GR program. The F_T values for all simple nodes appear as inputs to the algorithm – these values depend on the target architecture. The algorithm uses the reduced call graph, RCG, which contains the SCC's of the function call graph, CG. The SCC's are processed according to their order in V*, which is a reverse topological sort of E*. Thus, the callee of any external call in the current SCC (v_i^*) must belong to an SCC which has been processed earlier. The cost of an external call is the F_T value of the callee's GR graph.

Step 1 initialises c_{jh} and w_j for use in step 2. w_j stores the inverse of u_j, so that $w_{u_j} = j$. c_{jh} is set to zero $\forall\ 1 \leq j, h \leq k$ in step 1 and is incremented appropriately in step 2. Step 2 calls procedure InitCalls (Figure 3-5) to initialise the F_T values for all function calls contained in v_i^* and to determine the coefficients c_{ij}. Procedure InitCalls sets F_T to zero for all internal calls and uses the callee's F_T value for all external calls. The values j, u_j, v_i^*, w are all assumed to be available in procedure InitCalls. Step 3 then calls procedure AssignCosts (Figure 3-3) to determine $F_T(g_{u_j})$, the base cost for each function $u_j \in v_i^*$. In Steps 4 and 5, we set $B(j)$, t_j and i_j, using the results of steps 2 and 3. I' is computed in step 6. In step 7, procedure AssignInternalCalls (Figure 3-6) assigns F_T for all internal calls, according to $I(j) = I'$. Finally, all costs are reassigned in Step 8 by calling procedure AssignCosts. This should yield $F_T(g_{u_j}) = E(j)$, $\forall u_j \in v_i^*$, so that $F_T(g_{u_j})$ is the cost of an external call to function u_j.

The algorithm in Figure 3-4 has $O(\|PROG\| + NF^2)$ execution time, where $\|PROG\|$ is the total size of the GR program and NF is the number of functions in program PROG. The quadratic NF^2 term is due to the coefficient matrix c_{ij}, and can be reduced to a linear term by using a sparse adjacency list representation [Aho 74] instead. The full coefficient matrix was used in the presentation of the algorithm for the sake of clarity.

The general method of cost assignment described in this section may be used in any application which requires compile-time estimates of execution time in a program. We will, of course, use these execution time costs for partitioning and scheduling parallel programs.

1. A GR program, PROG = { (g_1, f_1), ..., (g_{NF}, f_{NF}) }.

2. F_T values for all simple nodes contained within PROG's GR function graphs.

3. CG's strongly connected components in a reduced call graph, RCG = (V^*, E^*).

Outputs:
1. F_T values for all nodes and GR graphs contained within P.

Algorithm:

for each SCC vertex $v_i^* \in V^*$ **do**
/* Recall that V^* is in a reverse topological sort order of E^*. */
/* Let $v_i^* = \{u_1, ..., u_k\}$ be the functions in the current SCC */

1. **for** $j \leftarrow 1$ **to** k **do**
    a. **for** $h \leftarrow 1$ **to** k **do** $c_{jh} \leftarrow 0$
    b. $w_{u_j} \leftarrow j$

2. **for** $j \leftarrow 1$ **to** k **do call** InitCalls$(g_{u_j}, 1)$

3. **for** $j \leftarrow 1$ **to** k **do call** AssignCosts(g_{u_j})

4. **for** $j \leftarrow 1$ **to** k **do**
    a. $B(j) \leftarrow F_T(g_{u_j})$
    b. $t_j \leftarrow f_{u_j}$

5. **for** $j \leftarrow 1$ **to** k **do**
    a. $i_j \leftarrow \sum_{1 \le i \le k} t_i\, c_{ij}$

6. **if** $\sum_{1 \le j \le k} \sum_{1 \le h \le k} c_{jh} = 0$ **then** $I' \leftarrow 0$
   else $I' \leftarrow \sum_{1 \le j \le k} i_j\, B(j)\ /\ \sum_{1 \le j \le k} \sum_{1 \le h \le k} c_{jh}$

7. **for** $j \leftarrow 1$ **to** k **do call** AssignInternalCalls(g_{u_j}, I')

8. **for each** function $u_j \in v_i^*$ **do call** AssignCosts(g_{u_j})
   /* $F_T(g_{u_j}) = E(j)$ should now be true */

Figure 3-4: Algorithm to compute F_T for an entire GR program

Inputs:
  1. A GR graph, $g = (N, \top, \bot, E_C, F_C, F_T)$.

  2. $f \in Q_0^+$ is the average number of times g is executed in a single call to function u_j.

Outputs:
  1. F_T is initialised for all function call nodes contained within g. For function call node n, $F_T(n)$ is set to zero when $n.u \in v_i^*$ (internal call), and to $F_T(g_{n.u})$ otherwise (external call).

  2. The coefficient of each internal call to function $u_h \in v_i^*$ is added to c_{jh}.

```
procedure InitCalls(g, f)
begin
for each node n ∈ N do
    1. if n is a function call node then
          a. if n.u ∈ v_i* then begin F_T(n) ← 0 ; c_{jw_{n.u}} ← c_{jw_{n.u}} + f end
          b. else F_T(n) ← F_T(g_{n.u})
    2. else if n is a parallel node then call InitCalls(n.g, f × n.f)
    3. else if n is a compound node then
       /* let n.s = {(g_1,f_1), (g_2,f_2), ..., (g_k,f_k)} */
       for each GR graph g_h in n do call InitCalls(g_h, f × f_h)
end
```

Figure 3-5: Procedure InitCalls

Inputs:
  1. A GR graph, $g = (N, \top, \bot, E_C, F_C, F_T)$.

  2. I', the cost of all internal calls in SCC v_i^*.

Outputs:
  1. For each internal function call node n contained within g, $F_T(n)$ is set to I'.

```
procedure AssignInternalCalls(g, I')
begin
for each node n ∈ N do
    1. if n is a function call node then
          a. if n.u ∈ v_i* then F_T(n) ← I'
    2. else if n is a parallel node then
       call AssignInternalCalls(n.g, I')
    3. else if n is a compound node then
       /* let n.s = {(g_1,f_1), (g_2,f_2), ..., (g_k,f_k)} */
       for each GR graph g_h in n do call AssignInternalCalls(g_h, I')
end
```

Figure 3-6: Procedure AssignInternalCalls

As an example of cost assignment, consider the Quicksort program presented in Figures 3-1 and 3-2. We used an array of 1023 integers to obtain the execution profile information consisting of frequencies and communication sizes. To simplify the following discussion, the input permutation was chosen so that the recursive call tree for QuickSort() is a complete, balanced, binary tree, e.g. for 7 integers, the input permutation would have been <4 2 1 3 6 5 7>.

From the execution profile information for this "balanced" input permutation of 1...1023, we see that functions QuickSort() and Split() were called 1023 and 511 times respectively. The *false* branch of the *if*-expression was selected with frequency, $511/1023 \approx 0.4995$. The average size of the input array to QuickSort() (over all 1023 calls) is $\sum_{0 \le i < 9}(2^{10-i}-1)2^i/1023 \approx 9.01$. The communication sizes for the other array edges can be similarly obtained and are shown in parentheses in Figure 3-2.

Due to the reverse topological sort order of the reduced call graph, the cost assignment algorithm of Figure 3-4 will first process function Split(). The average number of iterations in the Forall (over all 511 calls) is $\sum_{0 \le i < 8}(2^{10-i}-1)2^i/511 \approx 17.04$. Based on costs of 5 and 6 for the Forall body and the rest of the function respectively, the algorithm assigns a total cost of $5 \times 17.04 + 6 \approx 91.18$ to function Split().

We examine the cost assignment of function QuickSort() more closely, according to the steps performed by the algorithm in Figure 3-4. Note that QuickSort() is a recursive function in an SCC by itself. Step 2 sets $c_{11} = 1022/1023$. Steps 3 and 4 give $t_1 = 1023$ and

$$B(1) \approx 1 + 1 + (91.18 + 9.02 + 17.04) \times 511/1023 \approx 60.56$$

Step 5 gives $i_1 = t_1 \times c_{11} = 1022$, and step 6 gives[6] $I' = i_1 \times B(1)/c_{11} = 61950$. Step 7 assigns I'=61950 as the execution time for both recursive calls to function QuickSort(). Finally, in step 8, the execution time of the entire function is determined as

$$E(1) \approx 1 + 1 + (91.18 + 61950 + 61950 + 9.02 + 17.04) \times 511/1023 = 61950$$

So, we have the surprising result that the costs for internal and external calls to

---

[6]The 4-5 digit precision used here is insufficient to yield the value, 61950, exactly. However, the prototype implementation has a precision of about 15 digits, which was sufficient to obtain I'=61950 exactly.

QuickSort() are the same, I' = E(1) = 61950! We would normally expect the internal (recursive) calls to have a smaller cost, because they operate on smaller arrays than the external call. However, the internal calls are weighted by the frequency of the *false* subgraph, $511/1023 \approx 0.5$, so that their weighted execution time is less than the execution time of an external call, as expected. It can be easily proved, using equations (3.1) to (3.4), that I' = E(1) for any SCC containing exactly one function. If an SCC has more than one function, then I' < E(i) or I' > E(i) is also possible.

We conclude this section by summarising the important properties of F_T values in the following theorem:

Theorem 3-5: The F_T values assigned by the algorithm in Figure 3-4 satisfy the following properties:

1. $F_T(x) \geq 0$, for any GR graph or GR node x.

2. $F_T(g) = \sum_{n \in N} F_T(n)$, for any GR graph g with node set N.

3. $F_T(n_p) = n_p.f \times F_T(n_p.g)$, for any parallel node n_p.

4. $F_T(n_c) = \sum_i n_c.f_i \times F_T(n_c.g_i)$, for any compound node n_c.

5. $F_T(n_u) = F_T(g_{n_u.u})$, for any *external* function call node n_u (when the caller and callee functions belong to different SCC's).

6. For all functions in the same SCC $\{u_1, ..., u_k\}$

    a. $I(i) = I(j) \; \forall \; 1 \leq i, j \leq k$, so that all internal calls in the same SCC have the same cost.

    b. $\sum_{1 \leq j \leq k} e_j \, E(j) = \sum_{1 \leq j \leq k} t_j \, B(j)$ (see Equation (3.3)).

Proof: Properties 2, 3 and 4 are guaranteed by procedure AssignCosts (Figure 3-3). Property 5 is maintained by step 1.b in procedure InitCalls (Figure 3-5). Property 6 is guaranteed by the choice of I' in procedure AssignCosts.

Property 1 can be proved by induction on cost assignment. The base condition assumes that the starting F_T values for all simple nodes are ≥ 0. The induction step shows that any new cost must also be ≥ 0.

Q. E. D.

3.5. Multiprocessor Model

This section describes our abstraction of MIMD multiprocessor organisations, which is the target multiprocessor model used for partitioning and scheduling parallel programs. A multiprocessor is modelled as a collection of identical, communicating processing elements (PE's). The only inter-PE interaction considered by the model is task scheduling and data communication (synchronisation is treated as a special case of communication). Other inter-PE interactions which may arise in real multiprocessor systems, such as I/O, contention for system resources and distribution of program code are ignored.

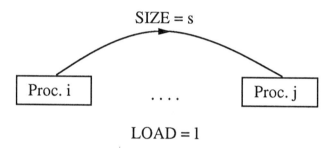

Figure 3-7: Inter-processor communication model

Definition 3-6: A multiprocessor model is a 6-tuple $M = (P, R_C, W_C, D_C, F_S, T_{sched})$, where

- P is the number of processors (or PE's) in the multiprocessor.

- $R_C : Z^+ \times Z^+ \times Q_0^+ \times Q_0^+ \rightarrow Q_0^+$ is the communication overhead function for *reading* data. $R_C(i,j,s,l)$ is the execution time incurred by processor j to receive s units[7] of data from processor i, $j \neq i$, assuming a communication load of l per processor (Figure 3-7).

- $W_C : Z^+ \times Z^+ \times Q_0^+ \times Q_0^+ \rightarrow Q_0^+$ is the communication overhead function for *writing* data. $W_C(i,j,s,l)$ is the execution time incurred by processor i to send s units of data to processor j, $i \neq j$, assuming a communication load of l per processor (Figure 3-7).

---

[7]The data size unit is assumed to be the same as that used by the GR communication cost function, F_C.

- $D_C:\mathbf{Z}^+\times\mathbf{Z}^+\times\mathbf{Q}_0^+\times\mathbf{Q}_0^+\to\mathbf{Q}_0^+$ is the communication *delay* overhead function. $D_C(i,j,s,l)$ is the delay time (in execution time units) which must elapse when processor i sends s units of data to processor j, $i \neq j$, assuming a communication load of l per processor (Figure 3-7). The delay overhead is a *lower bound* on the length of the latency period after processor i has incurred its output overhead, W_C, and before processor j has begun its input overhead, R_C. Processors i and j are free to execute other instructions during this latency period.

- $F_S:N\to\mathbf{Q}_0^+$ is the simple node execution time cost function. $F_S(n_s)$ gives the execution time of simple node n_s. F_S is used by the cost assignment algorithm to provide the F_T values of all simple nodes.

- $T_{sched}:\mathbf{Q}_0^+$ is the *scheduling overhead* (in execution time units) incurred by a processor when it begins execution of a new task.

For the sake of simplicity, T_{sched} is the only task management overhead parameter in the multiprocessor model. The T_{sched} parameter is used in the macro-dataflow model, where the tasks (or macro-actors) are scheduled by a run-time scheduler in the language system, rather than by the operating system. Thus, T_{sched} should be no greater (and probably much less) than the overhead of scheduling "lightweight" tasks in today's multiprocessor operating systems.

The multiprocessor model does not include any parameter for *context switching* overhead. If the context switching is due to inter-task synchronisation or communication, then the overhead can be included in the communication overhead parameter, R_C. Context switching for fairness (i.e. for an equitable time slicing of tasks on a processor) is essential for multiprogramming, but not necessary for multiprocessing where all tasks belong to the same program. Another possible source of context switching is the use of task priorities in the parallel program. However, the macro-dataflow model does not need any form of context switching because of the *convexity constraint* discussed later.

The cost functions R_C, W_C and D_C in a multiprocessor model describe communication overhead. Communication overhead is considered to have two components:

1. *Processor component* – the duration for which a processor participates in a communication. This component is expressed by the reading and writing cost functions, R_C and W_C.

2. *Delay component* – the fraction of communication time during which the producer and consumer processors are free to execute other instructions. This component is expressed by the delay cost function, D_C.

All communication cost functions have the source and destination processors as arguments, which can be used to describe inter-processor distances (number of hops) for communication overhead. The communication load argument in the cost functions is a very simple approximation of the effect of communication demand on communication overhead. It is an estimate of the communication demand rate per processor, at the time the specified communication is to be initiated. This estimate will be very crude at compile-time – the only way to accurately estimate the communication load is by actually executing (or simulating) the program. The effect of communication load on communication overhead depends on the target multiprocessor. Communication overhead will be independent of communication load if the peak communication load can be supported by the communication bandwidth provided in the multiprocessor.

A simple queuing theory model can be used to approximate the effect of communication load, when the communication bandwidth cannot support the peak communication load. Approximate the communication demand as a *Poisson process* with a mean arrival rate of λ. Therefore, the waiting time between successive arrivals (i.e. communication requests) is an exponential distribution with mean $1/\lambda$. Also assume that the communication bandwidth provides a fixed service rate of μ. λ and μ give the communication load and bandwidth in a unit like bytes/second. The *occupancy* is defined as $\rho = \lambda/\mu$. Then, the mean waiting time for a communication request in this model is given by $T_w = (1/\mu)\, 0.5\rho/(1-\rho)$ [Kleinrock 75][8]. The mean waiting time, T_w, does not include the fixed service time of $1/\mu$. T_w can be included appropriately in the communication overhead functions, R_C, W_C and D_C, by using the communication load argument as an estimate of λ. μ is determined by the communication bandwidth provided in the target multiprocessor.

Figure 3-8 plots the function $0.5\rho/(1-\rho)$ to show the behaviour of T_w as ρ increases from 0 to 1. Note that $T_w = 0$ when $\rho = 0$ and $T_w = \infty$ when $\rho = 1$. The important

---

[8]This is the Pollaczek-Khinchin mean value formula applied to a M/D/1 queueing system.

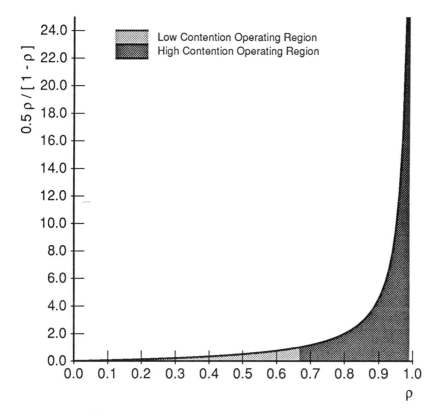

Figure 3-8: Behaviour of average waiting time, T_w

observation is that $T_w \leq 1/\mu$ when $\rho \leq 2/3$, even though $T_w \to \infty$ as $\rho \to 1$. We can consider the curve in Figure 3-8 to basically consist of a *low contention operating region* $(0 \leq \rho \leq 2/3)$ and a *high contention operating region* $(2/3 \leq \rho \leq 1)$. Though the value of ρ determined at compile-time is a crude estimate, it will probably be good enough to identify the correct operating region in Figure 3-8. This approximation is usually sufficient to avoid partitions and schedules which lead to large values of T_w.

The multiprocessor model described in this section is used by the partitioning and scheduling algorithms to estimate the parallel execution time of GR graphs, when taking communication and scheduling overhead into account.

4 Macro-Dataflow

In this chapter, we investigate the execution of parallel programs on multiprocessors, based on a model of compile-time partitioning and run-time scheduling. A GR program is partitioned into parallel *tasks* at compile-time; these tasks are mapped to processors as *macro-actors* at run-time, providing a concurrent execution of the program. There is a *scheduling overhead* involved in scheduling a macro-actor on a processor, and a *communication overhead* associated with communicating a macro-actor's inputs and outputs. It is demonstrated that there is an optimal task granularity which minimises parallel execution time in the presence of overhead. We introduce a performance model to evaluate the parallel execution time of a partitioned GR program, for a given target multiprocessor. An objective function, F(Π), is derived from the performance model to define the cost of partition Π. We show that the problem of building a partition with the smallest value of F(Π) is NP-complete in the strong sense. We present an efficient partitioning algorithm which is close to optimal in practise. Finally, we present performance results for benchmark programs written in the single-assignment language, SISAL [McGraw 85]. A preliminary report on this *macro-dataflow* model of compile-time partitioning and run-time scheduling was presented in [Sarkar 86a].

4.1. The Model

This section formally defines a *partition* of a GR program and the *macro-dataflow* model for its concurrent execution. We derive tight lower and upper bounds on the parallel execution time of the partitioned program, for a given multiprocessor. The analysis assumes run-time scheduling in the presence of communication and scheduling overhead. These bounds are used to derive the partition cost function, F(Π), where a smaller F(Π) value corresponds to a smaller parallel execution time. The bounds also help us understand the variation in parallel execution time with different multiprocessor parameters (e.g. scheduling overhead, communication overhead, number of processors).

Definition 4-1: A partition, $\Pi(g) = (PN, TP)$, of a GR graph, g, consists of:

1. A set of *primitive* nodes, PN, on which the task mapping is defined. PN is not allowed to contain any top ($\top$) or bottom ($\bot$) nodes.

   Define

   - SPN := $\{ n_a \mid (n_a \in^* n_b) \wedge (n_b \in PN) \wedge (n_a \neq n_b) \}$ is the set of *sub-primitive* nodes. A sub-primitive node must be properly contained within a primitive node.

   - EN := $\{ n_a \mid (n_b \in^* n_a) \wedge (n_b \in PN) \wedge (n_a \neq n_b) \} \cup$
     $\{ n_a \mid (n_a \notin SPN) \wedge (n_a$ is a top or bottom node$) \}$
     is the set of *expanded* nodes. An expanded node must properly contain a primitive node, or must be a non-sub-primitive top or bottom node.

   - EG := $\{ g'=(N', \top', \bot', E_C', F_C', F_T') \mid N' \subseteq PN \cup EN \}$ is the set of all *expanded graphs* contained within g.

   The sets SPN, EN and EG are uniquely determined by PN. The only constraint on PN is that the sets PN, SPN and EN must cover all nodes contained within g, i.e. $PN \cup SPN \cup EN = \{ n \mid n \in^* g \}$. Further, PN, SPN and EN are mutually disjoint by definition, so the three sets will properly partition the set of all nodes contained within g.

2. A *task partition* TP:PN$\rightarrow$Z$^+$. $TP(n_a) = TP(n_b)$ means that primitive nodes n_a and n_b belong to the same task. Task $\tau_i = TP^{-1}(i)$ is the set of all primitive nodes, n_a, with $TP(n_a) = i$. All nodes within a task will be executed sequentially – the only parallelism visible in the partition is between entire tasks. We impose a *convexity constraint* on TP so that

   - Primitive nodes n_a and n_b must belong to different tasks τ_i and τ_j if they belong to different GR graphs, i.e.

     $$PARENT(n_a) \neq PARENT(n_b) \Rightarrow TP(n_a) \neq TP(n_b).$$

   - There is no (n_a, n_b, n_c, n_d) which satisfies all the following conditions:

     a. n_a, n_b, n_c, n_d are GR nodes in the same GR graph.

     b. $(n_a, n_d \in \tau_i) \wedge (n_b, n_c \in \tau_j) \wedge (i \neq j)$, i.e. n_a, n_d and n_b, n_c belong to two distinct tasks τ_i and τ_j respectively.

     c. $(n_a \leq^* n_b) \wedge (n_c \leq^* n_d)$.

   This constraint guarantees that the task partition of any GR graph will always be acyclic.

The convexity constraint ensures that a macro-actor can run to completion once all its inputs are available, since all task partitions of GR graphs must be acyclic. Actually, the term *acyclic constraint* would be more accurate than *convexity constraint* because all convex partitions of a directed graph are not acyclic, though all acyclic partitions are convex. However, we will continue to use the terms *convexity constraint* and *convex partition* for the conditions in Definition 4-1, since that is the term originally used in [Sarkar 86a]. A further discussion of the convexity constraint and its implications appears at the end of this section.

The primitive nodes define a partial fringe of the GR graph structure tree. All sub-primitive nodes fall below the fringe, and all nodes above the fringe are expanded parallel or compound nodes. The only other nodes are expanded top and bottom nodes. Two nodes from different GR graphs can only be in the same task if they are sub-primitive nodes contained in primitive nodes which are in the same task (and also in the same GR graph).

For convenience in presenting the partitioning algorithms for macro-dataflow, we extend the definition of PARENT to tasks so that $PARENT(\tau_i) = PARENT(n_a)$, if $TP(n_a) = i$. $PARENT(\tau_i)$ is uniquely defined since all nodes in the same task belong to the same graph and have the same parent. We extend the task partition mapping to sub-primitive nodes, so that $TP(n_a) = TP(n_b)$, if n_a is a sub-primitive node contained within primitive node n_b.

The task partition TP also stores the following information for function call and parallel nodes:

- If function call node $n_u \in PN$ is in a task by itself, then $n_u.par = true$ indicates that the function call will be executed by using the parallelism in the callee function's partition. $n_u.par = false$ indicates that the function call will be executed sequentially. $n_u.par$ is ignored if any other primitive node is in the same task as n_u, since n_u must execute sequentially within task $TP(n_u)$ in that case[9].

- If parallel node $n_p \in PN$ is in a task by itself, then $n_p.size \in Z^+$ gives the number of iterations of n_p to be executed in a single macro-actor. $n_p.size$ is ignored if any other primitive node is in the same task as n_p, since n_p must execute sequentially within task $TP(n_p)$ in that case (just like function call nodes above).

---

[9]The convexity constraint prohibits task $TP(n_u)$ from spawning other tasks and suspending itself.

Note that partition $\Pi(g)$ has $O(\|g\|)$ size, where $\|g\|$ is the total size of GR graph g and all its subgraphs.

	Sub-primitive	Primitive	Expanded
Top & bottom nodes	X		X
Other simple nodes	X	X	
Function call nodes	X	X	
Parallel nodes	X	X	X
Compound nodes	X	X	X

Figure 4-1: Possible classifications of GR nodes for macro-dataflow

Figure 4-1 summarises the possible sub-primitive, primitive or expanded classifications for all GR nodes. A top (⊤) or bottom (⊥) node which is not sub-primitive is considered to be an expanded node. An expanded top (⊤) or bottom (⊥) node belongs to an expanded graph with tasks as sub-computations. Simple nodes can either be primitive or sub-primitive and are always executed sequentially. A function call node can be primitive or sub-primitive. Parallel nodes and compound nodes can be expanded, primitive or sub-primitive. Expanded parallel and compound nodes reveal the parallelism among their primitive sub-computations, whereas primitive and sub-primitive parallel and compound nodes are executed sequentially. The only exception is a primitive parallel node, n_p, in a task by itself. n_p is executed by creating a macro-actor for every n_p.size iterations in n_p.

> **Definition 4-2:** A partition π of an entire GR program, $\{(g_1,f_1),\ (g_2,f_2),\ ...,\ (g_{NF},f_{NF})\}$, is a set of partitions $\{\Pi(g_1),\ \Pi(g_2),\ ...,\ \Pi(g_{NF})\}$, one per function.

We now describe the macro-dataflow model for the parallel execution of a partitioned GR program. For convenience, a *macro-actor* is defined to be a dynamic invocation of a static task. The distinction between a macro-actor and a task is akin to the distinction between a process and a program. In the macro-dataflow model of concurrent execution, each processor repeatedly executes the following steps:

1. Pick a "ready" macro-actor.

2. Fetch the macro-actor's inputs.

3. Execute the macro-actor.

4. Store the macro-actor's outputs.

An important property of this scheduling model is that there is no *unforced idleness*. A processor never stays idle if there is a macro-actor ready for execution.

It is usually possible for a real multiprocessor system to find useful work (from another job, say) for an idle processor. A basic assumption throughout this dissertation is that the target multiprocessor executes one program at a time. Though this mode of execution is not necessarily recommended for real systems, the assumption is necessary to obtain useful definitions of the partitioning and scheduling problems in terms of a single program. Without this assumption, the partitioning and scheduling problems would depend on the job mix for the system, where the optimal solution could well be to execute each program sequentially on a separate processor!

The details of the run-time scheduler were deliberately left unspecified in the definition of the macro-dataflow model. The scheduler may be an active entity like a process, or it may just be a passive data structure shared by all the processors and updated by each processor in steps 1 and 4 above. The partitioning algorithm is only concerned with the scheduling overhead parameter, T_{sched}, which depends both on the target multiprocessor and on the scheduler. Usually, a *distributed* scheduler is most efficient for large scale multiprocessors. However, a *centralised* scheduler may be more appropriate for loosely-coupled systems or for master-slave organisations. The idea is to use the best scheduling strategy for the given multiprocessor, and then let the partitioner adapt to the scheduling overhead appropriately.

It is also important to observe that the scheduler is responsible for enforcing all the *data dependences* and *control dependences* among macro-actors. The *data dependences* are enforced by only declaring a macro-actor to be ready when all its inputs have been computed. The *control dependences* are enforced by only creating a macro-actor when the control condition for its parent graph becomes true, e.g. the scheduler examines the condition value of an IF statement before deciding whether the macro-actors in the THEN or ELSE parts should be created. However, any control flow *within* a macro-actor is performed by the macro-actor's sequential code and not by the scheduler.

Definition 4-3: Consider the execution of a partitioned GR program for a single set of inputs. Define

- A := set of all macro-actors created during the program execution.

- $T(a)$:= the total execution time (steps 1 to 4) of macro-actor $a \in A$. For simplicity, we assume that $T(a)$ does not depend on when macro-actor a was scheduled.

- $\leq^*_A \subseteq A \times A$, a partial order on A describing the precedence constraints among the macro-actors. $\leq^*_A$ is the *run-time* graph, defined for use in the proof of Theorem 4-4 below. This graph is never explicitly constructed by the partitioner. However, the scheduler maintains a dynamically changing *subgraph* of $\leq^*_A$ at run-time, for only those tasks which have been created and are waiting for their inputs.

- $T_{total} := \sum_{a \in A} T(a)$ is the total execution time of all macro-actors in A.

- $T_{par}(P)$:= parallel execution time of the program on P processors, using the run-time scheduling model outlined above. $T_{par}(P)$ can vary, depending on which ready macro-actor is chosen by the scheduler in each execution of step 1 of the model.

- T_{crit} := critical path length of the precedence graph $\leq^*_A$. Since $\leq^*_A$ is the *run-time* graph, its critical path length is the parallel execution time of the program on an infinite number of processors ($|A|$ processors are sufficient actually), i.e. $T_{par}(P) \rightarrow T_{crit}$ as $P \rightarrow \infty$.

Theorem 4-4: $max(T_{crit}, T_{total}/P) \leq T_{par}(P) \leq T_{crit} \times (P-1)/P + T_{total}/P$

Proof: For the lower bound on $T_{par}(P)$, we have

$$T_{par}(P) \geq T_{crit} \qquad (4.1)$$

since the critical path length is the (optimal) parallel execution time on an unbounded number of processors. Also

$$T_{par}(P) \geq T_{total}/P \qquad (4.2)$$

since there are only P processors available for parallel execution. Combining (4.1) and (4.2) gives the lower bound:

$$max(T_{crit}, T_{total}/P) \leq T_{par}(P) \qquad (4.3)$$

The proof for the upper bound is based on the proof of a similar upper bound in [Graham 69]. Let's say that a processor is executing an *idle task* when there are no macro-actors ready for execution. Define B to be the set of all such idle tasks during an execution of the program on P processors, and $T(b)$ to be the duration of idle task $b \in B$. We have

$$T_{par}(P) \times P = \sum_{a \in A} T(a) + \sum_{b \in B} T(b) \qquad (4.4)$$

since the macro-actors and idle tasks account for the total duration of $T_{par}(P)$ on P processors.

Next we see that there must be a chain of macro-actors

$$a_1 \leq^*_A a_2 \leq^*_A \cdots \leq^*_A a_k \qquad (4.5)$$

so that for any idle task $b \in B$, $\exists$ macro-actor a_i in the chain which is executing at the same time as b. If this were not the case, then the schedule must have some unforced idleness, thus contradicting the run-time scheduling model (see [Graham 69] for more details).

Since the chain of macro-actors covers all idle tasks, we have

$$\Sigma_{b \in B}\, T(b) \leq (P\text{-}1)\, \Sigma_{1 \leq i \leq k}\, T(a_i) \qquad (4.6)$$

as there are at most P-1 idle processors at any time. Also

$$\Sigma_{1 \leq i \leq k}\, T(a_i) \leq T_{crit} \qquad (4.7)$$

since the critical path length must at least be as large as the chain in (4.5). (4.6) and (4.7) imply

$$\Sigma_{b \in B}\, T(b) \leq (P\text{-}1) \times T_{crit} \qquad (4.8)$$

Finally, we substitute $T_{total} := \Sigma_{a \in A}\, T(a)$ in (4.4) to get

$$T_{par}(P) = T_{total}\,/\,P + \Sigma_{b \in B}\, T(b)\,/\,P$$

and use (4.8) to get

$$T_{par}(P) \leq T_{total}\,/\,P + (P\text{-}1) \times T_{crit}\,/\,P$$

which is the desired upper bound.

$$Q.\,E.\,D.$$

Theorem 4-4 is a general result for any system of tasks with precedence constraints and variable execution times. The only assumption made about the scheduling is that there was no unforced idleness. Even though different scheduling choices can yield different values of $T_{par}(P)$, the theorem provides a bound on the variation. For instance, if $T_{crit} \ll T_{total}/P$, then $T_{par}(P) \approx T_{total}/P$ for any schedule consistent with the run-time model.

The problem of finding a schedule with the smallest $T_{par}(P)$ is NP-complete [Graham 79]. Theorem 4-4 can be used to derive a *worst-case* performance bound for run-time scheduling, when compared with the optimal schedule, $T_{par}(P)|_{opt}$. Using (4.1) and (4.2) we have

$$T_{par}(P) \leq T_{crit} \times (P\text{-}1)/P + T_{total}/P$$
$$\Rightarrow T_{par}(P) \leq (1 + (P\text{-}1)/P) \times T_{par}(P)|_{opt}$$
$$\Rightarrow T_{par}(P) \leq (2 - 1/P) \times T_{par}(P)|_{opt}$$

which is a worst-case performance bound of (2 - 1/P). Therefore, the performance loss due to the NP-completeness of the scheduling problem is less than a factor of 2, and is not an impediment to achieving linear speed-up by run-time scheduling. Further, run-time scheduling is very close to optimal when $T_{crit} \ll T_{total}/P$ or $T_{total}/P \ll T_{crit}$.

Since

$$T_{par}(P) \leq T_{crit} \times (P-1)/P + T_{total}/P \Rightarrow T_{par}(P) < 2 \times max(T_{crit}, T_{total}/P),$$

Theorem 4-4 gives

$$max(T_{crit}, T_{total}/P) \leq T_{par}(P) < 2 \times max(T_{crit}, T_{total}/P) \qquad (4.9)$$

$max(T_{crit}, T_{total}/P)$ provides a tight lower and upper bound on $T_{par}(P)$. Our approach is to use $max(T_{crit}, T_{total}/P)$ to determine the cost of a partition at compile-time. For a given partition, the average value of T_{total} is computed by using average frequency, execution time and overhead values. An approximation to the average value of T_{crit} is also computed by using these average costs. Unlike T_{total}, the approximation for T_{crit} is not the true average because T_{crit} uses the *max* function, which does not preserve average values[10].

The multiprocessor model in Definition 3-6 consists of $M = (P, R_C, W_C, D_C, F_S, T_{sched})$. F_S is used by the cost assignment algorithm (page 46) to provide the costs of all simple nodes. Our run-time scheduling model does not offer any opportunity for overlapping communication delay with computation in a processor, since the next macro-actor to be executed on a processor is only determined after the processor completes executing its current macro-actor. Therefore we do not use the delay overhead function D_C in macro-dataflow, but instead assume that all the communication delay is included in the reading and writing overhead functions R_C and W_C. We also ignore the source and destination processor arguments in R_C and W_C, since the actual processors participating in the communication will only be known at run-time. At compile-time, we use average overhead values for all processor pairs, and write $R_C(s,l)$ or $W_C(s,l)$ for reading or writing s units of data, assuming an average communication load, l, per processor. The overhead functions R_C, W_C, D_C will be used in their full generality in the *compile-time scheduling* approach presented in Chapter 5.

> **Definition 4-5:** For a GR graph g, with partition $\Pi(g) = (PN, TP)$, and a multiprocessor model M, define
> - $T_{seq} := F_T(g)$, the average sequential execution time of GR graph g. T_{seq} does not contain any scheduling or communication overhead.

---

[10]In general, $E[max(x,y)] \neq max(E[x], E[y])$, where $E[\ ]$ stands for the expected value.

- $T(\tau_i) := \Sigma_{n \in \tau_i} F_T(n)$, the average sequential execution time of task $\tau_i \in TP$. Like T_{seq}, $T(\tau_i)$ does not contain any overhead.

- $Q(\tau_i) :=$ the average frequency of task τ_i in GR graph g. $Q(\tau_i)$ is the product of the frequencies of all GR graphs enclosing the primitive nodes in task τ_i. The properties of the cost assignment algorithm (Theorem 3-5, page 49) ensure that

$$T_{seq} = F_T(g) = \Sigma_{1 \leq i \leq NT} Q(\tau_i) \times T(\tau_i)$$

- $E_{IN}(\tau_i) := \{(n_a, p_a) \mid n_a \notin \tau_i \wedge n_b \in \tau_i \wedge (n_a, p_a, n_b, p_b) \in E_C\}$, is the set of input values needed by τ_i. Note that a value produced at a given port of a given node outside τ_i is only counted once even though it may be used more than once in τ_i.

- $E_{OUT}(\tau_i) := \{(n_a, p_a) \mid n_a \in \tau_i \wedge n_b \notin \tau_i \wedge (n_a, p_a, n_b, p_b) \in E_C\}$, is the set of output values produced by τ_i. Again, a value produced at a given port of a given node in τ_i is only counted once, even though it may be used more than once outside τ_i.

- $LOAD(\Pi) := \Sigma_{\tau_i \in TP} Q(\tau_i) \times (\Sigma_{(n_a, p_a) \in E_{IN}(\tau_i)} F_C(n_a, p_a)$
$$+ \Sigma_{(n_a, p_a) \in E_{OUT}(\tau_i)} F_C(n_a, p_a)) / T_{seq},$$
is a crude estimate of the average communication load per processor in the partitioned program. It is the ratio of the total, frequency-weighted size of all inter-task communication, to the total sequential execution time. Note that the ratio uses T_{seq} (without overhead) in the denominator, rather than $T_{total}(\Pi)$, making the ratio conservatively large.

- $T_{in}(\tau_i) := \Sigma_{(n_a, p_a) \in E_{IN}(\tau_i)} R_C(F_C(n_a, p_a), LOAD(\Pi))$, is the average input communication overhead for task τ_i.

- $T_{out}(\tau_i) := \Sigma_{(n_a, p_a) \in E_{OUT}(\tau_i)} W_C(F_C(n_a, p_a), LOAD(\Pi))$, is the average output communication overhead for task τ_i.

- $O(\tau_i) := T_{sched} + T_{in}(\tau_i) + T_{out}(\tau_i)$, is the total average overhead for task τ_i.

- $T_{total}(\Pi) := \Sigma_{1 \leq i \leq NT} Q(\tau_i) \times (T(\tau_i) + O(\tau_i))$
$= T_{seq} + \Sigma_{1 \leq i \leq NT} Q(\tau_i) \times O(\tau_i)$, is the average total execution time of all macro-actors created from the tasks in Π.

- $T_{crit}(\Pi)$ is the estimate of the critical path length of the macro-actors at run-time, using $T(\tau_i) + O(\tau_i)$ as the estimate of task τ_i's execution time (including overhead).

$T_{total}(\Pi)$ and $T_{crit}(\Pi)$ in Definition 4-5 are compile-time estimates of T_{crit} and T_{total}. Plugging them in (4.9) gives

$$max(T_{crit}(\Pi), T_{total}(\Pi)/P) \leq T_{par}(P) < 2 \times max(T_{crit}(\Pi), T_{total}(\Pi)/P) \qquad (4.10)$$

which motivates the following definition for the partition cost function:

Definition 4-6:

Let

$$F(\Pi) := max(T_{crit}(\Pi), T_{total}(\Pi)/P) / (T_{seq}/P)$$
$$= max(T_{crit}(\Pi)/(T_{seq}/P), 1 + \Sigma_{1 \leq i \leq NT} Q(\tau_i) \times O(\tau_i)/T_{seq})$$

be the cost of partition Π.

The cost function, $F(\Pi)$, is defined to be the maximum of two terms:

1. The *critical path* term, $T_{crit}(\Pi)/(T_{seq}/P)$, which is the estimated critical path length of the partitioned program, normalized to T_{seq}/P, the "ideal" parallel execution time on P processors. The critical path term can take on any value ≥ 0.

2. The *overhead* term, $1 + \Sigma_{1 \leq i \leq NT} Q(\tau_i) \times O(\tau_i)/T_{seq}$, which equals 1 plus the estimated total overhead in the program, normalized to T_{seq}. The overhead term will always be ≥ 1, because of the + 1 term in its definition. Therefore, $F(\Pi)$ will also always be ≥ 1.

$F(\Pi)$ in Definition 4-6 nicely expresses the trade-off between parallelism and overhead. If the partition is too fine, the overhead term, $1 + \Sigma_{1 \leq i \leq NT} Q(\tau_i) \times O(\tau_i)$, will be large causing $F(\Pi)$ to be large. If the partition is too coarse, then $T_{crit}(\Pi)$ will be large due to loss of parallelism, causing $F(\Pi)$ to be large once again. $F(\Pi)$ is minimised at an optimal intermediate granularity.

To emphasise the difference between the *actual* values of T_{crit} and T_{total} used in (4.9), and the *estimated* values used in (4.10) and Definition 4-6, we state the following theorem.

Theorem 4-7:

$$(1 - \varepsilon) \times F(\Pi) \times (T_{seq}/P) \leq T_{par}(P) < (1 + \varepsilon) \times 2 \times F(\Pi) \times (T_{seq}/P)$$

where ε is the relative error in the compile-time estimates, $T_{total}(\Pi)$ and $T_{crit}(\Pi)$, of the run-time values T_{total} and T_{crit}:

$$(1 - \varepsilon) \times T_{crit}(\Pi) < T_{crit} < (1 + \varepsilon) \times T_{crit}(\Pi)$$
$$(1 - \varepsilon) \times T_{total}(\Pi) < T_{total} < (1 + \varepsilon) \times T_{total}(\Pi)$$

Proof: Follows directly from (4.9) and Definition 4-6.

$Q.E.D.$

From Theorem 4-7, we see that the absolute value of $F(\Pi)$ represents the factor by which $T_{par}(P)$ is away from the ideal speed-up, T_{seq}/P. By definition, $F(\Pi) \geq 1$, and we would like to make $F(\Pi)$ as close to 1 as possible. $F(\Pi) = 1$ represents the "ideal" case in which $T_{crit}(\Pi) \leq T_{seq}/P$, and there is zero overhead in the partitioned program. In this ideal case, we will get a speed-up between $P/2$ and P, since $T_{seq}/P \leq T_{par}(P) < 2 \times T_{seq}/P$ (assuming $\varepsilon=0$ in Theorem 4-7).

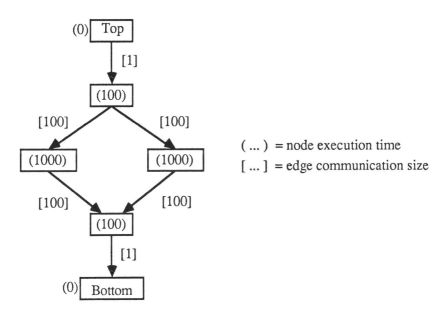

Figure 4-2: A simple GR graph

As an example of cost function usage, consider two different convex partitions of the simple GR graph shown in Figure 4-2:

1. Π_1 – the fine granularity partition which places each of the four primitive nodes in separate tasks.

2. Π_2 – the coarse granularity partition which places all four primitive nodes in the same task.

We also consider two different multiprocessor models:

1. M_1, with $T_{sched}=100$ and $R_C=W_C=0$.

2. M_2, with $T_{sched}=100$ and $R_C=W_C=10 \times size$.

We can think of M_1 as a tightly-coupled system with negligible communication overhead, and M_2 as a loosely-coupled system with significant communication overhead.

P	$F(\Pi_1)$ on M_1	$F(\Pi_2)$ on M_1	$F(\Pi_1)$ on M_2	$F(\Pi_2)$ on M_2
1	$2600/2200 \approx 1.18$	$2300/2200 \approx 1.05$	$10420/2200 \approx 4.74$	$2320/2200 \approx 1.05$
2	$1500/1100 \approx 1.36$	$2300/1100 \approx 2.09$	$7420/1100 \approx 6.75$	$2320/1100 \approx 2.11$

Figure 4-3: Sample partition cost values

Figure 4-3 displays the $F(\Pi)$ values obtained for the four possible combinations of partitions (Π_1, Π_2) and multiprocessors (M_1, M_2). For P=1, we see that the coarser partition Π_2 is better than Π_1 for both multiprocessors, consistent with the observation that the coarsest partition is optimal when there is only one processor. For P=2, Π_1 is better than Π_2 on multiprocessor M_1 which has no communication overhead, and Π_2 is better than Π_1 on multiprocessor M_1 which has large communication overhead.

An important point to remember about the cost function, $F(\Pi)$, is that a partition with the smallest $F(\Pi)$ value may not have the smallest parallel execution time. However, any optimal partition is guaranteed to have a parallel execution time which is within a factor of 2 from the optimal parallel execution time. Consider two partitions, Π_1 and Π_2, with cost function values, $F(\Pi_1) < F(\Pi_2)$, and parallel execution time values $T_{par}(\Pi_1) > T_{par}(\Pi_2)$ for some schedule of each partition on P processors. Assuming $\varepsilon=0$ in Theorem 4-7, we have

$T_{par}(\Pi_1) < 2 \times F(\Pi_1) \times T_{seq}/P$ (upper bound in Theorem 4-7)
$\Rightarrow T_{par}(\Pi_1) < 2 \times F(\Pi_2) \times T_{seq}/P$ (since $F(\Pi_1) < F(\Pi_2)$)
$\Rightarrow T_{par}(\Pi_1) < 2 \times T_{par}(\Pi_2)$ (lower bound in Theorem 4-7)

which shows why the anomaly cannot go beyond a factor of 2.

We conclude this section with a few words about the convexity constraint in Definition 4-1. The run-time scheduling model stipulated that each processor repeatedly executes the following steps:

1. Pick a "ready" macro-actor.

2. Fetch the macro-actor's inputs.

3. Execute the macro-actor.

4. Store the macro-actor's outputs.

The model implicitly assumed that a macro-actor could always uninterruptedly run to completion, once it was ready to start execution. This assumption was also necessary for the proof of Theorem 4-4.

The assumption was valid because of the convexity constraint imposed on task partitions in Definition 4-1. With the convexity constraint, all GR graph partitions are acyclic, and any task $\tau_a \in$ TP forms a *convex subgraph* of PARENT(τ_a), the GR graph containing the task. In general, a subgraph H of directed graph G is said to be *convex* [Pfaltz 77] if any path P(a,b), with a, b $\in$ H, is completely contained in H. This is analogous to convex geometrical figures which must completely contain all straight line paths between any two internal points.

Besides restricting the partitions of GR graphs, the convexity constraint also restricts the use of function call, parallel and compound nodes. If any such node contains one or more tasks, then the node itself is not allowed to belong to another task. If the node were allowed to belong to a parent task, then the parent task would have to remain suspended during the execution of the task(s) contained within the node itself. This suspension and resumption of the parent task violates the convexity constraint. Therefore, any node which contains a task must either be expanded (for compound or parallel nodes) or be in a task by itself (for parallel nodes, or function call nodes with n_u.par = true).

The convexity constraint guarantees that a macro-actor will be able to run to completion when all its inputs are available. With this constraint, our model of run-time scheduling is very similar to the dataflow model [Davis 82]. The only difference is that the dataflow model is traditionally defined at the granularity of instructions or dataflow operators. Our model of run-time scheduling is defined at the granularity of macro-actors, and can be called a *macro-dataflow* model.

In a general non-convex task partition, a macro-actor may have to start execution when some of its inputs are ready, and then wait for more inputs to become available. The run-time scheduling model for such a task partition must include a facility for *context switching* of macro-actors. In fact, the problem of scheduling and context switching macro-actors in a general partition is very much like the problem of process scheduling in a multiprocessor operating system. The major activities of the process scheduler in an operating system are typically:

1. Assign a new process to a processor based on some heuristic evaluation of the processor assignment. The operating system may continually need to perform some *load balancing* by *migrating* processes from busy processors to idle processors. Process migration can be very expensive

due to the amount of process state which has to be moved from one processor's local memory to the other processor's local memory. The cost is usually unacceptably high on loosely coupled, message-passing multiprocessors.

2. Perform a uniprocessor-like preemptive scheduling of processes on each processor, by context switching processes as necessary. A process waiting for a synchronisation event or a message will be held in a *wait* state till the corresponding event occurs. A process cannot be allowed to *busy-wait* indefinitely, since it could lead to deadlock in the system.

How can we compare the performance of convex partitions and general partitions? If we assume that the overhead of context switching and process migration is negligible, then a general partition can certainly be no worse than a convex partition. In fact, we could expect the convex partition to be worse, if the convexity constraint causes a noticeable loss of parallelism in the partitioned program. Neglecting the overhead of context switching and process migration is probably reasonable when scheduling a continuous stream of newly-created *independent* processes, since context switching is only necessary for timesharing (as in uniprocessors) and not for synchronisation, and since new processes can be assigned to idle processors obviating the need for process migration. The situation is less clear for *dependent* processes, and in particular, for the case when all processes belong to the same program. Suppose there are initially 100 processes, from the same program, to be scheduled on 10 processors. It is possible that, after some initialisations, most of the work in the program is done by 10 processes which were unfortunately assigned to the same processor. So, either the program is forced to execute entirely on 1 processor with 9 idle processors in the system, or the process scheduler must incur a large overhead in dynamically trying to maintain a balanced load on all processors. However, if the processes came from a convex partition, then the 10 major processes cannot be assigned to the same processor, since a processor only executes one process at a time.

The main advantages of the convexity constraint is its automatic load balancing, and the fact that the scheduling overhead incurred for the entire execution of a macro-actor is a bounded, one-time charge. The potential disadvantage is that the convexity restriction on task partitions may involve a significant loss of parallelism. We need to compare the performance of convex and general partitions of real programs, to observe whether the convexity constraint is a serious restriction. Looking at some SISAL benchmark programs (see Appendix A), it is clear that shortage of parallelism is not an issue. The real issue is achieving the right trade-off between parallelism and overhead. The partition cost function, $F(\Pi)$, keeps track of this trade-off so that the partitioning algorithm recognises when loss of parallelism outweighs the benefit of reduced overhead. For programs with lots of parallelism, it is unlikely that the loss of parallelism (if any) due to the convexity constraint will be a serious problem.

4.2. The Partitioning Problem

In this section, we examine the complexity of finding a partition $\Pi(g) = (PN, TP)$, with the smallest $F(\Pi)$.

Definition 4-8: The MACRO-DATAFLOW PARTITION problem, posed as a decision problem in yes-no form, is specified as:

INSTANCE: A GR graph g, a multiprocessor model M and a cost bound $CB \in Q_0^+$.

QUESTION: Is there a convex partition $\Pi(g)$ of GR graph g for multiprocessor M, with $F(\Pi) \leq CB$?

Definition 4-9: The 3-PARTITION problem is specified as [Garey 79]:

INSTANCE: Set A of 3m elements, a bound $B \in Z^+$, and a size $s(\dot{a}) \in Z^+$ for each $a_j \in A$ $(1 \leq j \leq 3m)$ such that $B/4 < s(a_j) < B/2$ and such that $\Sigma_{a_j \in A} s(a_j) = mB$.

QUESTION: Can A be partitioned into m disjoint sets $A_1, A_2, ..., A_m$ such that, for $1 \leq i \leq m$, $\Sigma_{a \in A_i} s(a) = B$ (note that each A_i must therefore contain exactly three elements from A)?

Theorem 4-10: The MACRO-DATAFLOW PARTITION problem is NP-complete in the strong sense.
Proof: It is easy to see that the problem is in NP, since a nondeterministic algorithm need only guess a partition $\Pi(g)$, evaluate $F(\Pi)$ in polynomial time and thus check in polynomial time if $F(\Pi) \leq CB$.

We now give a *pseudo-polynomial transformation* from the 3-PARTITION problem to the MACRO-DATAFLOW PARTITION problem. Consider an arbitrary instance of 3-PARTITION (Definition 4-9). The corresponding instance of MACRO-DATAFLOW PARTITION is given by

1. A GR graph $G = (N, T, \bot, E_C, F_C, F_T)$ with

   - $N := A \cup \{T, \bot\}$, where A is the set of elements in 3-PARTITION.

   - $E_C := \{(T, 1, a_j, 1)|a_j \in A\} \cup \{(a_j, 1, \bot, j)|a_j \in A\} \cup \{(T, 2, \bot, 3m+1)\}$, contains only the required precedence constraints that T precede all other nodes and $\bot$ follow all other nodes[11]. E_C does not impose any precedence constraints on the nodes corresponding to elements of A.

   - $F_C(n_a, p_a) := 0 \; \forall \; (n_a, p_a, n_b, p_b) \in E_C$.

   - F_T is defined as

     - $F_T(a_j) := s(a_j)$, if $a_j \in A$.

     - $F_T(T) := 0, F_T(\bot) := 0$.

     - $F_T(G) := \Sigma_{a_j \in A} s(a_j)$.

2. A multiprocessor model, $M = (P, R_C, W_C, D_C, F_S, T_{sched})$ with

   - $P = m$.

   - $R_C(s, l) = W_C(s, l) = 0, \forall \; s, l$, since all communication sizes in F_C are zero anyway.

   - The simple node execution time cost function F_S is the same as F_T for all simple nodes in G.

   - $T_{sched} = B$.

3. A cost bound CB = 2.

Thus each element in the 3-PARTITION problem corresponds to a simple node in the GR graph G, with an execution time equal to the size of the element.

This transformation can be performed in time polynomial in the input length of 3-PARTITION. Further, the length of the constructed MACRO-DATAFLOW PARTITION instance is polynomially related to the length of the 3-PARTITION instance, and the largest (cost) number in the MACRO-DATAFLOW PARTITION instance is the same as the largest number in the 3-PARTITION instance. With these conditions satisfied, all that remains in the proof of strong NP-completeness is to show that the 3-PARTITION instance (with A, B, $s(a_j)$) is a solution if and only if the MACRO-DATAFLOW PARTITION instance (with G, M, CB) is a solution.

Consider any convex partition $\Pi(G) = (PN, TP)$ on GR graph G in the constructed instance of MACRO-DATAFLOW PARTITION. All nodes in G

---

[11] $\{(T, 2, \bot, 3m+1)\}$ was added to E_C for the special case when $(m = 0) \wedge (A = \varnothing)$.

are simple nodes, so the primitive nodes must be $PN = N - \{T, \bot\} = A$. Let the task partition on PN be $TP = \{\tau_1, \tau_2, ..., \tau_{NT}\}$. Then the values introduced in Definition 4-5 are given by (for each $\tau_i \in TP$):

- $T_{seq} = F_T(G) = \Sigma_{a_j \in A} s(a_j) = m \times B$.
- $T(\tau_i) = \Sigma_{n \in \tau_i} F_T(n) = \Sigma_{n \in \tau_i} s(n)$.
- $Q(\tau_i) = 1$, since G has no subgraphs due to parallel or compound nodes.
- $T_{in}(\tau_i) = T_{out}(\tau_i) = 0$, since R_C and W_C are zero valued functions.
- $O(\tau_i) = T_{sched} + T_{in}(\tau_i) + T_{out}(\tau_i) = B$.
- $T_{total}(\Pi) = T_{seq} + NT \times T_{sched} = m \times B + NT \times B$.
- $T_{crit}(\Pi) = max(\{T(\tau_i) + T_{sched}\}) = max(\{\Sigma_{n \in \tau_i} s(n)\}) + B$, since there are no inter-task dependences.
- $F(\Pi) = max(T_{crit}(\Pi) \times P/T_{seq}, 1 + \Sigma_{1 \leq i \leq NT} Q(\tau_i) \times O(\tau_i)/T_{seq})$
  $= max((max(\{T(\tau_i)\}) + B) \times m/(m \times B), 1 + NT \times B/(m \times B))$
  $\Rightarrow F(\Pi) = 1 + max(max(\{\Sigma_{n \in \tau_i} s(n)\}) / B, NT / m)$ (4.11)

Using Equation (4.11), we have

$F(\Pi) \leq 2$ (4.12)

$\Leftrightarrow (NT \leq m) \wedge (\Sigma_{n \in \tau_i} s(n) \leq B) \ \forall \ 1 \leq i \leq NT$ (4.13)

But $NT < m$ in (4.13) implies that there must be at least one task τ_i with more than 3 nodes, which in turn implies that $\Sigma_{n \in \tau_i} s(n) > B$, contradicting (4.13).

$\therefore$ (4.13) $\Rightarrow NT = m$ (4.14)

Also

(4.13) $\Rightarrow \Sigma_{n \in \tau_i} s(n) = B \ \forall \ \tau_i \in TP$ (4.15)

otherwise

$\Sigma_{\tau_i \in TP} \Sigma_{n \in \tau_i} s(n) < m \times B,$

which contradicts

$\Sigma_{\tau_i \in TP} T(\tau_i) = T_{seq} = m \times B.$

Combining (4.14) and (4.15), we have

(4.13) $\Rightarrow (NT = m) \wedge (\Sigma_{n \in \tau_i} s(n) = B) \ \forall \ \tau_i \in TP$ (4.16)

The converse of (4.16) is trivially seen to be true, so the one-way implication ($\Rightarrow$) in (4.16) can be replaced by an equivalence ($\Leftrightarrow$), and then combined with the equivalence (4.12) $\Leftrightarrow$ (4.13) to give

$$F(\Pi) \leq 2 \Leftrightarrow (NT = m) \wedge (\textstyle\sum_{n \in \tau_i} s(n) = B) \; \forall \; \tau_i \in TP \qquad (4.17)$$

With (4.17), all the conditions are satisfied for a pseudo-polynomial transformation from 3-PARTITION to MACRO-DATAFLOW PARTITION. Since 3-PARTITION is NP-complete in the strong sense, we have proved that MACRO-DATAFLOW PARTITION is NP-complete in the strong sense as well.

Q. E. D.

Theorem 4-10 shows that a pseudo-polynomial time algorithm cannot exist for MACRO-DATAFLOW PARTITION unless P=NP. Any algorithm designed to solve MACRO-DATAFLOW PARTITION will take super-polynomial time in the size of the input (unless P=NP), even if the largest cost number is bounded by a polynomial in the length of the instance. Since typical GR graphs contain 100-10,000 nodes and edges, a super-polynomial algorithm is intractable.

We now investigate the *minimisation* problem for solution value $F(\Pi)$ corresponding to the MACRO-DATAFLOW PARTITION decision problem. Define $F(\Pi)|_{opt}$ to be the optimal (minimum) solution value over all possible candidate solutions, Π. Our goal is to find an efficient (up to $O(n^3)$, say) approximation algorithm which produces a partition with a $F(\Pi)$ value "close" to $F(\Pi)|_{opt}$. Let $PR := F(\Pi)/F(\Pi)|_{opt}$ be the *performance ratio* for partition Π produced by the approximation algorithm. We see that

$$F(\Pi) \geq 1 \Rightarrow F(\Pi)|_{opt} \geq 1 \Rightarrow PR \leq F(\Pi)$$

The value of $F(\Pi)$ directly gives an upper bound for PR, so a sufficiently small value of $F(\Pi)$ (e.g. 2 or 1.1) has a performance ratio which is at least as small. In the next section, we present an approximation algorithm for the $F(\Pi)$ minimisation problem.

The remainder of this section is devoted to special cases of the MACRO-DATAFLOW PARTITION problem. We discuss all known special cases for completeness, even though some of them are trivial. Various characteristics of execution times, overhead and precedence/communication edges are represented by a 4-field problem classification $\alpha|\beta|\gamma|\delta$, where

1. $\alpha \in \{1, \infty\}$ indicates constraints on node execution times and graph frequencies.

   - $\alpha = 1$: Each simple node has unit execution time and each GR graph has unit frequency.

- $\alpha = \infty$: General case.

2. $\beta \in \{0, \infty\}$ describes the scheduling overhead.
   - $\beta = 0$: Zero scheduling overhead ($T_{sched} = 0$).
   - $\beta = \infty$: General case.

3. $\gamma \in \{empty, seq, prec\}$ indicates the structure of $\leq^*$.
   - $\gamma = empty$: The GR graph contains only simple nodes with no communication edges, except for the required edges connected to $\top$ and $\bot$.
   - $\gamma = seq$: Sequential case. The precedence constraints in each GR graph is a total order and there are no parallel nodes.
   - $\gamma = prec$: General case.

4. $\delta \in \{0, \infty\}$ indicates constraints on communication edges.
   - $\delta = 0$: All communication edges have zero size and incur zero overhead.
   - $\delta = \infty$: General case.

$\infty|0|prec|0$

In this case, both scheduling and communication incur zero overhead so that $O(\tau_i) = 0, \forall \ \tau_i \in TP$. Therefore $F(\Pi) = max(T_{crit}(\Pi) \times P/T_{seq}, 1)$ and the finest granularity partition is optimal. A coarser granularity partition cannot possibly have a smaller value of $T_{crit}(\Pi)$ since it does not have any more parallelism or any less overhead than the finest granularity partition.

$\infty|\infty|seq|\infty$

In this case, all precedence constraints are sequential and there are no parallel nodes, so that $T_{crit}(\Pi) = T_{total}(\Pi)$. Therefore $F(\Pi) = max(T_{total}(\Pi) \times P / T_{seq}, T_{total}(\Pi) / T_{seq})$ and the coarsest granularity partition is optimal. The coarsest granularity partition has the smallest value of $T_{total}(\Pi)$ because the scheduling and communication overhead for the single task containing all nodes must be incurred by any other partition as well.

$1|\infty|empty|0$

In this case, the GR graph contains only simple nodes with unit execution times and no communication edges (except for edges due to $\top$ and $\bot$ which have zero overhead). Therefore $O(\tau_i) = T_{sched}$ and $T_{crit}(\Pi) = T_{sched} + max(\{T(\tau_i)\})$. Also, T_{seq} equals the total number of simple nodes (excluding $\top$ and $\bot$) in the GR graph, since each node has unit execution time. Any partition Π with NT tasks will have

$$F(\Pi) = max((max(\{T(\tau_i)\}) + T_{sched}) \times P / T_{seq}, 1 + NT \times T_{sched} / T_{seq})$$

We define a *balanced partition*, B(NT), with NT tasks such that

1. All NT tasks have exactly T_{seq}/NT nodes, if T_{seq} *mod* $NT = 0$.

2. $(T_{seq}$ *mod* $NT)$ tasks have $\lceil T_{seq}/NT \rceil$ nodes and the remaining tasks have $\lceil T_{seq}/NT \rceil - 1$ nodes, if T_{seq} *mod* $NT > 0$.

It is easy to see that any partition Π with NT tasks must have $F(\Pi) \geq F(B(NT))$, since $B(NT)$ has the smallest possible value of $max(\{T(\tau_i)\}) = \lceil T_{seq}/NT \rceil$ among all partitions with NT tasks. We only need to determine the optimal value of $NT = NT|_{opt}$ in the range $1 \leq NT \leq T_{seq}$ which minimises

$$F(B(NT)) = max(\ \lceil T_{seq}/NT \rceil + T_{sched}) \times P / T_{seq}, 1 + NT \times T_{sched} / T_{seq}) \quad (4.18)$$

and $B(NT|_{opt})$ will be an optimal partition. To determine $NT|_{opt}$, we first find an approximate solution, NT', by ignoring the ceiling function ($\lceil\ \rceil$) in (4.18), and instead minimising the following expression:

$$F(B(NT)) = max(\ (T_{seq}/NT + T_{sched}) \times P / T_{seq}, 1 + NT \times T_{sched} / T_{seq}) \quad (4.19)$$

As NT increases from 1 to T_{seq}, the *max* function's first argument monotonically decreases from $(T_{seq}+T_{sched}) \times P/T_{seq}$ to $(1+T_{sched}) \times P/T_{seq}$ (due to T_{seq}/NT), and the second argument monotonically increases from $1 + T_{sched}/T_{seq}$ to $1 + T_{sched}$ (due to $NT \times T_{sched}$). Therefore, the *max* function in (4.19) is minimised by equating the two arguments:

$$(T_{seq}/NT' + T_{sched}) \times P / T_{seq} = 1 + NT' \times T_{sched} / T_{seq}$$
$$\Rightarrow NT' = P$$

It is easy to verify that NT' = P is the solution to the above equation. This result seems intuitive as well, since we would expect the optimal partition to have P tasks for P processors, when there is no communication among the nodes[12].

While NT = P will always give an optimal parallel execution time for independent, unit execution time nodes on P processors, NT = P does not always minimise the partition cost function, $F(B(NT))$. This is because we ignored the ceiling function in $F(\Pi)$ when deriving NT' = P. The only $F(B(NT))$ value which may be smaller than $F(B(NT'))$ occurs when the $\lceil T_{seq}/NT \rceil$ drops to its next lower value as NT increases beyond NT'. Let NT" > NT' be the smallest NT value to have $\lceil T_{seq}/NT'' \rceil < \lceil T_{seq}/NT' \rceil$. Then

$$T_{seq}/NT'' \leq \lceil T_{seq}/NT' \rceil - 1$$

must be true, so that

---

[12]This is true even if the scheduling overhead, T_{sched}, is arbitrarily large. Our model assumes that every task incurs the same scheduling overhead, even if the entire program is contained within a single task.

$$NT'' \geq T_{seq}/(\lceil T_{seq}/NT' \rceil - 1) \tag{4.20}$$

The smallest NT'' to satisfy (4.20) will be (substitute NT' = P also)

$$NT'' = \lceil T_{seq} / (\lceil T_{seq}/P \rceil - 1) \rceil \tag{4.21}$$

Therefore, $NT|_{opt}$ is determined by evaluating F(B(NT)) at NT=NT'=P, and NT=NT'' from equation (4.21), and choosing the NT value which gives the smallest F(B(NT)).

As an example of when F(B(NT'')) is smaller than F(B(P)), consider

- $T_{seq} = 100$, $T_{sched} = 5$, $P = 9$
- $F(B(P=9)) = max(17/(100/9), 1 + 9 \times 5/100) = max(1.53, 1.45) = 1.53$
- $F(B(NT''=10)) = max(15/(100/9), 1 + 10 \times 5/100) = max(1.35, 1.5) = 1.5$

If $NT|_{opt} = NT'' > P$ is the optimal value for F(B(NT)), the partition, $B(NT|_{opt})$, will not usually have an optimal parallel execution time even though it minimises the cost function. As discussed earlier, this kind of anomaly is always possible. However, our guarantee is that the parallel execution time of an optimal partition will not be more than a factor of 2 away from the optimal parallel execution time obtained by any partition.

∞|∞|*empty*|0

This is an extension of the previous case by allowing arbitrary node execution times. The problem is now NP-complete in the strong sense; in fact the proof of Theorem 4-10 just used this restricted case to show that MACRO-DATAFLOW PARTITION is NP-complete in the strong sense. For partition Π with NT tasks τ_1, ..., τ_{NT}, the cost function becomes

$$F(\Pi) = max((max(\{T(\tau_i)\}) + T_{sched}) \times P / T_{seq}, 1 + NT \times T_{sched} / T_{seq})$$

If we restrict the problem to finding the optimal partition for a given value of NT (e.g. NT=P), then it becomes exactly the problem of multiprocessor scheduling with no precedence constraints on NT processors. Several approximation algorithms have been designed for this problem [Graham 79]. For example, a list scheduling algorithm which schedules nodes in LPT (largest processing time first) order has a guaranteed performance bound of 4/3, giving $F(\Pi) < F(\Pi)|_{opt} \times 4 / 3$.

4.3. Partitioning Algorithm

As discussed in the previous section, the problem of building a partition $\Pi(g) = (PN, TP)$, with the smallest $F(\Pi)$ is intractable. In this section, we present an approximation algorithm for the problem. Our approach is to start with an initial fine granularity partition, Π_0, and then iteratively merge tasks (chosen by heuristics) till we reach the coarsest partition, Π_n (with one task containing all nodes), after n iterations. The partition Π_{min} with the smallest $F(\Pi_i) \; \forall \; 0 \leq i \leq n$ is the selected partition for GR graph g.

Before we discuss the partitioning algorithm, let us consider the general behaviour of $F(\Pi_i)$ as i goes from 0 to n. Each partition Π_i is obtained by merging a group of tasks in the previous partition Π_{i-1}. The partition cost function $F(\Pi)$ is the *max* of two terms (Definition 4-6):

    1. The critical path term, $T_{crit}(\Pi) \times P / T_{seq}$.

    2. The overhead term, $1 + \Sigma_{\tau_i \in TP} \; Q(\tau_i) \times O(\tau_i) / T_{seq}$.

The overhead term is monotonically nonincreasing with i, since a move to a coarser granularity cannot increase the total overhead, $\Sigma_{\tau_i \in TP} \; Q(\tau_i) \times O(\tau_i)$. The critical path term is more erratic. Each critical task, τ_c, contributes $T(\tau_c) + O(\tau_c)$ to $T_{crit}(\Pi)$. As i increases, the $O(\tau_c)$ terms in critical tasks tend to decrease due to reduced overhead, but the $T(\tau_c)$ terms tend to increase due to sequentialisation.

Initially, when i = 0, the overhead term usually dominates the critical path term and determines the partition cost, $F(\Pi)$. The two terms cross over at an intermediate point, and the critical path term usually dominates the overhead term at the end when i = n. In fact, at i = n the entire program is contained within a single task, τ_1, with $T(\tau_1) = T_{seq}$, $Q(\tau_1) = 1$ and $T_{crit}(\Pi_n) = T_{seq} + O(\tau_1)$. In this case, the critical path term will be $(T_{seq} + O(\tau_1)) \times P / T_{seq}$, and the overhead term will be $(T_{seq} + O(\tau_1)) / T_{seq}$, so that $F(\Pi_n) \approx P$ if $O(\tau_1) << T_{seq}$. The lowest value of $F(\Pi_i)$ does not necessarily occur at the crossover point between the two terms, because of the non-monotonic behaviour of the critical path term.

Figure 4-4 shows this variation in $F(\Pi)$, obtained from an actual execution of our partitioning algorithm on function Conduct in the benchmark program, SIMPLE, with the following parameters:

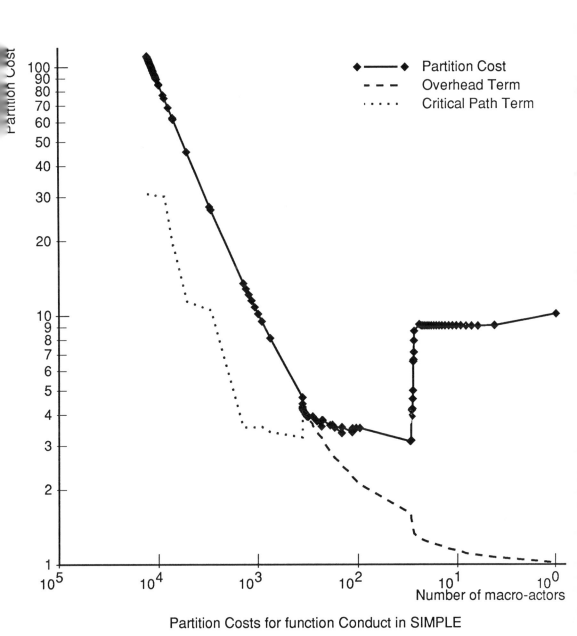

Partition Costs for function Conduct in SIMPLE

Figure 4-4: Variation in partition cost, $F(\Pi)$

- Sequential execution time, T_{seq} = 125,000 cycles.
- Number of processors, P = 10.
- Scheduling overhead, T_{sched} = 1000 cycles.
- Communication overhead functions, $R_C(size) = W_C(size) = size/8$, where *size* is in bytes and the overhead is in cycles.

The abscissa is the projected number of macro-actors, $\sum_{\tau_j \in \Pi_i} Q(\tau_j)$, and the ordinate is the partition cost, $F(\Pi)$. Each data point corresponds to an iteration in the partitioning algorithm in the range $0 \le i \le n$ (n = 104 in this case). The number of macro-actors, $\sum_{\tau_j \in \Pi_i} Q(\tau_j)$ (plotted on the x-axis), decreases from nearly 13,000 to 1 in this range. The curve plotted in dashes is the overhead term, which decreases monotonically from about 110.0 to 1.0. The dotted line is the curve for the critical path term, which varies approximately from 30.0 to 3.0 to 10.0. The partition cost values, $F(\Pi_i)$, is given by the solid line, which is the *max* of both terms. So, the solid line exactly overlaps parts of the two previous curves. In this case, the best partition Π_{min} is obtained at the 70th iteration when the number of macro-actors is $\sum_{\tau_i \in TP} Q(\tau_i)$ = 30, and the cost function value is $F(\Pi_{min})$ = 3.1. The crossover point occurred on the 52nd iteration with $\sum_{\tau_i \in TP} Q(\tau_i)$ = 316 and $F(\Pi)$ = 3.9. $F(\Pi_{min})$ = 3.1 suggests a speed-up in the range of 1.6 to 3.3 for 10 processors. The low speed-up is due to the small size of the program input used for the execution profile (see Appendix A), relative to the overhead values. This example was chosen to illustrate how the cost function behaves in general, rather than to demonstrate good speed-up values.

As discussed in the following presentation of the partitioning algorithm, the heuristic used for merging tasks in each step is to first select the task with the largest overhead, and then merge it with the task which gives the smallest increase in the critical path term. In this way, we hope to get a large reduction in the overhead term, without a significant increase in the critical path term. However, in our initial approach [Sarkar 86a], the heuristic used was to first select the task with the largest overhead (as done now), but then merge it with the task which gives the smallest increase in the cost function. After some experimentation, we discovered that minimisation of the cost function directly was a poor heuristic. When values of the overhead parameters were large, the cost of the initial fine grain partition would be much greater than the cost of the final sequential partition. By attempting to directly minimise the cost function, the partitioning algorithm would show an affinity for the trivial, sequential partition, which appeared to have a relatively low cost function value. Instead, by using the critical path heuristic as presented here, the partitioning algorithm is forced to avoid the sequential partition for as long as possible, and to step through a more promising range of intermediate partitions.

Inputs:
    1. A GR program with NF functions, PROG = { (g_1, f_1), (g_2, f_2), ..., (g_{NF}, f_{NF}) }.

Outputs:
    1. A set of partitions, { $\Pi(g_1)$, $\Pi(g_2)$, ..., $\Pi(g_{NF})$ }, one for each function.

procedure PartitionFunctions(PROG)
    1. Determine V^*, the strongly connected components (SCC's) of PROG's call graph, as in Figure 3-4, page 46. The SCC's in V^* = { v_i^* } are in a reverse topological sort order of the reduced call graph.

    2. **for each** strongly connected component $v_i^* \in V^*$ **do**
      /* Let $v_i^* = \{u_1, ..., u_k\}$ be the functions in the current SCC */
      a. **for** $j \leftarrow 1$ **to** k **do**
        /* Initialise CP and O, in case these values are needed by a recursive call in the same SCC. */
        i. $O(u_j.g) \leftarrow T_{sched} + T_{in}(u_j.g) + T_{out}(u_j.g)$
        ii. $CP(u_j.g) \leftarrow F_T(u_j.g) + O(u_j.g)$

      b. **for** $j \leftarrow 1$ **to** k **do**
        i. PN $\leftarrow$ **call** InitPrimitiveNodes($u_j.g$)

        ii. **for each** $n_a \in$ PN **do**
          1. $TP(n_a) \leftarrow id(n_a)$ /* $\tau_a = \{ n_a \}$ is a singleton task initially. */
          2. **call** SetTaskCosts(τ_a)

        iii. $\Pi_0(u_j.g) \leftarrow$ (PN, TP)

        iv. **call** PartitionGraph($u_j.g$, Π_0, O, CP)
        /* The reverse topological sort order guarantees that any function call in $u_j.g$ must be to some function $u_h \in \cup_{1 \leq i \leq j} v_i^*$. $\therefore$ $CP(u_h.g)$ and $O(u_h.g)$ are defined for all calls to function u_h contained in GR graph $u_j.g$, during PartitionGraph($u_j.g$). */
end procedure

Figure 4-5: Procedure PartitionFunctions

Procedure PartitionFunctions in Figure 4-5 outlines the algorithm used to partition all functions in a GR program. Because the O and CP values (*overhead* and *critical path* respectively) for a function call are obtained from the callee's partition, it is important to partition functions in a reverse topological sort order of the call graph.

This is exactly the approach we took when assigning execution time costs (Figure 3-4, page 46). As before, we use the strongly connected components (SCC's) of the call graph. Each iteration of step 2 processes an entire SCC. Step 2.a initialises $O(u_j.g)$ and $CP(u_j.g)$ values in case they are needed before $u_j.g$ is partitioned – this can only happen due to an internal (recursive) call to u_j. Each iteration of step 2.b processes one function (u_j) in the current SCC. Step 2.b.i calls procedure InitPrimitiveNodes (discussed later) to build PN, the set of primitive nodes for Π_0. Step 2.b.ii uses PN to build the trivial task partition TP for Π_0, and to initialise $O(\tau_a)$ and $CP(\tau_a)$. PN and TP are put together as Π_0 in step 2.b.iii. Finally, step 2.b.iv calls PartitionGraph to perform the actual partitioning algorithm.

Procedure PartitionGraph in Figure 4-6 outlines the partitioning algorithm. The algorithm takes the initial partition, $\Pi_0(g) = (PN, TP)$, as input. The issue of choosing an appropriate initial partition is addressed later. For now, we can think of Π_0 as some fine granularity partition. As mentioned earlier, the algorithm iteratively merges tasks to build successive partitions. This iteration is performed by the while loop in step 2, which terminates when no further merging is possible in the task partition, TP, i.e. when the partition is at the coarsest possible granularity. The iteration number with lowest $F(\Pi_i)$ is stored in BESTITER, so that partition Π_{min} can be reconstructed in step 3. The initial overhead and critical path length functions, O and CP, are inputs to procedure PartitionGraph. $O(\tau_i)$ gives task τ_i's total overhead. For task $\tau_i \in TP$, $CP(\tau_i) = T(\tau_i) + O(\tau_i)$ gives the total execution time. For an expanded graph or node, CP gives its estimated parallel execution time (including overhead) on an unbounded number of processors. Note that $Q(g')$, the average frequency in g of graph $g' \in {}^* g$, can be pre-computed in linear time for all expanded graphs g'. Thus $Q(\tau_a) = Q(PARENT(\tau_a))$ is directly available for any task τ_a in any partition Π_i.

The main issue in the partitioning algorithm is the choice of tasks to be merged. The task, τ_a, with the largest value of $Q(\tau_i) \times O(\tau_i)$ is chosen as the primary candidate for merging in step 2.b. This heuristic focuses on the task with the largest overhead in the hope of gaining the largest reduction in the overhead term. Steps 2.c and 2.d address special cases when there is only one way to "merge" task τ_a. Step 2.c handles the case when $\tau_a = \{ n_a \}$ is a single node. If n_a is a function call node with $n_a.par = true$, then step 2.c.ii.1 sets $n_a.par$ to *false*. This "merge" changes n_a from a parallel function call to a sequential function call, thus increasing its granularity and reducing its total

Inputs:

    1. A GR graph, $g = (N, \top, \bot, E_C, F_C, F_T)$.

    2. An initial partition, $\Pi_0(g) = (PN, TP)$.

    3. The initial overhead and critical path functions, O and CP.

Outputs:

    1. Partition $\Pi_{min}(g)$ with the smallest $F(\Pi_i)$.

procedure PartitionGraph(g, Π_0, O, CP)

    1. BESTITER $\leftarrow$ 0 ; CURITER $\leftarrow$ 0 ; BESTCOST $\leftarrow$ $F(\Pi_0)$;
       OVERHEADSUM $\leftarrow$ $\sum_{\tau_i \in TP} Q(\tau_i) \times O(\tau_i)$

    2. **while** TP has a task which can be further merged **do**

       a. CURITER $\leftarrow$ CURITER + 1 ; DONE $\leftarrow$ *false*

       b. $\tau_a \leftarrow$ task with largest $Q(\tau_i) \times O(\tau_i)$

       c. **if** $|\tau_a| = 1$ **then**
          /* τ_a is a singleton set. Let $\tau_a = \{ n_a \}$. */
          i. OLDOVERHEAD $\leftarrow$ $Q(\tau_a) \times O(\tau_a)$
          ii. **if** n_a is a function call node **then**
             1. **if** n_a.par = *true* **then**
                n_a.par $\leftarrow$ *false* ; DONE $\leftarrow$ *true* ; $\tau_{new} \leftarrow \tau_a$
          iii. **else if** n_a is a parallel node **then**
             1. **if** $2 \times n_a$.size $\leq n_a$.f **then**
                n_a.size $\leftarrow$ $2 \times n_a$.size ; DONE $\leftarrow$ *true* ; $\tau_{new} \leftarrow \tau_a$

       d. **else if** τ_a includes all nodes in PARENT(τ_a) **then**
          i. OLDOVERHEAD $\leftarrow$ $Q(\tau_a) \times O(\tau_a)$
          ii. $n_b \leftarrow$ PARENT(PARENT(τ_a)) ; PN $\leftarrow$ PN $\cup$ $\{n_b\}$ $- \tau_a$;
             TP(n_b) $\leftarrow$ *id*(n_b) ; DONE $\leftarrow$ *true* ; $\tau_{new} \leftarrow \{ n_b \}$
          iii. **if** n_b is a parallel node **then** n_b.size $\leftarrow$ 1

       e. **if** DONE = *false* **then** /* General case. */
          i. **call** SetupMerge(τ_a)
          ii. Determine τ_b with PARENT(τ_a) = PARENT(τ_b), which
             would give the smallest CP(g) at the end of step
             2.f if τ_a and τ_b were merged.
          iii. τ_{new}, OLDOVERHEAD $\leftarrow$ **call** MergeTasks(τ_a, τ_b)

       f. **call** SetTaskCosts(τ_{new}) ; $g' \leftarrow$ PARENT(τ_{new}) ;
       loop
          i. **call** SetGraphCP(g')
          ii. **if** ($g' = g$) $\vee$ (new CP(g') = old CP(g')) **then exit**
          iii. $n' \leftarrow$ PARENT(g') ; **call** SetENCP(n') ; $g' \leftarrow$ PARENT(n')
          iv. **if** new CP(n') = old CP(n') **then exit**

       g. OVERHEADSUM $\leftarrow$ OVERHEADSUM - OLDOVERHEAD + $Q(\tau_{new}) \times O(\tau_{new})$

       h. $F(\Pi_{CURITER}) \leftarrow$ *max*(CP(g)$\times P/F_T(g)$, 1 + OVERHEADSUM/$F_T(g)$)

       i. **if** $F(\Pi_{CURITER}) \leq$ BESTCOST **then**
          BESTITER $\leftarrow$ CURITER ; BESTCOST $\leftarrow$ $F(\Pi_{CURITER})$

    3. Reconstruct partition $\Pi_{BESTITER}$ as Π_{min}.

Figure 4-6: Procedure PartitionGraph

overhead. If n_a is a parallel node, then step 2.c.iii.1 attempts to double the size of n_a's macro-actors, $n_a.size$, provided the new $n_a.size$ does not exceed the number of iterations, $n_a.f$. This "merge" increases the granularity of n_a's macro-actors. Step 2.d handles the case when τ_a contains all the nodes (except top and bottom) in the graph PARENT(τ_a). The only way to "merge" τ_a in this case is to replace it by a task consisting of PARENT(PARENT(τ_a)), which is the expanded parallel or compound node containing τ_a.

Step 2.e handles the general case, where a second task τ_b is chosen to be merged with τ_a. The call to procedure SetupMerge in step 2.e.i pre-computes LOCALTP and PATH so that they do not need to be computed for every candidate task, τ_b. Step 2.e.ii only considers tasks in the same graph as τ_a (i.e. PARENT(τ_a) = PARENT(τ_b)) as candidates for merging. The task τ_b which yields the smallest value of CP(g) (or $T_{crit}(\Pi)$) is chosen for the merge. Thus τ_a was chosen to minimise the overhead term and τ_b is chosen to minimise the critical path term in F(Π). Steps 2.e.iii and 2.f are then performed to merge tasks τ_a and τ_b and to update the overhead and critical path values, O and CP. The critical path length of the new partition is given by CP(g) at the end of step 2.f. Step 2.e.ii chooses τ_b so that CP(g) will be minimised at the end of step 2.f. For the sake of brevity, we omitted a detailed description of step 2.e.ii, since steps 2.e.iii and 2.f make clear what needs to be done.

The merging of tasks τ_a and τ_b is performed by calling procedure MergeTasks in step 2.e.iii. The convexity constraint requires that all tasks in the convex hull of τ_a and τ_b be included in the new merged task, τ_{new}, so that τ_{new} forms a convex subgraph of PARENT(τ_{new}). Otherwise, a cycle could be introduced in the task partition. O(τ_{new}) and CP(τ_{new}) are set by the call to procedure SetTaskCosts in step 2.f. The CP values of enclosing graphs and nodes are then set by the loop in step 2.f. The loop exits if a new CP value is the same as the old one or if it reaches graph g at the outermost level. The new overhead sum, $\sum_{\tau_i \in TP} Q(\tau_i) \times O(\tau_i)$, is computed in step 2.g by incrementally updating the old overhead sum. Finally, step 2.h evaluates the cost of the new partition, F($\Pi_{CURITER}$), and step 2.i compares the new partition with the best partition seen so far.

Figure 4-7 contains procedures SetupMerge and MergeTasks. Procedure SetupMerge initialises LOCALTP and PATH for use in procedure MergeTasks. Steps

procedure SetupMerge (τ_a)
Inputs:
    1. Task $\tau_a \in$ TP, the primary candidate for merging.
Outputs:
    1. Procedure SetupMerge initialises LOCALTP and PATH for use by
       procedure MergeTasks, so that LOCALTP and PATH do not have to
       be recomputed for each candidate τ_b considered in step 2.e.ii.
begin
    1. $g = (N, \top, \bot, E_C, F_C, F_T) \leftarrow$ PARENT (τ_a)
    2. **for each** $n \in N - \{\top, \bot\}$ **do**
       /* Determine the local task partition, LOCALTP. */
        a. **if** $n \in$ PN **then** LOCALTP $(n) \leftarrow$ TP (n)

        b. **else** LOCALTP $(n) \leftarrow id(n)$
          /* LOCALTP places n in a local task by itself. n must be
          an expanded parallel or compound node. */
    3. PREC $\leftarrow$ { (LOCALTP (n_a), LOCALTP (n_b)) $|n_a,$ $n_b \in$ N-$\{\top, \bot\}$ $\wedge$
      LOCALTP $(n_a) \neq$ LOCALTP $(n_b) \wedge (n_a, p_a, n_b, p_b) \in E_C\}$
      /* The convexity constraint ensures that PREC is acyclic. */
    4. **for each** local task $\tau_i \in$ LOCALTP **do**
        a. PATH $(\tau_i) \leftarrow$ { τ_j | $\tau_j \in$ LOCALTP $\wedge \exists$ a path from τ_i to τ_j in
          PREC }
          /* PATH (τ_i) is the set of local tasks reachable from τ_i in
          PREC. We assume that $\tau_i \in$ PATH (τ_i). */
end procedure

procedure MergeTasks (τ_a, τ_b)
Inputs:
    1. Tasks $\tau_a, \tau_b \in$ TP with PARENT (τ_a) = PARENT (τ_b).
Outputs:
    1. τ_{new}, the new task which replaces τ_a, τ_b and all other tasks in
       their convex hull.
    2. OLDOVERHEAD $\in Q_0^+$, the overhead sum for the group of tasks
       replaced by τ_{new}.
begin
    1. $\tau_{new} \leftarrow \emptyset$; OLDOVERHEAD $\leftarrow$ 0
    2. **for each** local task $\tau_i \in$ LOCALTP **do**
        a. **if** $(\tau_i \in$ PATH $(\tau_a) \vee \tau_i \in$ PATH $(\tau_b)) \wedge (\tau_a \in$ PATH $(\tau_i) \vee \tau_b \in$ PATH $(\tau_i))$
         then
         /* τ_i is in the convex hull of τ_a and τ_b. Add τ_i to τ_{new}.
         */
           i. $\tau_{new} \leftarrow \tau_{new} \cup \tau_i$
           ii. OLDOVERHEAD $\leftarrow$ OLDOVERHEAD + $Q(\tau_i) \times O(\tau_i)$
end procedure

Figure 4-7: Procedures SetupMerge and MergeTasks

1, 2 and 3 take $O(|g|)$ time, but step 4 takes a total of $O(|g|^2)$ time. Step 4.a computes $PATH(\tau_i)$, the set of local tasks reachable from τ_i in PREC. This can be done in $O(|g|)$ time by performing a depth-first search [Tarjan 72] in PREC, starting at τ_i. Therefore step 4's total execution time is $O(|g|^2)$. Procedure MergeTasks uses LOCALTP and PATH to build τ_{new} in linear time. Though Figure 4-6 shows only one call to MergeTasks in step 2.e.iii, MergeTasks will in fact be performed $O(|g|)$ times in step 2.e.ii to choose the best τ_b, and the original task partition must be restored after each such call. These details were omitted in step 2.e.ii of PartitionGraph, for the sake of brevity.

Inputs:
   1. Task $\tau_a \in$ TP.

Outputs:
   1. Procedure SetTaskCosts sets $O(\tau_a)$ and $CP(\tau_a)$.

procedure SetTaskCosts (τ_a)
   1. **if** $\tau_a = \{n_a\} \wedge n_a$ is a function call node $\wedge$ n_a.par = *true* **then**
      /* τ_a is a singleton set containing a parallel function call
      node. Get O and CP values from the callee's graph, $g_{n.u}$. */
      a. $O(\tau_a) \leftarrow O(g_{n.u})$
      b. $CP(\tau_a) \leftarrow CP(g_{n.u})$
   2. **else if** $(\tau_a = \{n_a\}) \wedge (n_a$ is a parallel node) **then**
      /* τ_a is a singleton set containing a parallel node. Use
      n_a.size to determine $O(\tau_a)$ and $CP(\tau_a)$. */
      a. $T_{in}(\tau_a) \leftarrow \sum_{(n_b,p_b)\in IN_{partial}(n_a)} R_C(F_C(n_b,p_b)) \times n_a.size/n_a.f +$
         $\sum_{(n_b,p_b)\in IN(n_a)-IN_{partial}(n_a)} R_C(F_C(n_b,p_b))$
      b. $T_{out}(\tau_a) \leftarrow \sum_{(n_b,p_b)\in OUT_{partial}(n_a)} R_C(F_C(n_b,p_b)) \times n_a.size/n_a.f +$
         $\sum_{(n_b,p_b)\in OUT(n_a)-OUT_{partial}(n_a)} R_C(F_C(n_b,p_b))$
      c. $O(\tau_a) \leftarrow T_{sched} + T_{in}(\tau_a) + T_{out}(\tau_a)$
      d. $CP(\tau_a) \leftarrow n_a.size \times F_T(n_a.g) + O(\tau_a)$
   3. **else**
      a. $O(\tau_a) \leftarrow T_{sched} + T_{in}(\tau_a) + T_{out}(\tau_a)$
      b. $CP(\tau_a) \leftarrow \sum_{n\in\tau_a} F_T(n) + O(\tau_a)$
end procedure

Figure 4-8: Procedure SetTaskCosts

Figure 4-8 outlines procedure SetTaskCosts, which is called in step 2.f of procedure PartitionGraph. SetTaskCosts computes $O(\tau_a)$ and $CP(\tau_a)$, the overhead and critical path length of task τ_a respectively. The general case is handled in step 3. Step 1 checks for a singleton task containing a parallel function call node. The O and CP values are given by the callee's graph in this case. Step 2 checks for a singleton parallel node n_a, where n_a.size determines the O and CP values. The sets $IN_{partial}(n_a)$ and $OUT_{partial}(n_a)$ are used to obtain more accurate estimates of $T_{in}(\tau_a)$ and $T_{out}(\tau_a)$ for a parallel node, and are defined as:

- $IN(n_a) := \{ (n_b, p_b) \mid (n_b, p_b, n_a, p_a) \in E_C \}$ is the set of port values required as inputs to n_a.

- $OUT(n_a) := \{ p_a \mid (n_a, p_a, n_b, p_b) \in E_C \}$ is the set of n_a's output ports.

- $IN_{partial}(n_a) := \{ (n_b, p_b) \mid (n_b, p_b) \in IN(n_a) \wedge$ each iteration in n_a only needs $1/n_a.f^{th}$ the size of the value produced at $(n_b, p_b)\}$.

- $OUT_{partial}(n_a) := \{ p_a \mid p_a \in OUT(n_a) \wedge$ each iteration in n_a only produces $1/n_a.f^{th}$ the output size of the value produced at $(n_a, p_a)\}$.

Figure 4-9 contains procedures SetGraphCP and SetENCP, which are called to update CP values for all ancestors of task τ_{new} in step 2.f of procedure PartitionGraph. Procedure SetGraphCP(g) determines CP(g) by building the local task partition and evaluating its critical path length. Procedure SetENCP(n) determines CP(n) from the CP values of n's subgraphs. CP(n) = CP(n.g) for a parallel node, since all of n's iterations can be done in parallel. For a compound node, CP(n) is the weighted sum of $CP(n.g_i)$, since the subgraphs are executed in a sequential order.

A rudimentary worst case execution time analysis of the partitioning algorithm in procedure PartitionGraph (Figure 4-6) now follows. We first show that the while loop in step 2 has $O(|TP_0| + |EN_0|)$ iterations, where $|TP_0|$ and $|EN_0|$ are respectively the number of tasks and expanded nodes in the initial partition, Π_0. Steps i, ii and iii in 2.e are executed at most $|TP_0|$ times, since $|TP| = |TP_0|$ initially and each execution reduces the value of $|TP|$ till the while loop terminates with $|TP| = 1$. If i, ii and iii in 2.e are not executed, then DONE must have been set to *true* in an earlier step. 2.c.ii.1 sets DONE to *true* at most $|TP_0|$ times, since each execution makes $n_a.par = false$, which can be done at most once for each task in Π_0. 2.c.iii.1 sets DONE to *true* at most $(|TP_0| + |EN_0|) \times log_2(f_{max})$ times, where f_{max} is the largest frequency value among all *parallel* nodes contained in g. The $log_2(f_{max})$ factor is due to the doubling of the macro-actor size, performed each time step 2.c.iii.1 is executed. This is the only algorithm in which the execution time depends on a frequency value; all other algorithms have execution times which depend only on the size of the GR graph and, possibly, on the number of processors in the target multiprocessor. However, since the

```
procedure SetGraphCP(g)
Inputs:
    1. A GR graph, g = (N, T, ⊥, E_C, F_C, F_T).
Outputs:
    1. Procedure SetGraphCP sets the value of CP(g), using the CP
       values of all tasks and expanded nodes in N.
begin
    1. for each n ∈ N - {T, ⊥} do
       /* Determine the local task partition, LOCALTP. */

       a. if n ∈ PN then LOCALTP(n) ← TP(n)

       b. else LOCALTP(n) ← id(n)
          /* LOCALTP places n in a local task by itself.  n must be
          an expanded parallel or compound node. */

    2. PREC ← { (LOCALTP(n_a), LOCALTP(n_b)) | n_a, n_b ∈ N-{T, ⊥} ∧
       LOCALTP(n_a) ≠ LOCALTP(n_b) ∧ (n_a, p_a, n_b, p_b) ∈ E_C}
       /* The convexity constraint ensures that PREC is acyclic. */

    3. LIST ← topological sort of PREC
       /* LIST = (t_1, ..., t_k) is a sequence of local tasks in an order
       consistent with PREC. */

    4. for j ← 1 to k do
       a. START(t_j) ← max({ 0 } ∪ { START(t_i) + CP(t_i) | (i, j) ∈
          PREC })

    5. CP(g) ← max({ 0 } ∪ { START(t_i) + CP(t_i) | 1 ≤ i ≤ k })
end procedure


procedure SetENCP(n)
Inputs:
    1. n, an expanded node (parallel or compound)
Outputs:
    1. Procedure SetENCP sets the value of CP(n), using the CP values
       of n's subgraphs.
begin
    1. if n is a parallel node then
       a. CP(n) ← CP(n.g)

    2. else
       /* n is a compound node with n.s = { (g_1,f_1), (g_2,f_2), ...,
       (g_k,f_k) } */
       a. CP(n) ← Σ_{1≤i≤k} f_i × CP(n.g_i)
end procedure
```

Figure 4-9: Procedures SetGraphCP and SetENCP

dependence is logarithmic, we just consider the $\log_2(f_{max})$ factor to be a constant (e.g. $f_{max} \leq 1000 \Rightarrow \log_2(f_{max}) \leq 10$).

Step 2.d.ii sets DONE to *true* exactly $|EN_0|$ times since each execution makes some $n_b \in EN_0$ a primitive node, and all nodes in EN_0 must become primitive for the while loop to terminate with $|TP| = 1$. Combining the executions of steps 2.c.ii.1, 2.c.iii.1,

2.d.ii and 2.e, we see that the while loop in step 2 has $O(|TP_0| + |EN_0|)$ iterations. We also observe that $|TP|$ is monotonically nonincreasing from $|TP_0|$ to 1, and only stays the same when DONE is set to *true* in 2.c.ii.1, 2.c.iii.1 or 2.d.ii.

2.b, 2.e and 2.f are the only steps which do not take constant time for a single iteration of the while loop. Step 2.b takes $O(\log |TP_0|)$ time if we store the $Q(\tau_i) \times O(\tau_i)$ values as a *heap* [Floyd 64]. The heap will have a total of $O(|TP_0| + |EN_0|)$ insertions and deletions, each of which takes $O(\log |TP_0|)$ time, giving an amortised cost of $O(\log |TP_0|)$ per iteration.

Step 2.e.i takes $O(|PARENT(\tau_a)|^2)$ time and step 2.e.iii takes $O(|PARENT(\tau_a)|)$ time, based on our earlier discussions of procedures SetupMerge and MergeTasks. The call to procedure SetTaskCosts in 2.f also takes $O(|PARENT(\tau_a)|)$ time, whereas the loop takes $O(\sum_{\tau_a \in *g'} |g'|)$ time for all graphs g' which enclose τ_a. Step 2.e.ii effectively executes steps 2.e.iii and 2.f $O(|PARENT(\tau_a)|)$ times to choose τ_b. Therefore steps 2.e and 2.f have an execution time of $O(H \times |g'|^2)$, where $|g'|$ is the size of the largest expanded graph in Π_0 and H is the average number of iterations in the loop in 2.f. In the worst case, H is the height of the graph structure tree rooted at g.

So the entire partitioning algorithm has $O((|TP_0|+|EN_0|) \times (\log |TP_0| + H \times |g'|^2)) = O(\|g\| \times (\log\|g'\| + H \times |g'|^2))$ execution time. Depending on the graph structure, the execution time falls between $O(\|g\| \log \|g\|)$ and $O(\|g\|^3)$. The execution time will be $O(\|g\|^3)$ if g has no subgraphs (i.e. $|g'| = \|g\|$ and H = 1). Instead, if g has several subgraphs of constant size and has height H = $O(\log \|g\|)$, then the execution time will be $O(\|g\| \log \|g\|)$. H can vary from $O(1)$ to $O(\|g\|)$, depending on the graph structure. Figure 6-3 in the Conclusions chapter presents actual execution time data for the prototype implementation. It suggests that the execution time for the macro-dataflow partitioning algorithm is approximately $O(\|g\|^{1.2})$ in practise.

The last issue to be settled in the partitioning algorithm is the choice of the initial partition, $\Pi_0(g) = (PN, TP)$. Ideally, we would like to use the finest granularity partition as the initial partition, so as to get the widest range of merging choices in the partitioning algorithm. However, for large programs, the super-linear execution time of the partitioning algorithm will make it expensive to start at the finest granularity. We want the initial set of primitive nodes to be large enough to expose sufficient parallelism, but small enough so that the execution time of procedure PartitionGraph does not become intractable.

Inputs:
> 1. A GR graph g' = (N', T', ⊥', E_C', F_C', F_T') contained within GR graph g.

Outputs:
> 1. Procedure InitPrimitiveNodes adds new primitive nodes to the set, PN, for use in the initial partition, Π_0(g).

```
procedure InitPrimitiveNodes(g')
begin
for each node n' ∈ N' do
    1. if F_T'(n') < T_min then
       /* Don't expand n' further. */
         a. PN ← PN ∪ { n' } /* Add n' to PN. */

         b. if n' is a function call node then n'.par ← false

         c. else if n' is a parallel node then n'.size ← ⌈ n'.f ⌉

    2. else if n' is a simple node then
         a. /* n' has to be a primitive node - we have no choice. */
            PN ← PN ∪ { n' }

    3. else if n' is a function call node then
         a. /* Again n' has to be a primitive node. */
            PN ← PN ∪ { n' }

         b. n'.par ← true

    4. else if n' is a parallel node then
         a. call InitPrimitiveNodes(n'.g)

         b. n'.size ← 1

    5. else /* n' must be a compound node. */
       /* Let n'.s = { (g_1,f_1), (g_2,f_2), ..., (g_k,f_k) } */
         a. for i ← 1 to k do
              i. call InitPrimitiveNodes(g_i)
end procedure
```

Figure 4-10: Procedure InitPrimitiveNodes

Procedure InitPrimitiveNodes in Figure 4-10 outlines a simple solution to the problem of selecting the initial partition. A *granularity threshold value*, T_{min}, is used to control the granularity of the initial partition. Only nodes with execution times of at least T_{min} are allowed to be expanded. Increasing T_{min} will yield an initial partition of smaller size, leading to a decrease in the execution time of the partitioning algorithm. Later, in Section 5.2, we present a more sophisticated solution to the problem of determining the initial set of primitive nodes, for the *compile-time scheduling* approach. In that solution, we also consider the amount of parallelism available in different parts of the program, and allow in-line expansion of selected (possibly recursive) function calls, to arrive at the initial set of primitive nodes. These techniques for determining the initial set of primitive nodes are essential for compile-time scheduling (where all parallelism has to be exposed statically), but may also improve the quality of the partition produced by macro-dataflow.

4.4. Performance Results

In this section, we present some performance results of our partitioning algorithm for the macro-dataflow problem. The benchmark programs used are described in Appendix A. Figure 4-11 gives an overview of the implementation of the partitioning and simulation system used to obtain these performance results. A SISAL program goes through the following phases in the implementation:

1. **Translation to optimised IF1:**
   IF1 [Skedzielewski 85a] is a graphical intermediate form based on SISAL, with a hierarchical structure like GR. However, it does not contain any of the cost functions defined in GR. A front-end which translates SISAL to IF1 and an IF1 optimiser are used in this phase. The optimisations performed by the IF1 optimiser include [Skedzielewski 85b]:

   • Common subexpression elimination.

   • Loop invariant removal.

   • Loop-test inversion.

   • In-line expansion of function calls (optional).

   Both the front-end and the IF1 optimiser were obtained from Livermore.

2. **Profile Generation:**
   We extended Livermore's IF1 level debugger and interpreter (DI) so that it could generate an execution profile of a SISAL program for one or more sets of inputs. Execution profile information is used to derive average frequency values and data sizes, as was described in Section 3.3. The frequency values and data sizes are attached to IF1 nodes and edges as attributes (called *pragmas* in IF1).

3. **Cost Assignment:**
   This phase implements the cost assignment algorithm described in Figure 3-4. The inputs are:

   • An IF1 program, annotated with execution profile information.

   • Multiprocessor parameters to define the cost of all simple nodes in the program.

   After this cost assignment phase, the estimated execution time costs are also stored as IF1 node attributes.

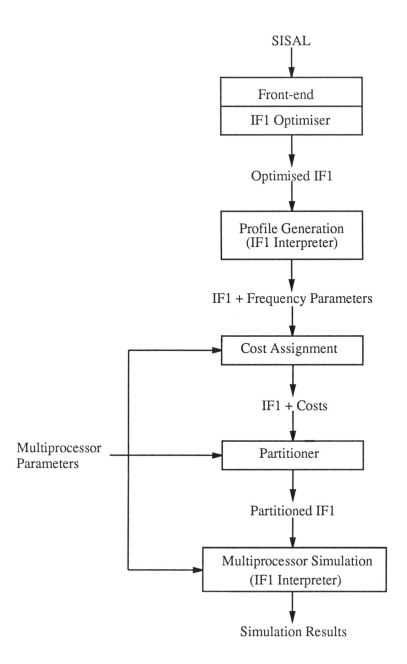

Figure 4-11: Overview of Partitioning and Simulation system

4. **The partitioner:**
   This phase is a complete implementation of the partitioning algorithm for macro-dataflow described in this chapter. Its inputs are:

   - An IF1 program produced by the cost assignment phase, with the appropriate frequency and cost attributes.

   - Multiprocessor parameters to define the number of processors and the scheduling and communication overhead (see Definition 3-6) in the target system.

   The partitioner's output is a partition for each function, as described in procedure PartitionFunctions (Figure 4-5). A special node attribute is used in IF1 to store the task partition, TP.

5. **Multiprocessor simulation:**
   The final phase is an actual macro-dataflow simulation of the partitioned program. We extended the IF1 interpreter so that it could perform this multiprocessor simulation as well. The simulation consists of two steps:

   a. A depth-first, sequential execution of the partitioned program by the IF1 interpreter, for a given set of inputs. The input set can be different from the inputs used to obtain the execution profile. This execution produces dynamic trace files at the level of macro-actors, containing dependences, execution times and data sizes.

   b. A second pass which reads in the trace files and builds the run-time graph of macro-actors. A breadth-first traversal of this graph simulates a parallel execution of the program. We assumed a simple FIFO scheduling policy for ready macro-actors, with no priorities. This pass can be repeated on the same trace files with different multiprocessor parameters for scheduling and communication overhead functions and the number of processors. The simulation outputs give the parallel execution time and the speed-up observed. A profile of the number of active processors over time can also be produced.

The main purpose of this implementation was to build a prototype of the partitioner as well as a simulation system to test the effectiveness of the partitioning algorithms presented in this chapter. However, this prototype implementation can be easily augmented to build a macro-dataflow system for SISAL on real multiprocessors. The additional pieces needed in a real implementation are:

1. A compiler which translates SISAL (or IF1) to *sequential* machine code for the target multiprocessor.

2. A compiler option to emit extra code to generate execution profile information. It would be impractical to depend on the interpreter for this purpose in a real system.

3. A run-time mechanism for scheduling macro-actors. Macro-dataflow needs the full generality of tagging outputs as in a dynamic tagged token dataflow machine [Gurd 85]. The difference is that the matching of inputs and the scheduling of macro-actors can be done in software.

4. An extension to the sequential SISAL compiler, so that each task in the partitioned program can be compiled separately with the necessary interface for the run-time scheduling mechanism.

There is a project under way at Stanford to use this prototype implementation to build SISAL and SAL compilers for shared-memory multiprocessors like the Encore Multimax and the MIPS-X-MP [Hennessy 86], and possibly for a loosely-coupled cluster of workstations running the Stanford V system [Cheriton 87].

Of the issues outlined above for a real implementation, the most important is the run-time mechanism for scheduling macro-actors. We do not address the run-time scheduling problem in this dissertation, beyond requiring that it be non-preemptive and have no unforced idleness. The only knowledge that the partitioner needs from the run-time scheduler is an estimate of the average scheduling overhead, T_{sched}. Clearly, a *centralised* scheduler will become a performance bottleneck as the number of processors increases. A *distributed* scheduler would be more desirable; but it is an open problem as to how a distributed scheduler should be implemented, especially on a loosely-coupled, message-passing multiprocessor. Different multiprocessor systems have different kinds of hardware and operating systems support to ease the scheduling bottleneck. The goal is to tune the scheduler to the target multiprocessor, so that the scheduler does not become a bottleneck and the scheduling overhead remains low.

As a final note on the prototype implementation, here is an estimate of the amount of software effort which went into it. Figure 4-12 gives rough estimates of the number of lines (Pascal) for each phase[13]. Though the number of lines *per se* has little meaning, it is interesting to compare the amount of software which had to be produced from scratch with the amount of software imported from outside (i.e. Livermore). There was an obvious advantage in using software which was "not invented here"!

The following parameters were used in these simulation experiments:

---

[13]The entry labelled *Compile-time Scheduler* is for a complete implementation of the compile-time scheduling approach discussed in the next chapter.

Phase	Lines imported	Lines produced
IF1 Utilities	10,000	0
Front-end + IF1 optimiser	24,000	0
IF1 interpreter	20,000	0
Extensions to the IF1 interpreter	0	2,000
(For profile generation and multiprocessor simulation)		
Cost Assignment	0	2,000
Macro-Dataflow Partitioner	0	5,000
Compile-time Scheduler	0	7,000
Total	54,000	16,000

Figure 4-12: Software line count of prototype implementation

- The number of processors, P, was varied in the range 1 - 20.

- The scheduling overhead, T_{sched}, was taken to be 0, 10 and 100 cycles. These values were intentionally adjusted to be smaller than realistic values, because of the small input sizes used for the benchmark programs (which led to small simulated sequential execution times). As explained in Appendix A, we were forced to use small input sizes because of the slow speed of the IF1 interpreter, compared to compiled code.

- Communication overhead for macro-dataflow was assumed to be entirely in the input and output components, R_C and W_C, with no delay component D_C. R_C and W_C were assumed to be linearly proportional to the size argument s. Thus

  - $R_C(s, 1) = k \times s$
  - $W_C(s, 1) = k \times s$
  - $D_C(s, 1) = 0$

  where k is some constant. These experiments used $k = 0$, 0.125 and 1 cycles/byte.

- The execution profile used to generate the partition was varied as SMALL, CORRECT and LARGE, with sequential execution times increasing by approximately a factor of 2, as the inputs were changed from SMALL to CORRECT and from CORRECT to LARGE. Naturally, the actual inputs needed for each case depends on the benchmark program e.g. for MM, the matrix sizes used for SMALL, CORRECT, LARGE were 15×15, 20×20, 25×25 respectively.

- The initial partition used was simply the finest granularity partition, obtained by setting $T_{min}=0$ in procedure InitPrimitiveNodes. No in-line expansion of function calls was performed.

Figures 4-13 to 4-17 contain speed-up plots for different simulation experiments. The speed-up is the ratio of the program's sequential execution time to the parallel execution time (including overhead) on P processors. Appendix B contains all the raw simulation data for these experiments and describes how the simulated speed-up value was computed.

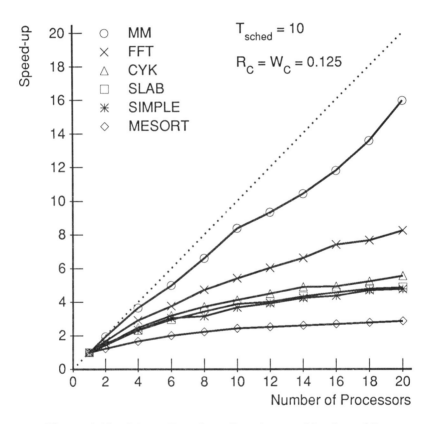

Figure 4-13: Macro-Dataflow: Speed-up vs. Number of Processors

Figure 4-13 shows the variation in speed-up as the number of processors is increased from 1 to 20. The scheduling overhead, T_{sched}, was assumed to be 10 cycles, and the input and output communication overhead functions, R_C and W_C were assumed to be 0.125 cycles/byte (i.e. a throughput of 8 bytes/cycle per processor).

All the speed-up curves in Figure 4-13 are monotonically non-decreasing. The fact that the speed-up curves for SIMPLE and SLAB flatten out approximately at 4.8 is discouraging, since they represent the kind of programs we would like to run efficiently on multiprocessors. However, this is most probably due to the unrealistically small input sizes used in the simulations (see Appendix A). Previous work on SIMPLE [Gilbert 80] indicates that the program has lots of parallelism at the outer level. Increasing the input size should give a partition with relatively less overhead and a larger speed-up. We have to wait till the programs can be compiled and run on real multiprocessors, to confirm this conjecture.

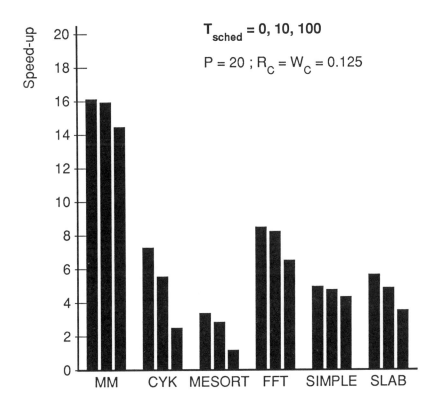

Figure 4-14: Macro-Dataflow: Speed-up vs. Scheduling Overhead

Figure 4-14 shows the variation in speed-up as the scheduling overhead, T_{sched}, is increased through 0, 10 and 100 cycles. The speed-ups were measured for 20 processors, assuming a communication overhead of 0.125 cycles/byte, as before.

For each benchmark in Figure 4-14, the speed-up falls as the scheduling overhead is increased. CYK and MESORT are the worst affected. This is because they have an outer sequential loop with inner-level parallelism, forcing a partition with smaller granularity, in which the relative effect of a constant scheduling overhead is more pronounced.

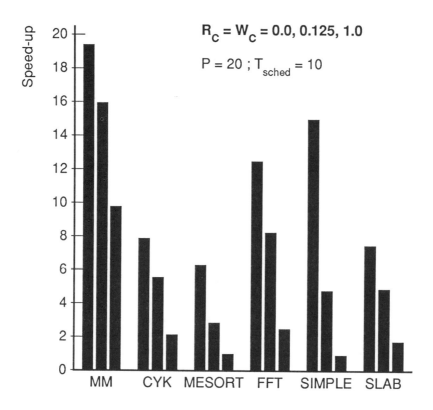

Figure 4-15: Macro-Dataflow: Speed-up vs. Communication Overhead

Figure 4-15 shows the variation in speed-up as the communication overhead is increased through 0.0, 0.125 and 1.0 cycles/byte. The speed-ups were measured for 20 processors, assuming a scheduling overhead of 10 cycles.

Figure 4-15 shows that communication overhead is a more serious concern than scheduling overhead. The speed-up falls dramatically as the communication overhead increases. According to these benchmark programs, a throughput of 8 bytes/cycle per processor (corresponding to $R_C = W_C = 0.125$ cycles/byte) should be considered a minimum requirement for macro-dataflow on a multiprocessor. If the processors have small cycle times, it is important to make the inter-processor communication correspondingly fast as well.

An important issue in Figures 4-14 and 4-15 is: how will they look for realistic larger size inputs? This depends on how the ratio of overhead to sequential execution time varies in a macro-actor. For a constant scheduling overhead, the ratio should decrease if increasing the input size increases the granularity of parallelism. The answer is less clear for communication overhead. If the communication size increases at the same rate as the sequential execution time, then the ratio will be the same and the speed-up variation should be just like Figure 4-15. Since many programs (e.g. all the benchmarks except MM) have this property, this is another reason why communication overhead is of greater concern than scheduling overhead.

Figure 4-16 shows the variation in speed-up for 3 different partitions; the partitions were generated for 3 sets of overhead parameters:
   1. LOW: $T_{sched} = 0$ cycles, $R_C = W_C = 0.0$ cycles/byte.
   2. MEDIUM: $T_{sched} = 10$ cycles, $R_C = W_C = 0.125$ cycles/byte.
   3. HIGH: $T_{sched} = 100$ cycles, $R_C = W_C = 1.0$ cycles/byte.
Each partition was then simulated on the MEDIUM overhead multiprocessor (with $P = 20$). The purpose of this experiment was to observe how the partitioner adapts to the input multiprocessor parameters. We expect the MEDIUM (middle) partition to have the best speed-up, since it was generated using the correct multiprocessor parameters. This is true for all benchmarks except MM and SLAB. On further investigation of both programs, it was discovered that this anomaly is due to the factor of 2 variation in parallel execution time discussed earlier (e.g. see Theorem 4-7). The MEDIUM partition had a smaller value of $F(\Pi)$ than the HIGH partition (assuming MEDIUM overhead parameters), but the HIGH partition gave a larger speed-up. This anomalous variation in the speed-ups for MM and SLAB is well within the factor of 2 bound.

Another observation in Figure 4-16 is that the HIGH partition had a better speed-up than the LOW partition in most cases (MESORT is the only exception). This indicates that in case of a doubt in which partition to choose, it is safer to choose the coarser

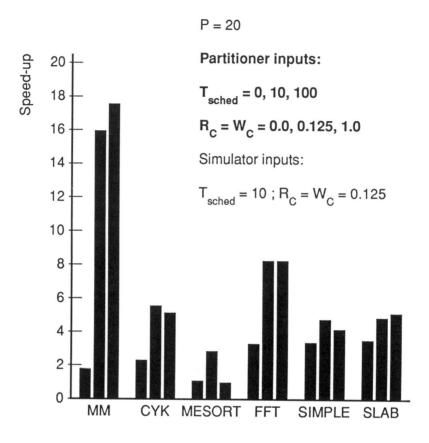

Figure 4-16: Macro-Dataflow: Speed-up for different Multiprocessor Inputs

granularity (corresponding to HIGH overhead) partition. The algorithm in procedure PartitionGraph (Figure 4-6) is consistent with this observation, since it chooses the coarser partition if two partitions have the same value of the cost function, $F(\Pi)$.

Figure 4-17 shows the results of an experiment similar to that of Figure 4-16. The 3 partitions were instead generated for different execution profile inputs:

1. SMALL: using an input size with approximately 0.5 times the sequential execution time of the correct input size.

2. CORRECT: using the correct input size, as described in Appendix A. This is the profile input which was used in all the previous experiments.

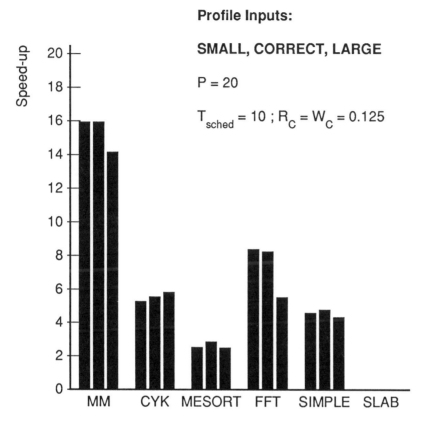

Figure 4-17: Macro-Dataflow: Speed-up for different Profile Inputs

3. LARGE: using an input size with approximately 2.0 times the sequential
   execution time of the correct input size.

Each partition was simulated with the CORRECT input (for P = 20 and MEDIUM
overhead)[14]. The variation is much less than for Figure 4-16, which shows that the
partition is not closely tied to the execution profile inputs. Of course, the reason why
we see this low sensitivity to execution profile inputs is that the benchmark programs

---

[14]There's no data presented for SLAB, because the program did not run correctly for a larger input
size. This is a bug which may get fixed in a later release from Livermore. The program runs correctly for
the inputs used in the other experiments, so this bug does not affect the other results. In any case, there is
certainly no harm in attempting to speed up a program with bugs!

used are reasonably "predictable" i.e. different program inputs essentially follow the same execution paths in these programs. For less predictable programs, it is important to use an execution profile which represents an *average* of different program inputs, as discussed earlier in Section 3.3, page 39.

5 Compile-time Scheduling

The macro-dataflow model described in the previous chapter is based on a model of compile-time partitioning and run-time scheduling. In this chapter, we take compile-time analysis one step further to include scheduling at compile-time as well. A *schedule* of a GR program for a multiprocessor model consists of P sequential threads for P processors. Compared to macro-dataflow, compile-time scheduling does not incur any scheduling overhead at run-time and offers many more opportunities to optimise inter-processor communication. As with a GR program's partition in macro-dataflow, we introduce an execution model to evaluate the parallel execution time of a GR program's schedule for a given target multiprocessor. We show that the problem of finding a schedule with the smallest parallel execution time is NP-complete in the strong sense, even for an unbounded number of processors, and present an efficient scheduling algorithm which is close to optimal in practise. Finally, we present performance results for benchmark programs written in the single-assignment language, SISAL [McGraw 85]. A preliminary report on this approach to *compile-time scheduling* was presented in [Sarkar 86b].

There are three basic steps in the compile-time scheduling approach:

1. Node Expansion (Section 5.2) – expand the main program's GR graph to reveal sufficient parallelism for the number of processors available. The expansion includes in-line expansion of selected (possibly recursive) function calls.

2. Internalisation Pre-pass (Section 5.3) – schedule the primitive nodes on an unbounded number of *virtual* processors. This phase can *internalise* a communication edge by assigning its source and destination nodes to the same virtual processor.

3. Processor Assignment (Section 5.4) – assign the virtual processors produced by the internalisation pre-pass to real processors, thus yielding a complete schedule for the expanded graph.

5.1. The Model

This section describes the execution model for a scheduled GR program on a given multiprocessor. The model is used for estimating the program's parallel execution time, as well as for parallel code generation.

Definition 5-1: A schedule $\Sigma(g) = (PN, PA, \leq)$ of GR graph g consists of:

1. A set of *primitive* nodes, PN. Primitive, sub-primitive and expanded nodes have similar properties as in Definition 4-1 for macro-dataflow. The main difference is that only compound nodes are allowed to be expanded in compile-time scheduling. Let ECN be the set of *expanded compound nodes* in $\Sigma(g)$. Also, let EG be the set of all *expanded graphs*, where $g' = (N', \top', \bot', E_C', F_C', F_T')$ is an *expanded graph* if and only if $N' \subseteq PN \cup ECN$.

2. A *processor assignment*, PA:$(PN \cup ECN) \rightarrow Z^+$. PA(n) is the processor on which node n is executed. We impose two constraints on PA:

   a. If $\top'$ and $\bot'$ are (primitive) top and bottom nodes from the same expanded graph $g' \in EG$, then they must be assigned to the same processor, $PA(\top') = PA(\bot')$.

   b. If an expanded compound node $n_c \in ECN$ has k subgraphs, $g_1, g_2, \ldots g_k$, with (primitive) top nodes, $T_1, T_2, \ldots, T_k$, then $PA(T_1) = PA(T_2) = \ldots = PA(T_k) = PA(n_c)$, so that all the branching code for an expanded compound node can be executed on one processor. The first constraint ensures that all bottom nodes are assigned to the same processor as well.

   These constraints on PA cannot worsen the parallel execution time, since a bottom node always follows the corresponding top node $(\top \leq^* \bot)$ and since the subgraphs of a compound node are executed sequentially. We also define PA's inverse, PA^{-1}, where $PA^{-1}(i) := \{ n \mid (n \in PN \cup ECN) \wedge (PA(n) = i) \}$ is the set of primitive and expanded nodes assigned to processor i.

3. A *node sequence* mapping, $\leq$. For every expanded graph, $g' = (N', \top', \bot', E_C', F_C', F_T') \in EG$, $\leq(g') = (n_1, n_2, \ldots, n_k)$ gives a *sequence* of N''s nodes. We take many notational liberties with the symbol $\leq$. We write $n_a \leq(g') n_b$ if n_a appears before (or is the same as) n_b in the sequence $\leq(g')$. We also drop the argument g' when it is clear from the context which GR graph we mean. The only constraint on $\leq(g')$ is that it must be consistent with E_C'. There must be no communication edge $(n_a, p_a, n_b, p_b) \in E_C'$ with $n_b \leq(g') n_a$.

   The processor assignment PA partitions $\leq(g')$ into a family of sequences $\{\leq_i(g')\}$, one per processor, such that $n_a' \leq_i(g') n_b'$ if and only if $(n_a', n_b' \in PA^{-1}(i)) \wedge (n_a \leq(g') n_b)$. Therefore, $\leq_i$ is the sequence obtained by restricting $\leq$ to only the nodes assigned to processor i. Sometimes we use $\leq_i(g')$ to represent the *set* of nodes, $PA^{-1}(i) \cap N'$, leaving it to the context to determine if we mean a set or a sequence.

Note that schedule $\Sigma(g)$ has $O(\|g\|)$ size, where $\|g\|$ is the total size of GR graph g and all its subgraphs.

	Sub-primitive	Primitive	Expanded
Top & bottom nodes	X	X	
Other simple nodes	X	X	
Function call nodes	X	X	
Parallel nodes	X	X	
Compound nodes	X	X	X

Figure 5-1: Possible classifications of GR nodes for compile-time scheduling

Figure 5-1 summarises the possible classifications of GR nodes as sub-primitive, primitive or expanded, for the case of compile-time scheduling. The important differences from the classifications for macro-dataflow (Figure 4-1) are:

- Top ($\top$) and bottom ($\bot$) nodes can be sub-primitive or primitive, but never expanded, in compile-time scheduling.

- Function call nodes and parallel nodes can never be expanded in compile-time scheduling. As explained in the next section, the expansion of function call nodes and parallel nodes is instead done statically in the program text.

- There is no notion of a *parallel* function call, as in macro-dataflow when $n_u.par = true$. In compile-time scheduling, a function call is either executed sequentially or expanded in-line.

- Similarly, a parallel node is either executed sequentially or expanded in-line into NC *concurrent* nodes which can be assigned to different processors at compile-time. In macro-dataflow, a primitive parallel node, n_p, dynamically spawned a macro-actor for every $n_p.size$ iterations.

Inter-processor communication for compile-time scheduling is defined by a simple message-passing protocol, using *send* and *receive* commands. These commands can be implemented on shared-memory or message-passing multiprocessors, with an overhead described by the communication overhead functions in the multiprocessor model

(Definition 3-6). A message identifier is used to match *send* and *receive* messages. The compile-time scheduling model ensures that there will never be more than one active message with the same destination processor and the same message identifier. The following functions are assumed to provide unique message identifiers:

- *start_id*(i, n) gives a unique identifier for a *start* message to processor i, used to control the execution of expanded compound node $n \in$ ECN.

- *port_id*(n_a, p_a) gives a unique identifier for the data produced on port p_a of node n_a.

Therefore, the number of identifiers needed is bounded by the *static* (rather than *dynamic*) size of the program.

The message-passing commands themselves are defined as:

- *send*(j, id, data) executed on processor i initiates the communication of data from processor i to processor j as a message with the given id. The send is *asynchronous*; processor i does not have to wait till processor j has received the message.

- *receive*(id) executed on processor j waits for a message with the given id. This is a *blocking* receive. Processor j can only continue after the message has arrived.

- *data*(id) is a function which returns the data received on the most recent *receive* command with the specified id. This is a notational convenience to represent local access of data which was received from another processor by a prior *receive* command.

For convenience, we assume that the function, *data*(*port_id*(n_a, p_a)), can also be used by all nodes following n_a on processor PA(n_a), to access the value produced at output port (n_a, p_a). This is a notational convenience to represent local access of data which was generated on the same processor.

Let g be a GR graph which is to be executed on the target multiprocessor using schedule $\Sigma(g) = (PN, PA, \leq)$. Typically, g is the GR graph of the "main program" function, so that Σ gives a schedule for the entire program. Schedule $\Sigma(g)$ is implemented by performing the steps specified by procedure ExecuteGraph(i, g, Σ) on processor i, $\forall\ 1 \leq i \leq P$.

Procedure ExecuteGraph(i, g', Σ), in Figure 5-2, is a recursive procedure which specifies the execution of any expanded graph g' $\in$ EG (including g'=g) on processor i. Procedure ExecuteGraph is a general interpretive procedure used to define the

Inputs:
  1. A processor number, i.

  2. A GR graph g' = (N', T', ⊥', E_C', F_C', F_T') ∈ EG.

  3. A schedule Σ(g) = (PN, PA, ≤), where g' ∈* g.

Outputs:
  1. Procedure ExecuteGraph describes the steps which need to be
     performed on processor i for the execution of expanded graph
     g' ∈ EG, according to schedule Σ.

procedure ExecuteGraph(i, g', Σ)
for each node n' ∈ N' s.t. ∃ n" ∈* n' with PA(n") = i **do**

  1. **if** n' ∉ ECN **then**
     /* Node n' is not an expanded compound node. */
       a. /* Wait for n''s inputs as specified by COMM. */
          for each (n_a, p_a, n') ∈ COMM(g', Σ) **do**
             i. *receive*(*port_id*(n_a, p_a))

       b. Execute node n'.

       c. /* Send n''s outputs as specified by COMM. */
          for each (n', p', n_b) ∈ COMM(g', Σ) **do**
             i. *send*(PA(n_b), *port_id*(n', p'), *data*(*port_id*(n', p')))

  2. **else if** PA(n') = i **then**
     /* n' ∈ ECN has subgraphs g_1, ..., g_k (say). */
       a. /* Wait for n''s inputs as specified by COMM. */
          for each (n_a, p_a, n') ∈ COMM(g', Σ) **do**
             i. *receive*(*port_id*(n_a, p_a))

       b. **loop**
             i. Pick the next subgraph, g_j (1 ≤ j ≤ k), to be
                executed in n', according to the n''s control flow.
                Set j = 0 if there is no next subgraph.

            ii. /* Send j to other procs working on n'. */
                for each processor ii≠i s.t. ∃ n"∈*n' ∧ PA(n")=ii
                do *send*(ii, *start_id*(ii, n'), j)

           iii. **if** j = 0 **then exit loop**

            iv. Recursively perform the steps dictated by
                ExecuteGraph(i, g_j, Σ).
          end loop

       c. /* Send n''s outputs as specified by COMM. */
          for each (n', p', n_b) ∈ COMM(g', Σ) **do**
             i. *send*(PA(n_b), *port_id*(n', p'), *data*(*port_id*(n', p')))

  3. **else** /* (n' ∈ ECN) ∧ (PA(n')≠i), but ∃ n"∈*n' with PA(n")=i */
       a. **loop**
             i. *receive*(*start_id*(i, n')) ; j ← *data*(*start_id*(i, n'))

            ii. /* Exit if compound node n' has completed. */
                if j = 0 **then exit loop**

           iii. Recursively perform the steps dictated by
                ExecuteGraph(i, g_j, Σ).
          end loop
end procedure

Figure 5-2: Procedure ExecuteGraph

execution model, and in fact describes a code generation scheme for compile-time scheduling. The outer for-loop in procedure ExecuteGraph is performed for each node $n' \in N'$ which contains a node assigned to processor i. As described later, the set COMM(g', Σ) is used to identify the communication edges for which *receive* and *send* commands must be executed.

Step 1 covers the simple case when n' is not an expanded compound node, and is thus entirely executed on processor i (= PA(n')). Step 1.a waits for n''s inputs, step 1.b executes n' and step 1.c stores n''s outputs.

The next case (step 2) is when n' is an expanded compound node and PA(n') = i. Let n''s subgraphs be $g_1, \ldots, g_k$. In this case, we know that $PA(T_1) = PA(\perp_1) = \ldots = PA(T_k) = PA(\perp_k) = i$, and that processor i is responsible for managing compound node n''s control structure . Step 2.a waits for n''s inputs, just like step 1.a. The loop in step 2.b represents n''s control structure. Step 2.b.i picks g_j, the next subgraph to be executed in n'. In step 2.b.ii, the value of j is sent in a start message to all other processors responsible for part of n''s execution. Step 2.b.iii checks if n' has completed execution, in which case j would have been set to zero in 2.b.i. Otherwise, step 2.b.iv recursively performs ExecuteGraph on g_j. Note that the recursive call is also performed on processor i. Step 2.c stores n''s outputs, just like step 1.c.

Finally, step 3 covers the case when n' is an expanded compound node and PA(n') $\neq$ i. Therefore there is at least one node $n'' \in^* n'$ such that PA(n'') = i. In this case, processor i needs directions from processor PA(n') as to which subgraph of n' should be executed. The loop in 3.a is structured like the loop in 2.b. Step 3.a.i waits for the *start* message from processor PA(n'). Step 3.a.ii exits the loop if there is no subgraph to be executed (i.e. j = 0). As in step 2.b.iv, step 3.a.iii recursively performs ExecuteGraph on g_j.

Note that all the for-loops in procedure ExecuteGraph will be unrolled and the if-conditions in steps 1 and 2 will be eliminated in the *compiled* code for scheduled graph g. The only control information which must remain are the **loop** constructs in 2.b and 3.a which describe the control structure of expanded compound node n'.

Steps   1.a,   1.c,   2.a   and   2.c   in   procedure   ExecuteGraph   use

COMM(g', Σ) ⊆ N'×Z^+×N' to identify the edges for which *receive* and *send* commands must be executed. We could require that COMM(g', Σ) be specified as part of the schedule, Σ(g), but that is unnecessary. There is a unique, minimal COMM(g', Σ) which is sufficient to support all edges in E_C', and can be efficiently constructed from the schedule.

Definition 5-2: Let

- DATA(n', COMM) := { (n_a, p_a) | $(PA(n_a) = PA(n') \land n_a \leq_{PA(n')}(g')$ n')
  $\lor$ $((n_a, p_a, n_b) \in$ COMM(g', Σ) $\land n_b \leq_{PA(n')}(g')$ n') }, so that
  DATA(n', COMM) is the set of all port values, (n_a, p_a), for which
  data(*port_id*(n_a, p_a)) is defined on processor PA(n') before n' is
  executed in step 3 of procedure ExecuteGraph.

- IN(n') := { (n_a, p_a) | $(n_a, p_a, n', p') \in E_C$' }, so that IN(n') is the set of
  all port values required as inputs to node n'.

- FIRST(n_a, p_a, i) := the first node, n_b, in the sequence $\leq_i(g')$, such that
  ∃ $(n_a, p_a, n_b, p_b) \in E_C$'. FIRST($n_a, p_a$, i) is the first node (according to
  $\leq_i(g')$) on processor i which uses the value at port (n_a, p_a) as an input,
  and is undefined if there is no such node.

COMM(g', Σ) is said to be *complete* if and only if
IN(n') ⊆ DATA(n', COMM) ∀ n' ∈ N'. Procedure ExecuteGraph must use a
COMM(g', Σ) which is complete, otherwise all of n''s inputs will not be
available when node n' is executed in step 1.b or 2.b.

The derivation of the minimal COMM(g', Σ) is based on two observations for
communication edge $(n_a, p_a, n_b, p_b) \in E_C$':

1. If PA(n_a) = PA(n_b) then no inter-processor communication is necessary,
   since n_a and n_b are assigned to the same processor.

2. If ∃ $(n_a, p_a, n_c, p_c) \in E_C$' s.t. (PA($n_c$) = PA($n_b$)) ∧ ($n_c \leq_{PA(n_c)} n_b$), then no
   inter-processor communication is necessary for (n_a, p_a, n_b, p_b) since the
   value produced at (n_a, p_a) must already have been communicated to
   PA(n_b) for use by n_c.

Theorem 5-3: $COMM_{min}$(g', Σ) := { (n_a, p_a, n_b) | PA(n_a) ≠ PA(n_b) ∧
n_b = FIRST(n_a, p_a, PA(n_b)) } is the unique, minimal COMM(g', Σ), which is
complete.

Proof: We first show that $COMM_{min}$(g', Σ) is complete. Consider
(n_a, p_a) ∈ IN(n'). We prove that (n_a, p_a) ∈ DATA(n', $COMM_{min}$), so that
IN(n') ⊆ DATA(n', $COMM_{min}$).

- **Case 1:** $PA(n_a) = PA(n')$

  $\Rightarrow n_a \leq_{PA(n')} n'$ since $(n_a, p_a) \in IN(n')$.

  $\Rightarrow (n_a, p_a) \in DATA(n', COMM)$, for any $COMM(g', \Sigma)$, by the definition of DATA.

  $\therefore (n_a, p_a) \in DATA(n', COMM_{min}(g', \Sigma))$

- **Case 2:** $PA(n_a) \neq PA(n')$

  Let $n_b = FIRST(n_a, p_a, PA(n'))$. n_b must exist since there is at least one node (n') on processor $PA(n')$, which uses the value (n_a, p_a) as an input.

  $\Rightarrow n_b \leq_{PA(n')} n'$, by the definition of FIRST.

  Also, $(n_a, p_a, n_b) \in COMM_{min}(g', \Sigma)$, by the definition of $COMM_{min}(g', \Sigma)$.

  $\therefore (n_a, p_a) \in DATA(n', COMM_{min}(g', \Sigma))$, by the definition of DATA.

For the second part of the proof, we prove that $COMM_{min}(g', \Sigma) \subseteq COMM(g', \Sigma)$, for all complete $COMM(g', \Sigma)$'s. We assume that $\exists\ (n_a, p_a, n_b)$ s.t. $(n_a, p_a, n_b) \in COMM_{min}(g', \Sigma) \wedge (n_a, p_a, n_b) \notin COMM(g', \Sigma)$, for some $COMM(g', \Sigma)$ which is complete, and derive a contradiction to prove the desired result.

$(n_a, p_a, n_b) \in COMM_{min}(g', \Sigma)$
$\Rightarrow PA(n_a) \neq PA(n_b) \wedge n_b = FIRST(n_a, p_a, PA(n_b))$,
by the definition of $COMM_{min}(g', \Sigma)$.

Also $(n_a, p_a, n_b) \notin COMM(g', \Sigma) \Rightarrow (n_a, p_a) \notin DATA(n_b, COMM)$, by the definition of DATA and $PA(n_a) \neq PA(n_b)$.

But $n_b = FIRST(n_a, p_a, PA(n_b)) \Rightarrow \exists\ (n_a, p_a, n_b, p_b) \in E_{C'}$
$\Rightarrow (n_a, p_a) \in IN(n_b)$
$\therefore IN(n_b) \not\subset DATA(n_b, COMM)$ and COMM is not complete. Contradiction.

$Q.E.D.$

Note that $COMM_{min}(g', \Sigma)$ can be efficiently computed in linear time by a depth-first traversal of g's graph hierarchy.

All inter-processor communication in compile-time scheduling is performed by the *send* and *receive* commands outlined in procedure ExecuteGraph. These commands incur a communication overhead, which has a processor component and a delay component. Consider the communication of some data from processor j to processor j:

- Processor i executes *send*(j, id, data).

- Processor j executes *receive*(id).

The processor component of communication overhead is given by the overhead functions R_C and W_C (Definition 3-6). Processor i spends W_C(i, j, *datasize, load*) time to initiate the communication and processor j spends R_C(i, j, *datasize, load*) time to complete the communication, *after the data reaches processor j.* The delay overhead function, D_C, expresses the delay component. D_C(i, j, *datasize, load*) is the minimum delay which must elapse after processor i has spent W_C(i, j, *datasize, load*) time to initiate the communication, and before processor j begins the R_C(i, j, *datasize, load*) time to complete the communication. Our compile-time scheduler uses the processor and delay components of the communication overhead functions to help overlap computation with communication delays. This model can be applied to a wide range of multiprocessors, from shared-memory to message-passing systems, by an appropriate choice of overhead functions. As mentioned earlier, the major simplification in the model is its gross approximation of the effect of communication demand on communication overhead (the load parameter in the overhead functions).

The choice of the schedule, $\Sigma(g) = (PN, PA, \leq)$ can have a dramatic influence on the parallel execution time for the following reasons:
- There is a loss in parallelism when two potentially parallel nodes are assigned to the same processor.

- Communication overhead is incurred for communication edge (n_a, p_a, n_b, p_b) if and only if $(n_a, p_a, n_b) \in COMM_{min}(g', \Sigma)$.

- A good choice of the node sequence, $\leq$, can often eliminate the effect of the delay component by overlapping the delay with other useful work.

Having defined our model for program execution (procedure ExecuteGraph) and communication overhead (functions R_C, W_C and D_C) for compile-time scheduling, we now use the model to estimate the parallel execution time of a scheduled program. A compile-time estimate of parallel execution time is based on compile-time estimates of node execution times and edge communication sizes. The major problem is in handling expanded compound nodes, where each subgraph may be executed several times. Though it is possible, we certainly do not want to make several in-line copies of each subgraph, according to its frequency (e.g. full loop unrolling). Such copying would make the cost of compile-time scheduling proportional to the *dynamic* size of the program, rather than the *static* size. Our approach is to approximate the execution time of an expanded compound node by the frequency-weighted sum of its subgraphs' parallel execution times. The ordering of subgraphs is unimportant in this approximation since there is no parallelism among subgraphs of a compound node in GR.

To estimate the parallel execution time of schedule $\Sigma(g)$, we will first build a *primitive graph*, with the set of primitive nodes, PN, as its nodes. The primitive graph has a single level, unlike the hierarchical structure in GR graphs. An execution time mapping, TIME:PN$\rightarrow Q_0^+$, gives the sequential execution time (weighted by frequencies of enclosing subgraphs) of each primitive node, for a single execution of GR graph g. EDGES $\subseteq$ PN $\times$ PN is the set of communication edges in the primitive graph. A communication size mapping, SIZE:EDGES$\rightarrow Q_0^+$, gives the total size (weighted by frequencies of enclosing subgraphs) of the data transferred along a communication edge. Finally, PREC $\subseteq$ PN $\times$ PN is a set of precedence edges necessary to enforce the sequencing of primitive nodes on the same processor and the sequencing of subgraphs in an expanded compound node. Section 5.4 later gives the details of procedure BuildPrimitiveGraph (Figure 5-13, page 132), which shows how the primitive graph can be constructed from a given schedule, $\Sigma(g)$.

Procedure DetermineTimes in Figure 5-3 is a general procedure to determine the following values for the input graph:

1. PARTIME is the parallel execution time. If procedure DetermineTimes is called for the primitive graph produced by BuildPrimitiveGraph, PARTIME is an estimate of the parallel execution time of the scheduled program.

2. The earliest start times. EST(n) is the earliest time (≥ 0) at which node n can start execution, with the given communication and precedence edges.

3. The latest completion times. LCT(n) is the latest time ($\leq$ PARTIME) at which node n can complete execution with the given communication and precedence edges.

4. The total execution times. TOTALTIME(n) is the total execution time of node n, including the processor component of all non-local communications.

5. TOTALORDER is a total order on all the nodes, which is consistent with the communication and precedence edges.

Procedure DetermineTimes is an efficient linear time algorithm and an important subroutine in compile-time scheduling. The output, PARTIME, is the sole cost value

Inputs:

1. A set of nodes N.

2. An execution time mapping TIME:N→Q_0^+.

3. A set of communication edges, EDGES ⊆ N×Z^+×N.

4. A communication size mapping, SIZE:EDGES→Q_0^+.

5. A set of precedence edges, PREC ⊆ N×N.

6. A processor assignment, PA:N→Z^+.

7. The communication overhead functions, R_C, W_C, D_C. If i = j then R_C(i, j, s, l) = W_C(i, j, s, l) = D_C(i, j, s, l) = 0.

Outputs:

1. The parallel execution time, PARTIME:Q_0^+.

2. An *earliest start time* mapping, EST:N→Q_0^+.

3. A *latest completion time* mapping, LCT:N→Q_0^+.

4. A *total execution time* mapping, TOTALTIME:N→Q_0^+.

5. A *total order* mapping, TOTALORDER:N→Z^+.

procedure DetermineTimes(N, TIME, EDGES, SIZE, PREC, PA, R_C, W_C, D_C)

1. $COMM_{min}$(g) ← { (n_a, p_a, n_b) | (n_a, p_a, n_b) ∈ EDGES ∧ PA(n_a) ≠ PA(n_b) ∧ n_b = FIRST(n_a, p_a, PA(n_b)) }
   /* See Definition 5-2. In this case, FIRST is determined by PREC and PA(n_b'), rather than by $≤_i$(g'). */

2. PAIRS ← { (n_a, n_b) | ∃ (n_a, p_a, n_b) ∈ $COMM_{min}$ }
   /* PAIRS = $COMM_{min}|_{N×N}$ is a projection of $COMM_{min}$. */

3. **for each** (n_a, n_b) ∈ PAIRS **do**
   a. TOTALSIZE(n_a, n_b) ← $\sum_{(n_a, p_a, n_b) \in COMM_{min}}$ SIZE((n_a, p_a, n_b))

4. LOAD ← $\sum_{(n_a, n_b) \in PAIRS}$TOTALSIZE($n_a$, n_b) / $\sum_{n \in N}$TIME(n)
   /* Crude estimate of communication load. */

5. LIST ← topological sort of PAIRS ∪ PREC
   /* LIST = (n_1, n_2, ..., n_k) is a sequence of nodes in N. */

6. **for** j ← 1 **to** k **do**
   a. TOTALTIME(n_j) ← TIME(n_j) +
      $\sum_{(n_i, n_j) \in PAIRS}$ R_C(PA(n_i), PA(n_j), TOTALSIZE(n_i,n_j), LOAD) +
      $\sum_{(n_j, n_i) \in PAIRS}$ W_C(PA(n_j), PA(n_i), TOTALSIZE(n_j,n_i), LOAD)

7. **for** j ← 1 **to** k **do**
   a. EST(n_j) ← *max*({ 0 } ∪ {EST(n_i) + TOTALTIME(n_i) +
      D_C(PA(n_i),PA(n_j),TOTALSIZE(n_i,n_j),LOAD) | (n_i,n_j) ∈ PAIRS}
      ∪ { EST(n_i) + TOTALTIME(n_i) | (n_i, n_j) ∈ PREC })

8. PARTIME ← *max*({EST(n) + TOTALTIME(n) |n ∈ N})

9. **for** j ← k **downto** 1 **do**
   a. LCT(n_j) ← *min*({ PARTIME } ∪ {LCT(n_i) - TOTALTIME(n_i) -
      D_C(PA(n_j),PA(n_i),TOTALSIZE(n_j,n_i),LOAD) | (n_j, n_i) ∈ PAIRS}
      ∪ { LCT(n_i) - TOTALTIME(n_i) | (n_j, n_i) ∈ PREC })

10. **for** j ← 1 **to** k **do** /* Set TOTALORDER according to LIST. */
    a. TOTALORDER(n_j) ← j
end procedure

Figure 5-3: Procedure DetermineTimes

used to compare two schedules. If the target multiprocessor has additional resource constraints which are not expressed in the multiprocessor model, it may be possible to still use the compile-time scheduling algorithms by incorporating the resource constraints in procedure DetermineTimes.

Step 1 initialises $COMM_{min}$ to contain those communication edges which actually incur a communication overhead (see Theorem 5-3). Steps 2 and 3 compute PAIRS and TOTALSIZE, the projections from $N \times \mathbf{Z}^+ \times N$ to $N \times N$ of EDGES and SIZE respectively. Step 4 estimates the average communication load per processor as the ratio of the total communication size to the total execution time. This value will be conservatively large if the processors have significant idle times. Step 5 performs a *topological sort* [Horowitz 76] on the edges in PAIRS $\cup$ PREC to build a priority list, LIST, of all the primitive nodes in PN. Step 6 determines TOTALTIME, where TOTALTIME(n) is the sum of TIME(n) and the processor component for all of n's external input and output edges. The earliest start times (EST) are determined by a forward scan of the topological sort list in step 7. The delay component of communication overhead is enforced as a constraint on start times. The largest value of EST(n)+TOTALTIME(n) gives the parallel execution time, PARTIME, in step 8. The latest completion times (LCT) are determined by a backward scan of the topological sort list in step 9. Finally, LIST is used to return the total order mapping, TOTALORDER, in step 10.

The execution model for compile-time scheduling was defined to support both message-passing and shared-memory target multiprocessors. However, inter-processor communication in a shared-memory multiprocessor is intrinsically different from message-passing communication, since the synchronisation operations and the data access operations are performed separately in a shared-memory multiprocessor. For example, a data communication between processors i and j can be achieved by performing the following steps on a shared-memory multiprocessor:

1. Processor i writes the data to shared memory.

2. Processor i performs a *signal* (or equivalent) synchronisation operation.

3. Processor j performs a *wait* synchronisation operation, and stays suspended till processor i's *signal* operation is performed (assuming that there is no other work for processor j to do).

4. Processor j reads the data from shared memory

It is possible to eliminate some of the synchronisation operations described in steps 2 and 3, without giving up any parallelism. A simple optimisation is to remove redundant synchronisation operations due to communicating different values between the same pair of nodes, or due to transitive dependence edges in the GR graph. Further optimisation is possible by using *counting* semaphores instead of *binary* semaphores [Sarkar 88].

Inputs:
    1. A GR program with NF functions, PROG = { (g_1, f_1), (g_2, f_2), ..., (g_{NF}, f_{NF}) }. Graph g_{main} is identified as the "main program" function graph.

Outputs:
    1. Schedule $\Sigma(g_{main})$ = (PN, PA, ≤) of GR graph g_{main} on P processors.

procedure ScheduleProgram(PROG)
    1. PN ← **call** DeterminePrimitiveNodes(g_{main}, P, T_{min})
       /* See Figure 5-5, section 5.2. */

    2. PA^∞, $\leq^\infty$, T_{par} ← **call** PartitionGraph(g_{main}, $id(T_{main})$)
       /* See Figure 5-12, section 5.3. */

    3. Σ ← **call** ScheduleGraph(g, Σ^∞=(PN, PA^∞, $\leq^\infty$))
       /* See Figure 5-15, section 5.4. */
end procedure

Figure 5-4: Procedure ScheduleProgram

Finally, procedure ScheduleProgram in Figure 5-4 outlines the three major phases in compile-time scheduling:

1. **Node Expansion:** The call to procedure DeterminePrimitiveNodes in step 1 performs a node expansion phase, as described in Section 5.2. It should be pointed out that in-line expansion of function calls is essential for compile-time scheduling, compared to macro-dataflow. The only way in which parallelism within a function call can be utilised in compile-time scheduling is by in-line expansion, so that the parallelism becomes visible in the static, expanded graph. In macro-dataflow, it is possible to partition the function body into concurrent tasks, to be spawned as macro-actors with each dynamic function call.

2. **Internalisation Pre-pass:** Step 2 calls procedure PartitionGraph which schedules the primitive graph on an unbounded number of virtual processors. The output schedule can also be viewed as partition of the set of primitive nodes along with a specified sequence. This phase is described in Section 5.3.

3. **Processor Assignment:** Step 3 calls procedure ScheduleGraph to assign the virtual processors generated by the internalisation pre-pass to real processors in the target multiprocessor. This phase is described in Section 5.4.

5.2. Node Expansion – Selection of Primitive Nodes

The first step in building a schedule $\Sigma(g) = (PN, PA, \leq)$ is to select the set of primitive nodes, PN. PN must form a complete fringe of the graph structure tree, so that any node contained within g falls into one of three disjoint sets:

1. PN, the set of primitive nodes.

2. ECN = $\{ n_a \mid (\exists n_b \in PN) \wedge (n_b \in^* n_a) \wedge (n_a \neq n_b)\}$, the set of expanded compound nodes.

3. SPN = $\{ n_a \mid (\exists n_b \in PN) \wedge (n_a \in^* n_b) \wedge (n_a \neq n_b)\}$, the set of sub-primitive nodes.

We want PN to be large enough to expose sufficient parallelism for P processors, but small enough so that the $O(|PG|^2)$ processor assignment algorithm presented later does not become prohibitively expensive ($|PG|$ is the size of the primitive graph constructed by procedure BuildPrimitiveGraph in Figure 5-13).

```
Inputs:
    1. A GR graph g = (N, T, ⊥, E_C, F_C, F_T).
    2. P, the number of processors in the multiprocessor model.
    3. T_min, the granularity threshold value.

Outputs:
    1. PN, the set of primitive nodes to be used in any schedule of g
       on P processors, Σ(g) - (PN, PA, ≤_i(g')).

procedure DeterminePrimitiveNodes(g, P, T_min)
begin
    1. for each function call node n_u ∈ N do
          a. PARENTCOST(n_u) ← ∅
             /* Initially, no node has any ancestor calls. */
    2. PN ← N
       /* Start with PN = N. */
    3. call ExpandNodes(PN, g, 0, 1)
end
```

Figure 5-5: Procedure DeterminePrimitiveNodes

Our approach in determining the primitive graph is to initially set PN = N at the top level, and then to recursively "expand" nodes in PN when appropriate. This expansion algorithm is described by procedure DeterminePrimitiveNodes in Figure 5-5.

All the work in procedure DeterminePrimitiveNodes is done by the call to procedure ExpandNodes in step 3. Procedure ExpandNodes is a recursive procedure described in

Inputs:

    1. PN, the current set of primitive nodes.

    2. A GR graph $g' = (N', \top', \bot', E_C', F_C', F_T')$, with $N' \subseteq PN$.

    3. PARWORK, the total "work" available to be done in parallel with g'. PARWORK $= \Sigma_{n \in PN-N' \wedge \neg(n \leq *\top \vee \bot' \leq *n)}$ (frequency of n in g) $\times F_T(n)$.

    4. $f \in Q_0^+$ is the average number of times g' is executed in a single execution of GR graph g.

Outputs:

    1. PN, the updated set of primitive nodes.

procedure ExpandNodes(PN, g', PARWORK, f)
begin
LIST $\leftarrow$ sequence containing all nodes from N'.

while LIST is not empty **do**

    1. n' $\leftarrow$ first node in LIST.

    2. LIST $\leftarrow$ remaining nodes in LIST.

    3. OKFLAG $\leftarrow$ f $\times$ $F_T'(n') \geq T_{min}$
       /* T_{min} is a granularity threshold value used for efficiency. */

    4. **if** n' is a simple node **then** OKFLAG $\leftarrow$ *false*

    5. **if** n' is a function call node $\wedge$ OKFLAG **then**
       call PreprocessFunctionCall(n', f)
       /* Procedure PreprocessFunctionCall sets OKFLAG to *false* if n' cannot be expanded. Otherwise, it initialises I' to be used later in procedure ExpandFunctionCall, if n' does get expanded. */

    6. **if** OKFLAG **then** LOCALPARWORK $\leftarrow \Sigma_{n \in N' \wedge \neg(n \leq *n' \vee n' \leq *n)}$ f $\times$ $F_T(n)$

    7. **if** n' is a parallel node $\wedge$ OKFLAG **then**

       a. NC $\leftarrow \lceil P \times f \times F_T'(n') \ / \ (f \times F_T'(n') + PARWORK + LOCALPARWORK) \rceil$

       b. **if** NC = 1 **then** OKFLAG $\leftarrow$ *false*

    8. **if** (PARWORK + LOCALPARWORK $< (P-1) \times f \times F_T'(n'))$ $\wedge$ OKFLAG **then**

       a. /* n' is a bottleneck node and OKFLAG = *true*. $\therefore$ Expand node n'. */
       if n' is a compound node **then**
       /* Let n'.s = { (g_1, f_1), (g_2, f_2), ..., (g_k, f_k) } */
          i. **for** i $\leftarrow$ 1 **to** k **do**
             1. PN $\leftarrow$ PN $\cup$ N_i
             2. **call**
               ExpandNodes(PN, g_i, PARWORK+LOCALPARWORK, f $\times f_i$)
       else if n' is a function call node **then**
          i. **call** ExpandFunctionCall(n', I')
       else
          i. **call** ExpandParallelNode(n', NC)

       b. /* Remove node n' from PN. */
       PN $\leftarrow$ PN $-$ { n' }

end procedure

Figure 5-6: Procedure ExpandNodes

Figure 5-6. Procedure ExpandNodes considers each node in N' as a possible candidate for expansion, according to the following rules:

- A candidate for expansion must be a *bottleneck node*. Node n' in procedure ExpandNodes is a bottleneck node if and only if (see step 8)

$$PARWORK + LOCALPARWORK < (P-1) \times f \times F_T'(n')$$

i.e. when all the primitive nodes which can be executed in parallel with n' contain insufficient work to keep P-1 processors busy during node n''s execution.

- A candidate for expansion must satisfy (step 3)

$$f \times F_T(n') \geq T_{min}$$

The *granularity threshold value*, T_{min}, ensures that PN will not grow too large due to expansion, especially for programs with little parallelism. Any node with $f \times F_T(n') < T_{min}$ is considered too small for further expansion to be worthwhile (note that the *frequency-weighted* cost of node n' is used in the threshold condition). A typical value for T_{min} is $0.01 \times T_{seq}/P$ (= 1% of the *ideal* parallel execution time). Programs with sufficient coarse-grain parallelism are unaffected by T_{min}. A few expansions remove all bottleneck nodes causing procedure ExpandNodes to terminate before primitive nodes reach the granularity threshold size.

- A simple node cannot be expanded (step 4).

- Function call node, n', will be considered for in-line expansion if n' satisfies the other conditions, and if the call to procedure PreprocessFunctionCall in step 5 (discussed later) does not set OKFLAG to *false*.

- Step 7 determines if parallel node n' should be considered for expansion. The actual expansion is done later by procedure ExpandParallelNode. The expansion of a parallel node replaces the node, n', by a *scatter* node, a *gather* node and NC *concurrent* nodes. n''s parallel iterations are distributed evenly among the NC concurrent nodes. Each concurrent node is assumed to have an execution time of $F_T'(n')/NC$. The value of NC is chosen to ensure that no concurrent node will be a bottleneck node, i.e. NC must satisfy the following condition:

$$PARWORK + LOCALPARWORK + (NC - 1) \times f \times F_T'(n') / NC \geq$$
$$(P - 1) \times f \times F_T'(n') / NC$$
$$\Leftrightarrow NC \geq$$
$$(P \times f \times F_T'(n')) / (f \times F_T'(n') + PARWORK + LOCALPARWORK)$$

The ceiling function $(\lceil \; \rceil)$ is used to set NC in step 7.a to the smallest integer value which satisfies this condition. The granularity threshold value, $T_{min} > 0$, ensures that $f \times F_T'(n') > 0$. Therefore $1 \leq NC \leq P$. Parallel node n' is considered for expansion if NC > 1.

All primitive nodes which obey these rules are expanded by procedure ExpandNodes in step 8.a. A compound node is expanded by recursively calling procedure ExpandNodes for each of its subgraphs. A function call node is expanded by calling procedure ExpandFunctionCall, as described later. Similarly, a parallel node is expanded by calling procedure ExpandParallelNode.

The total execution time of all steps except step 6 in procedure ExpandNodes, including all recursive calls, is $O(\|g\|)$, i.e. linear in the *final* size of GR graph g and all its subgraphs. Note that procedures ExpandFunctionCall and ExpandParallelNode modify g and its subgraphs; they can increase $\|g\|$ during the execution of procedure ExpandNodes. The increase in size due to procedure ExpandFunctionCall could be exponential in the worst case. Most often, the bottleneck and granularity threshold conditions prevent a large expansion due to function calls. The amount of expansion can be controlled by the granularity threshold value, T_{min}. More seriously, the increase in size due to procedure ExpandParallelNode may approach the factor (P + 2), since parallel node n_p is replaced by at most P+2 simple nodes. We performed an explicit expansion of a parallel node, for the sake of simplicity in presenting the later scheduling algorithms. In practise, if the number of processors is large, the scheduling algorithms should be modified so as to use one parallel node to implicitly represent P concurrent nodes, instead of explicitly replacing the parallel node by (P+2) primitive nodes.

The computation of LOCALPARWORK in step 6 is the most expensive computation in procedure ExpandNodes and contributes a total of $O(|N'| \times (|N'| + |E'|))$ time to the execution of a single call to procedure ExpandNodes. This contribution would have been $O(|N'| \times \|g\|)$ if the parameter PARWORK was unavailable in procedure ExpandNodes and had to be computed from scratch instead, and would have forced an $O(\|g\|^2)$ total execution time for procedure ExpandNodes. With parameter PARWORK available, the execution time is $O(\sum_{g' \in {}^* g} |N'| \times (|N'| + |E'|))$, which falls between $O(\|g\|)$ and $O(\|g\|^2)$ depending on g's graph structure. It would be $O(\|g\|^2)$ if g has no subgraphs, and $O(\|g\|)$ if g contains several subgraphs each of constant size. In practise, we observe an execution time which is linear, i.e. $O(\|g\|)$. Therefore, combining the PARWORK parameter with only local computation of LOCALPARWORK exploits the hierarchical graph structure in GR, and leads to a significant improvement in execution time. This is the optimisation which was discussed earlier on page 26.

Procedure PreprocessFunctionCall(n', f) in Figure 5-7 determines if primitive function call node n' should be considered for expansion. The actual expansion is done

```
Inputs:
    1. A function call node, n' ∈ N' in GR graph g' = (N', T', ⊥', E_C', F_C',
       F_T'), with PARENTCOST(n') defined.

    2. f ∈ Q_0^+, the average number of times node n' is executed in a
       single execution of GR graph g.

Outputs:
    1. OKFLAG is set to false if node n' cannot be expanded.

    2. I', the cost which should be assigned to all internal calls
       contain within n', if node n' is expanded.

procedure PreprocessFunctionCall(n', f)
begin
    1. if ∃ (n'.u, t_i) ∈ PARENTCOST(n') then

        a. if f × F_T'(n') = t_i then OKFLAG ← false
           /* Node n' should not be expanded, otherwise procedure
           ExpandNodes will get into an infinite series of
           expansions.
           WARNING: take adequate precautions to guard against
           round-off errors in this equality test of floating-point
           numbers, e.g. test the absolute value of the difference.
           */

    2. /* Determine I' = (F_T(n') - B(n'.u)) / Σ_h c_jh, based on Equation
       (3.4), page 43. */
       if Σ_h c_jh = 0 then
        a. I' ← 0
       else
        a. I' ← (F_T(n') - B(n'.u)) / Σ_h c_jh

    3. /* Node n' should not be expanded if I' < 0. */
       if I' < 0 then OKFLAG ← false
end procedure
```

Figure 5-7: Procedure PreprocessFunctionCall

later by procedure ExpandFunctionCall, if all the expansion conditions are satisfied. The expansion of a function call node replaces the node by a copy of the callee's GR graph (excluding top and bottom nodes). Unlike the expansion of compound nodes which only changes the set of primitive nodes, PN, the expansion of function call nodes also modifies the GR graph structure. In fact, a corresponding change must be made in all other representations of the parallel program to reflect the in-line expansion of the function call.

Let $PN^* := \{ n_a \mid n_a$ is a function call node $\wedge$

$n_a \in PN$ at some time before the call to PreprocessFunctionCall $\}$

be the set of all function call nodes which belong to PN, or used to belong to PN and were expanded in-line. $n_a \in PN^*$ is an *ancestor* of $n_b \in PN^*$, $n_a <_A n_b$, if $n_b \neq n_a$ was created by a sequence of function call expansions starting from n_a. Define

- PARENT(n', u_i) := the singleton set containing n''s closest ancestor in $<_A$, say n_a, with $n_a.u = u_i$. If no such n_a exists, then PARENT(n', u_i) is the empty set.

- PARENTCOST(n') = { (u_i, t_i) | PARENT(n', u_i) = {n_a} $\wedge$ t_i = n_a's total cost, $f \times F_T(n_a)$ }, is a set of function-time pairs with at most one entry for each function in the program. Each $(u_i, t_i) \in$ PARENTCOST(n') contains a parent function, u_i, along with the corresponding total cost, t_i.

The sets PARENT(n', u_i) and PARENTCOST(n') are efficiently stored in a *call expansion tree*, which is the transitive reduction of the *ancestor* relation, $<_A$. The call expansion tree contains a node for each entry in PN*. An internal node represents a function call which was expanded by procedure ExpandFunctionCall. The children of the internal node are the new function call nodes created due to the expansion. To determine PARENT(n', u_i), we follow the *parent* pointers in the call expansion tree till we find a node corresponding to function u_i or till we reach the root. We also store execution time information with each node in the call expansion tree, to facilitate the computation of the set, PARENTCOST(n').

Procedure PreprocessFunctionCall (Figure 5-7) sets OKFLAG to *false* in two cases, both of which can only arise in a program with recursive function calls:

1. If $f \times F_T'(n') = t_i$ in step 1.a. In this case, node n' has the same total cost as an ancestor recursive call to the same function, n'.u. Since the entire cost of the ancestor call has been passed down to n', further expansion of n' will not expose any parallelism and will instead lead to an infinite series of expansions.

2. If I' < 0 in step 3 $\Rightarrow$ $F_T'(n') < B(n'.u)$. Further expansion of node n' is forbidden because the new cost of internal call nodes will have to be negative. This situation may arise when the static expansion depth reaches the average value of the dynamic recursion depth, after successive expansions of recursive function calls.

If OKFLAG remains equal to *true* in procedure ExpandNodes and n' is later expanded by a call to procedure ExpandFunctionCall, then the value assigned to I' in step 2 of procedure PreprocessFunctionCall is used to set the cost of all new internal call nodes.

Procedure ExpandFunctionCall in Figure 5-8 describes the in-line expansion of a primitive function call node. The call node is replaced by a copy of the callee's GR graph (excluding the top and bottom nodes). Step 1 assigns a copy of the callee's *original* GR graph, $g_{n'.u}$, to g''. For a recursive call, we have to be careful that the

```
Inputs:
    1. A function call node, n' ∈ N' in GR graph g' = (N', T', ⊥', E_C', F_C',
       F_T').
    2. I', the cost of a new internal call node.

Outputs:
    1. n' is replaced by a copy of the callee's GR graph g_{n'.u} in g'.
    2. The new nodes are added to PN and LIST (in procedure
       ExpandNodes).

procedure ExpandFunctionCall(n', I')
begin
    1. g" = (N", T", ⊥", E_C", F_C", F_T") ← copy of original GR graph g_{n'.u}
    2. /* Add the new nodes to N'. */
       N' ← N' ∪ N"
    3. /* Add new edges to connect nodes from old N' to N". */
       E_C' ← E_C' ∪ E_C" ∪
       { (n_a, p_a, n_b, p_b) | ( (n_a,p_a,n',p') ∈ E_C' ∧  (T",p',n_b,p_b) ∈ E_C" ) ∨
       ( (n',p',n_b,p_b) ∈ E_C' ∧  (n_a,p_a,⊥",p') ∈ E_C" ) }
    4. Remove the nodes {n', T", ⊥"} from N' and all the edges connected
       to them from E_C'.
    5. for each function call node n" ∈* g" do
       a. PARENTCOSTS(n") ← PARENTCOSTS(n') - { (n'.u, t_i) |
          (n'.u, t_i) ∈ PARENTCOSTS(n') } ∪ { (n'.u, f × F_T'(n')) }
       b. if n".u is in the same SCC as n'.u (i.e. an internal call)
          then F_T'(n") ← I'
       /* The new F_T' values guarantee that the sum of the execution
       times of the new nodes equals the execution time of the
       original function call node. */
    6. for each n" ∈ N" - {T", ⊥"} do
       a. PN ← PN ∪ { n" }
       b. Add n" to the end of LIST.
end procedure
```

Figure 5-8: Procedure ExpandFunctionCall

original GR graph is used in the substitution, rather than the graph currently being
expanded. In step 2, N' is updated to include all the new nodes from N". The following
disjoint sets are added to E_C' in step 3:

- $E_C"$, the set of new edges.
- { (n_a, p_a, n_b, p_b) | ($(n_a, p_a, n', p') \in E_C' \land (T", p', n_b, p_b) \in E_C"$) ∨
  ($(n', p', n_b, p_b) \in E_C' \land (n_a, p_a, \perp", p') \in E_C"$) }
  This set consists of edges which directly wire n''s inputs and outputs to the
  corresponding nodes in N".

Step 4 removes the nodes {n', T", ⊥"} from N" and all edges connected to them from
E_C', since they are not needed after the function call expansion. Step 5.a initialises

120

PARENTCOSTS(n") for each new function call node $n'' \in^* g''$. Step 5.b sets $F_T'(n'')$ to I' for each internal call node, $n'' \in^* g''$. Finally, the new nodes from N" are added to PN and LIST in steps 6.a and 6.b respectively. The addition to LIST causes the new nodes to be themselves considered for expansion within the **while** loop of procedure ExpandNodes.

Procedure ExpandParallelNode in Figure 5-9 describes the expansion of a primitive parallel node. As mentioned earlier, a parallel node is replaced by NC+2 simple nodes, $\{n_{scatter}, n_1, \ldots, n_{NC}, n_{gather}\}$. The new simple nodes are added to N' in step 1. Step 2 sets $F_T'(n_{scatter})$ and $F_T'(n_{gather})$ to $T_{scatter}(n', NC)$ and $T_{gather}(n', NC)$, which represent the execution times of the scatter and gather computations respectively. n"'s input edges are copied as inputs to $n_{scatter}$, with the same F_C' values, in step 3. The ith iteration of step 4 processes the ith concurrent node, n_i. Step 4.a sets $F_T'(n_i)$ to $F_T'(n')/NC$, since the concurrent nodes are assumed to equally share the work in n'. Define

- MAXINPUTPORT(n') := $max(\{0\} \cup \{p_b \mid (n_a, p_a, n', p_b) \in E_C'\})$, is n"'s largest input port number used in a communication edge (assumed to be 0, if n' has no input communication edges).

- MAXOUTPUTPORT(n') := $max(\{0\} \cup \{p_a \mid (n', p_a, n_b, p_b) \in E_C'\})$, is n"'s largest output port number used in a communication edge (assumed to be 0, if n' has no output communication edges).

In step 4.b.i, n_i's input edge on port p_b is wired to output port $i \times (MAXINPUTPORT(n')+1) + p_b$ on $n_{scatter}$. The output port numbering on $n_{scatter}$ provides each concurrent node with a different set of inputs. In step 4.b.ii, the size of each of n_i's input edges is set to the original size, and is divided by NC if $(n_a, p_a) \in IN_{partial}(n')$. $IN_{partial}$ and $OUT_{partial}$ were previously defined in the macro-dataflow approach for use in procedure SetTaskCosts (Figure 4-8, page 84). In step 4.c, n_i's output edge on port n_a is wired to input port $i \times (MAXOUTPUTPORT(n')+1) + p_a$ on n_{gather}. The input port numbering allows n_{gather} to receive a different set of outputs from each concurrent node. The size of each of n_i's output edges is set to the original size, and is divided by NC if $p_b \in OUT_{partial}(n')$. n"'s output edges are copied as outputs from n_{gather} with the same F_C' values in step 5. The new simple nodes are added to PN and LIST in steps 6 and 7 respectively. Finally, step 8 removes node n' and all the edges connected to it from graph g'.

The execution time values $T_{scatter}$, T_{gather} and the sets $IN_{partial}$, $OUT_{partial}$ are input parameters required by procedure ExpandParallelNode. For simplicity, they were omitted from the input argument list in Figure 5-9.

Inputs:

1. A parallel node, $n' \in N'$ in GR graph $g' = (N', \top, \bot', E_C', F_C', F_T')$.

2. NC = number of concurrent nodes to replace n'.

Outputs:

1. Parallel node n' is replaced by a set of simple nodes $\{n_{scatter}, n_1, \ldots, n_{NC}, n_{gather}\}$ in g'.

2. The new nodes are added to PN and LIST (in procedure ExpandNodes).

procedure ExpandParallelNode(n', NC)
begin

1. $N' \leftarrow N' \cup \{n_{scatter}, n_1, \ldots, n_{NC}, n_{gather}\}$

2. $F_T'(n_{scatter}) \leftarrow T_{scatter}(n', NC)$; $F_T'(n_{gather}) \leftarrow T_{gather}(n', NC)$

3. **for each** $(n_a, p_a, n', p_b) \in E_C'$ **do**

    a. $E_C' \leftarrow E_C' \cup \{(n_a, p_a, n_{scatter}, p_b)\}$

4. **for** $i \leftarrow 1$ **to** NC **do**

    a. $F_T'(n_i) \leftarrow F_T'(n') / NC$

    b. **for each** $(n_a, p_a, n', p_b) \in E_C'$ **do**

        i. $E_C' \leftarrow E_C' \cup \{(n_{scatter}, i \times (MAXINPUTPORT(n')+1) + p_a, n_i, p_b)\}$

        ii. **if** $(n_a, p_a) \in IN_{partial}(n')$ **then**

            1. $F_C'(n_{scatter}, i \times (MAXINPUTPORT(n')+1) + p_a) \leftarrow F_C'(n_a, p_a) / NC$

        else

            1. $F_C'(n_{scatter}, i \times (MAXINPUTPORT(n')+1) + p_a) \leftarrow F_C'(n_a, p_a)$

    c. **for each** p_a s.t. $\exists (n', p_a, n_b, p_b) \in E_C'$ **do**

        i. $E_C' \leftarrow E_C' \cup \{(n_i, p_a, n_{gather}, i \times (MAXOUTPUTPORT(n')+1) + p_a)\}$

        ii. **if** $p_a \in OUT_{partial}(n')$ **then**

            1. $F_C'(n_i, p_a) \leftarrow F_C'(n', p_a) / NC$

        else

            1. $F_C'(n_i, p_a) \leftarrow F_C'(n', p_a)$

5. **for each** $(n', p_a, n_b, p_b) \in E_C'$ **do**

    a. $E_C' \leftarrow E_C' \cup \{(n_{gather}, p_a, n_b, p_b)\}$

    b. $F_C'(n_{gather}, p_a) \leftarrow F_C'(n', p_a)$

6. PN $\leftarrow$ PN $\cup \{n_{scatter}, n_1, \ldots, n_{NC}, n_{gather}\}$

7. Add each $n'' \in \{n_{scatter}, n_1, \ldots, n_{NC}, n_{gather}\}$ to the end of LIST.

8. Remove parallel node n' from N', and all the edges connected to n' from E_C'.

end procedure

Figure 5-9: Procedure ExpandParallelNode

We end this section by mentioning a possible optimising post-pass to node expansion, which could reduce the size of the primitive graph, ‖g‖, and hence reduce the execution time of compile-time scheduling. This optimisation could also be used after node expansion in macro-dataflow.

In general, it may be possible to reduce ‖g‖ after calling procedure DeterminePrimitiveNodes by replacing a set of primitive nodes $\{n_1, ..., n_k\}$ in an expanded graph $g \in EG$ by a new single primitive node n', if $\Sigma_i F_T(n_i) < T_{min}$. This *merging* of primitive nodes could be beneficial if there are several primitive nodes with small execution times ($<< T_{min}$). The merging process cannot go beyond a single level of expanded graphs, because the expanded compound node containing g must have an execution time $\geq T_{min}$ to have been expanded by procedure ExpandNodes.

The conditions under which $\{n_1, ..., n_k\}$ can be safely replaced by n' are:
- $\Sigma_i F_T(n_i) < T_{min}$, so that the execution time of the new primitive node is also less than the granularity threshold value.

- $\{n_1, ..., n_k\}$ must be a *convex* subgraph of g, so that g remains acyclic when $\{n_1, ..., n_k\}$ is replaced by n'.

- $\{n_1, ..., n_k\}$ must be a *connected* subgraph of g, so that replacing $\{n_1, ..., n_k\}$ by n' does not destroy any parallelism outside n' in g.

5.3. Internalisation Pre-pass

Once the primitive nodes have been established, we would like to assign them to processors in a schedule $\Sigma(g) = (PN, PA, \leq)$ which has the smallest parallel execution time. However, a single pass scheduling algorithm is unsuitable for handling communication overhead. Consider primitive nodes n_a and n_b, assigned to different processors $PA(n_a) \neq PA(n_b)$, with communication edges (n_a, p_a, n_c, p_c) and (n_b, p_b, n_c, p_c') connected to input ports p_c and p_c' of node n_c (Figure 5-10). After assigning n_a and n_b to separate processors (say), a single pass algorithm would be forced to make $PA(n_c) \neq PA(n_a)$ or $PA(n_c) \neq PA(n_b)$, and thus incur the communication overhead of at least one of the two communication edges mentioned earlier. This is inevitable no matter how large $F_C(n_a, p_a)$ and $F_C(n_b, p_b)$ may be and can thus lead to an arbitrarily large parallel execution time. We do not want to consider backtracking on previous assignments because of the worst case exponential execution time of backtracking algorithms. Our solution is to break the scheduling process into two phases:

- Internalisation pre-pass – scheduling on an unbounded number of *virtual* processors.

- Processor assignment – scheduling on the P *real* processors, using the partition produced by the internalisation pre-pass.

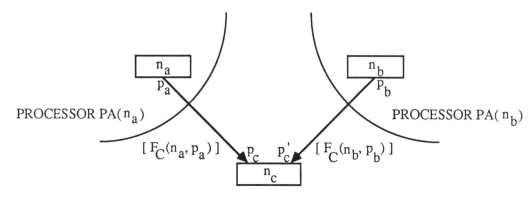

PROCESSOR PA(n_a)   PROCESSOR PA(n_b)

[...] = edge communication size

Figure 5-10: Counter-example for single-pass scheduling

The *internalisation pre-pass* builds a schedule $\Sigma^\infty(g) = (PN, PA^\infty, \leq^\infty)$ of the primitive nodes, with the goal of minimising the parallel execution time on an unbounded (i.e. up to |PN|) number of processors. Of course, if the multiprocessor has no communication overhead then the trivial partition, which assigns each primitive node to a separate virtual processor, is an optimal solution for the internalisation pre-pass. But communication overhead cannot be ignored in the realistic case. The communication overhead values used for an unbounded number of processors in the internalisation pre-pass are the smallest possible for two processors in the target multiprocessor. The main observation is that if two nodes are assigned to the same processor in this best case situation with an unbounded number of processors available and the lowest possible overhead, then they should be assigned to the same processor in any schedule $\Sigma(g)$ on the target multiprocessor. The *processor assignment* phase described in section 5.4 then builds a schedule on P processors, $\Sigma(g) = (PN, PA, \leq)$, so that PA maps PN to $\{1, ..., P\}$ and PA includes PA^∞, i.e. $PA^\infty(n_a) = PA^\infty(n_b) \Rightarrow PA(n_a) = PA(n_b)$.

We do not claim that this approach can always yield an optimal schedule. In fact, it may not be possible to obtain an optimal schedule for P processors by merging virtual processors from an optimal schedule on an unbounded number of processors. However, we conjecture that the best possible parallel execution time obtained by merging virtual processors, will be at most a factor of 2 larger than the optimal parallel execution on P processors.

We discuss the internalisation pre-pass in this section by first examining the complexity of the problem, and then presenting our approximation algorithm to solve the problem.

Definition 5-4: The INTERNALISATION problem, posed as a decision problem in yes-no form, is specified as:

INSTANCE: A GR graph G, a multiprocessor model M, a set of primitive nodes, PN and a completion time $T \in Q_0^+$.

QUESTION: Is there a schedule $\Sigma^\infty(g) = (PN, PA^\infty, \leq^\infty)$ of the primitive nodes on an unbounded number of processors with parallel execution time $\leq$ T?

Theorem 5-5: The INTERNALISATION problem is NP-complete in the strong sense.

Proof: It is easy to see that the problem is in NP, since a non-deterministic algorithm need only guess a schedule, $\Sigma^\infty(g)$, evaluate the parallel execution time in polynomial time and thus check in polynomial time if it is $\leq$ T.

As with the MACRO-DATAFLOW PARTITION problem, we give a *pseudo-polynomial transformation* from the 3-PARTITION problem to the INTERNALISATION problem. Consider an arbitrary instance of 3-PARTITION (Definition 4-9, page 69). The corresponding instance of INTERNALISATION is given by

1. A GR graph $G = (N, T, \perp, E_C, F_C, F_T)$ with
   - $N := A \cup \{b_1, ..., b_m\} \cup \{c_0, c_1, ..., c_m\}$, where A is the set of elements in 3-PARTITION. All nodes in N are simple nodes.
   - $T := c_0$
   - $\perp := c_m$
   - $E_C := \{(T, 3, a_i, 1)|a_i \in A\} \cup \{(a_i, 1, \perp, i+2)|a_i \in A\} \cup \{(c_j, 1, b_{j+1}, 1)|0 \leq j < m\} \cup \{(c_j, 2, c_{j+1}, 2)|0 \leq j < m\} \cup \{(b_j, 1, c_j, 1)|1 \leq j \leq m\}$

Figure 5-11 illustrates the set of communication edges, E_C, in the constructed instance of INTERNALISATION.

- The communication cost function, F_C, is defined as
  - $F_C(\top, 3) := 2mB.$
  - $F_C(a_i, 1) := 2mB, \forall\ 1 \le i \le 3m.$
  - $F_C(c_j, 1) := 0, \forall\ 0 \le j < m.$
  - $F_C(c_j, 2) := 2mB, \forall\ 0 \le j < m.$
  - $F_C(b_j, 1) := 0, \forall\ 1 \le j \le m.$
- The execution time cost function, F_T, is defined as
  - $F_T(a_i) := s(a_i), \forall\ 1 \le i \le 3m.$
  - $F_T(b_j) := B, \forall\ 1 \le j \le m.$
  - $F_T(c_j) := 0, \forall\ 0 \le j \le m.$

2. A multiprocessor model, $M = (P, R_C, W_C, D_C, F_S, T_{sched})$ with
   - The processor component functions, R_C and W_C, are zero valued, so that $R_C(i, j, size, load) = W_C(i, j\ size, load) = 0$, for all inputs.
   - The delay component function, $D(i, j, size, load)$, is defined as
     - $D_C(i, j, size, load) = size$, if $i \ne j$.
   - Since G has only simple nodes, the cost function for simple nodes, F_S, is identical to F_T defined above.
   - The number of processors, P, is not used in the INTERNALISATION problem.
   - T_{sched} is not used in compile-time scheduling.

3. A set of primitive nodes, PN = N. (This is the only possible definition for PN when all nodes in N are simple nodes.)

4. A completion time, T = mB.

Thus each element in the 3-PARTITION problem corresponds to a simple node in the GR graph G, with an execution time equal to the size of the element. G has two other sets of nodes, $\{b_1, ..., b_m\}$ and $\{c_0, c_1, ..., c_m\}$.

This transformation can be performed in time polynomial in the input length of 3-PARTITION. Further, the length of the constructed INTERNALISATION instance is polynomially related to the length of the 3-PARTITION instance, and the largest (cost) number in the INTERNALISATION instance is the same as the largest number in the 3-PARTITION instance. With these conditions satisfied, all that remains in the proof of strong NP-completeness is to show that the 3-PARTITION instance (with A, B, s(a)) is a solution if and only if the INTERNALISATION instance (with G, M, PN, T) is a solution.

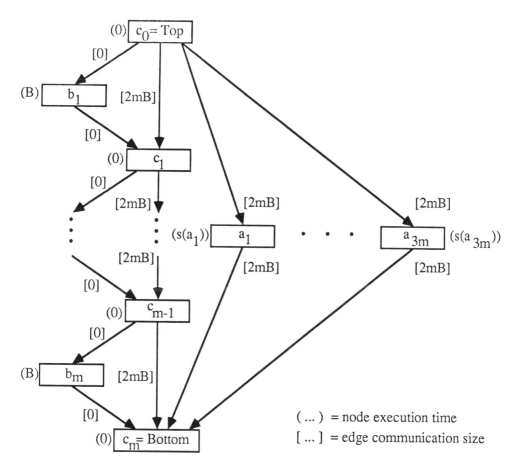

Figure 5-11: The constructed instance of INTERNALISATION

We first assume that the 3-PARTITION instance is a solution with $\sum_{a \in A_i} s(a) = B$, $\forall\ 1 \leq i \leq m$. Then the following schedule $\Sigma^{\infty}(g) = (PN, PA^{\infty}, \leq_i^{\infty})$ is a solution of the corresponding instance of INTERNALISATION:

- $PA^{\infty}(a_i) = PA^{\infty}(c_j) = 1$, $\forall\ 1 \leq i \leq m$, $0 \leq j \leq m$, and $PA^{\infty}(b_i) = 2$, $\forall\ 1 \leq i \leq m$.

- $\leq^{\infty} = (c_0, A_{1,1}, A_{1,2}, A_{1,3}, b_1, c_1, ..., c_{m-1}, A_{m,1}, A_{m,2}, A_{m,3}, n_m, c_m)$, where $A_i = \{A_{i,1}, A_{i,2}, A_{i,3}\}$ is the ith set in the 3-PARTITION solution. Therefore $\leq^{\infty}_1 = (c_0, A_{1,1}, A_{1,2}, A_{1,3}, c_1, ..., c_{m-1}, A_{m,1}, A_{m,2}, A_{m,3}, c_m)$, and $\leq^{\infty}_2 = (b_1, b_2, ..., b_m)$

It is easy to verify that this schedule has a parallel execution time of mB (= T in our constructed instance of INTERNALISATION).

Now we assume that the INTERNALISATION instance is a solution and show that the corresponding 3-PARTITION instance is also a solution. The only way that the INTERNALISATION instance can be a solution with parallel execution time $\leq mB$, is if all communication edges with F_C values of $2mB$ are internalised, because of the delay overhead they would incur otherwise. Therefore $PA^{\infty}(a_i) = PA^{\infty}(c_j) = 1$ (say), $\forall\ 1 \leq i \leq m, 0 \leq j \leq m$. Now, $\sum_{a_i \in A} F_T(a_i) + \sum_{0 \leq j \leq m} F_T(c_j) = mB$, so none of the remaining b_i nodes (with execution time $= B$) can also be assigned to processor 1; otherwise we would get a parallel execution time which exceeds $m \times B$. , when we have a parallel execution time $\leq mB$. Therefore $\leq_1^{\infty}$ is a sequence of the nodes from $A \cup \{c_0, ..., c_m\}$, such that $c_0 \leq_1^{\infty} c_1 \leq_1^{\infty} ... \leq_1^{\infty} c_m$. Let $A_i = \{a \mid a \in A \wedge c_{i-1} \leq_1^{\infty} a \leq_1^{\infty} c_i\}$ be the set of nodes which lie between c_{i-1} and c_i in $\leq_1^{\infty}$. Then

$$start(c_i) = start(c_{i-1}) + max(\sum_{a \in A_i} F_T(a), F_T(b_i))$$

$$= start(c_{i-1}) + max(\sum_{a \in A_i} s(a), B)$$

where $start(c_i)$ is c_i's starting time (and completion time, since $F_T(c_i) = 0$). Also $start(c_i) = iB$, since $start(c_0) \geq 0 \Rightarrow start(c_i) \geq iB$, and $start(c_m) \leq mB \Rightarrow start(c_i) \leq iB$, by induction on i and the definition of max. Therefore $\forall\ 1 \leq i \leq m, \sum_{a \in A_i} s(a) \leq start(c_i) - start(c_{i-1}) \Rightarrow \sum_{a \in A_i} s(a) = B$. Since $\sum_i \sum_{a \in A_i} s(a) = mB$, this can only be satisfied if $\sum_{a \in A_i} s(a) = B\ \forall\ 1 \leq i \leq m$. Therefore the corresponding 3-PARTITION instance is a solution.

$$Q.E.D.$$

Theorem 5-5 shows that a pseudo-polynomial time algorithm cannot exist for INTERNALISATION unless P=NP. Any algorithm designed to solve INTERNALISATION will take super-polynomial time in the size of the input (unless P=NP), even if the largest cost number is bounded by a polynomial in the length of the instance. Since typical GR graphs contain 100-10,000 nodes and edges, a super-polynomial algorithm is intractable. Theorem 5-5 is also valid for the INTERNALISATION problem on just 2 processors, and shows that the problem of building a schedule with the optimal parallel execution time on a bounded number of processors, $P \geq 2$, is also NP-complete in the strong sense.

Since the exact INTERNALISATION decision problem is intractable, let's consider the corresponding minimisation problem for the parallel execution time. Define T_{opt} to be the optimal (minimum) solution value over all possible schedules, $\Sigma^{\infty}(g)$. Our goal is to find an efficient (up to $O(n^3)$, say) approximation algorithm which produces a schedule with parallel execution time "close" to T_{opt}.

Inputs:

1. A GR graph, $g = (N, \top, \bot, E_C, F_C, F_T)$.

2. $P_{\top,\bot} \in \mathbf{Z}^+$, the processor number for $\top$ and $\bot$.

Outputs:

1. A processor assignment $PA^\infty: (PN \cup EN) \rightarrow \mathbf{Z}^+$.

2. A node sequence mapping $\leq^\infty(g')$ defined for all expanded GR graphs $g' \in EG \land g' \in^* g$.

3. $T_{par}(g)$, the parallel execution time of GR graph g.

procedure PartitionGraph(g, $P_{\top,\bot}$)

1. $PA^\infty(\top) \leftarrow P_{\top,\bot}$; $PA^\infty(\bot) \leftarrow P_{\top,\bot}$; $\leq_{P_{\top,\bot}}^\infty \leftarrow (\top, \bot)$

2. **for each** $n \in N - \{\top, \bot\}$ **do**

   a. $PA^\infty(n) \leftarrow id(n)$; $\leq_{id(n)}^\infty \leftarrow (n)$

3. **for each** $n \in N$ **do**
   if $n \in ECN$ (i.e. n is an expanded compound node) **then**
   /* Let $n.s = \{(g_1, f_1), (g_2, f_2), \ldots, (g_k, f_k)\}$ */

   a. TIME(n) $\leftarrow 0$

   b. **for** $j \leftarrow 1$ **to** k **do**

   i. **call** PartitionGraph(g_j, $PA^\infty(n)$)

   ii. TIME(n) $\leftarrow$ TIME(n) + $f_j \times T_{par}(g_j)$

   else TIME(n) $\leftarrow F_T(n)$

4. PARTIME, EST, LCT, TOTALTIME, TOTALORDER $\leftarrow$
   call DetermineTimes(N, TIME, $E_C|_{N \times \mathbf{Z}^+ \times N}$, F_C,
   $\{(n_a, n_b) \mid PA^\infty(n_a) = PA^\infty(n_b) = i \land n_a \leq_i^\infty(g)n_b\}$, PA^∞, R_C^∞, W_C^∞, D_C^∞)

5. EDGES $\leftarrow$ elements of E_C sorted in descending order of F_C values
   /* $\forall\ e_i, e_j \in$ EDGES, $F_C(e_i) \geq F_C(e_j) \Rightarrow i \leq j$ */

6. **for** $j \leftarrow 1$ **to** $|$EDGES$|$ **do** /* Let $e_j = (n_a, p_a, n_b, p_b)$. */
   if $PA^\infty(n_a) \neq PA^\infty(n_b)$ **then**

   a. $\{ \leq_i^{new} \} \leftarrow \{ \leq_i^\infty \}$

   b. $\leq_{PA^\sim(n_a)}^{new} \leftarrow$ interleave sequences $\leq_{PA^\sim(n_a)}^\infty$ and $\leq_{PA^\sim(n_b)}^\infty$, in order of increasing (LST, TOTALORDER)

   c. $PA^{new} \leftarrow$ merge $PA^\infty(n_a)$ and $PA^\infty(n_b)$ in PA^∞

   d. PARTIME$_{new}$, EST$_{new}$, LCT$_{new}$, TOTALTIME$_{new}$, TOTALORDER$_{new}$ $\leftarrow$
   call DetermineTimes(N, TIME, $E_C|_{N \times \mathbf{Z}^+ \times N}$, F_C,
   $\{(n_a, n_b) \mid PA^{new}(n_a) = PA^{new}(n_b) = i \land n_a \leq_i^{new}(g)n_b\}$, PA^{new}, R_C, W_C, D_C)

   e. **if** PARTIME$_{new} \leq$ PARTIME **then**

   i. $\{ \leq_i^\infty \} \leftarrow \{ \leq_i^{new} \}$; $PA^\infty \leftarrow PA^{new}$

   ii. EST $\leftarrow$ EST$_{new}$; LCT $\leftarrow$ LCT$_{new}$;
   PARTIME $\leftarrow$ PARTIME$_{new}$; TOTALTIME $\leftarrow$ TOTALTIME$_{new}$;
   TOTALORDER $\leftarrow$ TOTALORDER$_{new}$;

7. Build the sequence $\leq^\infty(g)$ according to TOTALORDER.

8. $T_{par}(g) \leftarrow$ PARTIME
end procedure

Figure 5-12: Procedure PartitionGraph

Procedure PartitionGraph(g, $P_{\top,\perp}$) in Figure 5-12 outlines the approximation algorithm used in the internalisation pre-pass. We assume that $id(n)$ gives a unique virtual processor number ($> P$) for each node $n \in PN \cup ECN$, contained within g. Then PA^∞ and $\leq^\infty$ are determined by the call, PartitionGraph(g, $id(T_g)$). In steps 1 and 2, procedure PartitionGraph begins by assigning each node to a separate processor, except for $\top$ and $\perp$ which must go together (Definition 5-1). Step 3 contains a recursive call to PartitionGraph, so that all subgraphs contained within g are partitioned before g itself is partitioned. Step 3.b.i forces the top and bottom nodes of each subgraph to be assigned to the same processor as n itself. The execution time, TIME(n), of expanded compound node n is estimated in step 3.b.ii by adding the *parallel* execution times of n's subgraphs, weighted by their frequencies. Therefore, we can treat expanded compound node n as a single node with execution time TIME(n), when partitioning g for an unbounded number of processors.

Procedure DetermineTimes (Figure 5-3) is called to set PARTIME and other values in step 4. The communication overhead functions R_C^∞, W_C^∞ and D_C^∞ represent the lowest possible overhead, e.g. $R_C^\infty(i, j, size, load) = min_{k \neq l}(\{R_C(k, l, size, load)\})$. The set $\{(n_a,n_b) \mid PA^\infty(n_a)=PA^\infty(n_b)=i \wedge n_a\leq_i^\infty(g)n_b\}$ contains the precedence constraints enforced by $\leq_i^\infty$, and is passed to procedure DetermineTimes as the argument, PREC.

Steps 5 and 6 outline the greedy algorithm actually used for internalisation. The communication edges are first sorted in decreasing order of F_C in step 5. Step 6 examines edges in this sorted order, and internalises every external edge whose internalisation does not cause an increase in the parallel execution time. Steps 6.a and 6.b build the new node sequence family, $\{\leq^{new}\}$, which will be used if processors $PA^\infty(n_a)$ and $PA^\infty(n_b)$ are merged (i.e. edge (n_a, p_a, n_b, p_b) is internalised).

The new sequence, $\leq_{PA^\infty(n_a)}^{new}$, is determined in step 6.b by interleaving the two old sequences in increasing order of (LST, TOTALORDER)[15]. LST(n) = LCT(n) - TOTALTIME(n), is the *latest starting time* of node n. The heuristic of placing the node with the smallest LST value first in the sequence, is based on Jackson's rule for optimal sequencing in the absence of release times: *schedule the*

---

[15] Assume lexicographic comparison for ordered pairs, with the first element being the most significant.

nodes according to nondecreasing deadlines [Jackson 55]. The output sequence is guaranteed to be consistent with the precedence constraints, because we use TOTALORDER as the secondary key when two nodes have the same LST value.

The new processor assignment, PA^{new}, is determined in step 6.c by merging virtual processors $PA^{\infty}(n_a)$ and $PA^{\infty}(n_b)$. Step 6.d calls procedure DetermineTimes to compute $PARTIME_{new}$, EST_{new}, LST_{new} and $TOTALTIME_{new}$, based on $\leq^{new}$. The set, $\{(n_a,n_b) \mid PA^{new}(n_a)=PA^{new}(n_b)=i \wedge n_a \leq_i^{new}(g)n_b\}$, contains the precedence constraints enforced by $\{\leq_i^{new}\}$. The internalisation does not cause an increase in the parallel execution time if and only if $PARTIME_{new} \leq PARTIME$, which is the condition in 6.e. Steps i and ii in 6.e perform the internalisation when the condition is true. Step i updates PA^{∞} and $\{\leq_i^{\infty}\}$ and step ii stores $PARTIME_{new}$ and other new values for use in the next iteration. PartitionGraph's outputs are then available after step 6, as described in steps 7 and 8.

PartitionGraph takes $O(|g|^2)$ time, if we ignore the contribution of the recursive calls in step 3.b.i. Step 6 is the most expensive step, since the **for** loop has $O(|g|)$ iterations, and each iteration takes $O(|g|)$ time. The sorting of the edges in step 5 can be done in $O(|g| \log |g|)$ time, though an $O(|g|^2)$ algorithm can also be used without changing the execution time complexity of procedure PartitionGraph. If we consider the recursive calls in step 3.b.i, then the total execution time for PartitionGraph is $O(\sum_{g'} |g'|^2)$, over all expanded GR graphs $g' \in EG$. Depending on the graph structure, the sum falls between $O(\|g\|)$ and $O(\|g\|^2)$, where $\|g\|$ is the total size of g and all its subgraphs. The execution time is $O(\|g\|^2)$ if g has no subgraphs, and $O(\|g\|)$ if g contains several subgraphs each of constant size. Measurements of actual execution times of the prototype implementation suggest an $O(\|g\|)$ execution time in practise for the internalisation pre-pass. The execution time of compile-time scheduling is dominated by the processor assignment phase described in the next section.

5.4. Processor Assignment

The internalisation pre-pass builds a schedule $\Sigma^{\infty}(g) = (PN, PA^{\infty}, \leq^{\infty})$ on an unbounded number of processors. The communication overhead values $(R_C^{\infty}, W_C^{\infty}$ and $D_C^{\infty})$ used in the internalisation pre-pass were the smallest overhead values for any pair of processors in the multiprocessor model. If two nodes were assigned to the same processor in this best case situation with an unbounded number of processors and the lowest possible overhead, then they should be assigned to the same processor in the realistic case of P processors and varying overhead. Thus, the processors used in the internalisation pre-pass are *virtual* processors which must be mapped to the set of *real* processors, $\{1, ..., P\}$. For convenience, the internalisation pre-pass guarantees that none of the virtual processor numbers are in $\{1, ..., P\}$.

The first step is to construct the *primitive graph* corresponding to the schedule, $\Sigma^{\infty}(g)$, produced by the internalisation pre-pass. The primitive graph has a single level, unlike the hierarchical structure in GR Graphs. Procedure BuildPrimitiveGraph(g, Σ) in Figure 5-13 outlines the algorithm used to construct the primitive graph corresponding to schedule $\Sigma(g)$. Most of the work is done in step 2 by the call to procedure ProcessGraph.

```
Inputs:
    1. A GR graph g = (N, T, ⊥, E_C, F_C, F_T).
    2. Schedule Σ(g) = (PN, PA, ≤).

Outputs:
A graph on PN consisting of:
    1. An execution time mapping, TIME:PN→Q₀⁺.
    2. A set of communication edges, EDGES ⊆ PN × Z⁺ × PN.
    3. A communication size mapping SIZE:EDGES→Q₀⁺.
    4. A set of precedence edges, PREC ⊆ PN × PN.
    5. A priority list on PN, PRIORITYLIST = (n₁, ..., nₖ).

procedure BuildPrimitiveGraph(g, Σ)
begin
    1. EDGES ← Ø ; PREC ← Ø
    2. call ProcessGraph(g, 1)
    3. PRIORITYLIST ← LIST(g)
end procedure
```

Figure 5-13: Procedure BuildPrimitiveGraph

Inputs:

    1. A GR graph $g' = (N', T', \perp', E_C', F_C', F_T')$.

    2. $f \in Q_0^+$ is the average number of times g' is executed in a single execution of GR graph g.

Outputs:

    1. Procedure ProcessGraph recursively adds TIME, PREC, EDGES and SIZE values for all primitive nodes contained within g'.

    2. LIST(g'), a priority list of all primitive nodes contained within g'.

procedure ProcessGraph(g', f)

    1. LIST(g') $\leftarrow$ ( )

    2. /* Let $\leq(g') = (n'_1, ..., n'_k)$ be the given node sequence on N'. */
    for $j \leftarrow 1$ **to** k **do**

        a. /* Add communication edges to EDGES. */
            for each $(n_a, p_a, n'_j, p') \in E_C'$ **do**
            if (SOURCE(n_a), p_a, SINK(n'_j)) $\notin$ EDGES **then**

                i. EDGES $\leftarrow$ EDGES $\cup$ { (SOURCE(n_a), p_a, SINK(n'_j)) }.

                ii. SIZE((SOURCE(n_a), p_a, SINK(n'_j))) $\leftarrow$ $f \times F_C$(SOURCE(n_a), p_a)

        b. **if** $n'_j \in$ ECN **then**
            /* Let $n'_j.s = \{ (g_1, f_1), (g_2, f_2), ... \}$ */
            for each GR graph g_i in n'_j **do**

                i. **call** ProcessGraph(g_i', $f \times f_i'$)

                ii. /* Add precedence edges to sequentialise n'_j's subgraphs. */
                    if $i > 1$ **then** PREC $\leftarrow$ PREC $\cup$ { $(\perp_{i-1}, T_i)$ }

                iii. /* Append LIST(g_i) to LIST(g'). */
                    LIST(g') $\leftarrow$ LIST(g') $\cdot$ LIST(g_i)

        c. **else**

                i. TIME(n) $\leftarrow$ $f \times F_T$(n).

                ii. /* Append node n'_j to LIST (g'). */
                    LIST(g') $\leftarrow$ LIST(g') $\cdot$ (n'_j)

end procedure

/* Assume $n.s = \{ (g_1, f_1), (g_2, f_2), ..., (g_k, f_k) \}$,
   when $n \in$ ECN in the functions SOURCE and SINK. */

function SOURCE(n) = **if** $n \in$ ECN **then** $\perp_k$ **else** n **end function**

function SINK(n) = **if** $n \in$ ECN **then** T_1 **else** n **end function**

Figure 5-14: Procedure ProcessGraph

Procedure ProcessGraph(g', f) is described in Figure 5-14. Functions SOURCE and SINK (defined at the bottom of Figure 5-14) are used to identify the top ($\top$) or bottom ($\bot$) primitive node corresponding to an expanded compound node in g'. Step 1 of procedure DetermineTimes initialises LIST to an empty list. Step 2 visits g''s nodes in the order specified by $\leq$(g'). Step 2.a incrementally updates EDGES and SIZE. The precedence edges required for sequentialising subgraphs of an expanded compound node are added to PREC in step 3.b.ii. For simplicity, we neglect the overhead of the *start_id* messages (steps 2.b.ii and 3.a.i in procedure ExecuteGraph, Figure 5-2) and do not include them in EDGES. The self-recursive call to ProcessGraph, due to expanded compound nodes, is done in step 2.b.i. Step 2.c sets the execution time value, TIME, for each primitive node in g'.

Procedure BuildPrimitiveGraph performs a linear time, pre-order traversal (down to the level of primitive nodes only) of g's graph hierarchy. The primitive graph produced by procedure BuildPrimitiveGraph can now be used to determine the parallel execution time. The parallel execution time is simply the primitive graph's critical path length (or $\bot_g$'s completion time), while taking into account the processor and delay components of communication overhead.

Procedure ScheduleGraph in Figure 5-15 outlines the algorithm used for processor assignment. Its input is a GR graph g with a schedule Σ^∞(g) on an unbounded number of processors, created by the internalisation pre-pass. ScheduleGraph is structured as a list scheduling algorithm [Graham 69]. Nodes are assigned to processors in the order given by PRIORITYLIST. If node n_j is assigned to processor i, then all following nodes on virtual processor PA(n_j) must also be assigned to processor i. This property makes our processor assignment algorithm more complex than the standard list scheduling algorithm. In list scheduling, the usual criterion for choosing n_j's processor is to pick the one which minimises n_j's start time, EST(n_j). Depending on the other nodes on the same virtual processor as n_j, the real processor which gives the smallest EST(n_j) value could in fact be the worst choice. We have to watch the new parallel execution time as well. Therefore, the criterion used in procedure ScheduleGraph is to choose PA(n_j) so that the pair (PARTIME, EST(n_j)) is minimised[16].

---

[16]As before, assume lexicographic comparison for ordered pairs, with the first element being the most significant.

Inputs:

   1. A GR graph $g = (N, \top, \perp, E_C, F_C, F_T)$.

   2. A schedule of g on an unbounded number of processors, $\Sigma^\infty(g) =$ $(PN, PA^\infty, \leq^\infty)$.

Outputs:

   1. Schedule $\Sigma(g) = (PN, PA, \leq)$ of GR graph g on P processors.

procedure ScheduleGraph(g, $\Sigma^\infty(g)$)

   1. PA $\leftarrow$ PA$^\infty$ /* Assume PA$^\infty(n) \notin \{1, ..., P\}$ $\forall$ $n \in$ PN. */

   2. TIME, EDGES, SIZE, PREC, PRIORITYLIST $\leftarrow$
      call BuildPrimitiveGraph(g, $\Sigma^\infty(g)$)
      /* Let PRIORITYLIST = $(n_1, ..., n_k)$. */

   3. **for** proc $\leftarrow$ 1 **to** P **do** LIST(proc) $\leftarrow$ ( )

   4. **for** j $\leftarrow$ 1 **to** k **do**
      if PA(n_j) $\notin \{1, ..., P\}$ **then**

        a. (PARTIME$_{min}$, EST$_{min}$) $\leftarrow$ ($+\infty$, $+\infty$)

        b. **for** proc $\leftarrow$ 1 **to** P **do**

          i. PA$_{new}$ $\leftarrow$ PA ;
            for each $n \in$ PA^{-1}(PA(n_j)) **do** PA$_{new}$(n) $\leftarrow$ proc

          ii. LIST$_{new}$ $\leftarrow$ LIST ;
            LIST$_{new}$(proc) $\leftarrow$ interleave sequences LIST(proc) and
            $\leq^\infty$(PA(n_j)), in order of increasing (LST, PRIORITYLIST)

          iii. PREC$_{new}$ $\leftarrow$ PREC ;
            for each non-empty LIST$_{new}$(i) = $(n'_1, ..., n'_{k_i})$ **do**
              1. **for** h $\leftarrow$ 1 **to** k_i-1 **do**
                PREC$_{new}$ $\leftarrow$ PREC$_{new}$ $\cup$ $\{(n'_h, n'_{h+1})\}$

          iv. PARTIME$_{new}$, EST$_{new}$, LCT$_{new}$, TOTALTIME$_{new}$, TOTALORDER$_{new}$
            $\leftarrow$ **call** DetermineTimes(PN, TIME, EDGES, SIZE, PREC$_{new}$, PA$_{new}$)

          v. **if** (PARTIME$_{new}$, EST$_{new}$(n_j)) < (PARTIME$_{min}$, EST$_{min}$)
            then
              1. (PARTIME$_{min}$, EST$_{min}$) $\leftarrow$ (PARTIME$_{new}$, EST$_{new}$(n_j))

              2. p_{min} $\leftarrow$ proc

        c. /* Map virtual processor PA(n_j) to real processor p_{min}. */
          i. LIST(p_{min}) $\leftarrow$ interleave sequences LIST(p_{min}) and
            $\leq^\infty$(PA(n_j)), in order of increasing (LST, PRIORITYLIST)

          ii. **for each** $n \in$ PA^{-1}(PA(n_j)) **do** PA(n) $\leftarrow$ p_{min}

end procedure

Figure 5-15: Procedure ScheduleGraph

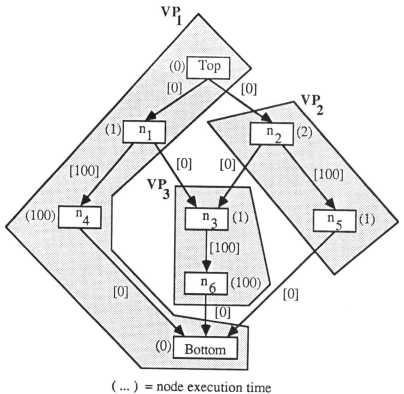

(...) = node execution time
[...] = edge communication size

PA(n₃)	EST(n₃)	PARTIME
P_1	1	202
P_2	2	104

Figure 5-16: Counter-example for simple list scheduling

Figure 5-16 gives an example to show how the minimum $EST(n_j)$ criterion may perform badly, compared to the minimum $(PARTIME, EST(n_j))$ criterion. The original GR graph has been scheduled[17] on three virtual processors – VP_1, VP_2 and VP_3.

---

[17]We can assume any communication overhead model in which the communication edges with *size*=0 incur no communication overhead, and the edges with *size*=100 incur an overhead substantially larger than the total sequential execution time of the program.

PRIORITYLIST, and in general any topological sequence of the nodes, must have nodes n_1 and n_2 before node n_3. Consider the processor assignment problem for 2 processors. Both the minimum $EST(n_j)$ and the minimum $(PARTIME, EST(n_j))$ criteria would assign nodes n_1 and n_2, and hence virtual processors VP_1 and VP_2, to separate real processors, say P_1 and P_2 respectively. When considering which processor node n_3 should be assigned to, we see the difference between the two criteria. The table at the bottom of Figure 5-16 shows the values for $EST(n_3)$ and PARTIME, for the cases $PA(n_3)=P_1$ and $PA(n_3)=P_2$. Therefore, node n_3 (and hence virtual processor VP_3) would be assigned to real processor P_1 with PARTIME=202, according to the minimum $EST(n_j)$ criterion, and to real processor P_2 with PARTIME=104, according to the minimum $(PARTIME, EST(n_j))$ criterion. Clearly, the minimum $(PARTIME, EST(n_j))$ is the better choice, since the minimum $EST(n_j)$ criterion sequentialises almost the entire program. This example can be easily extended to P processors, where the PARTIME ratio for the two criteria approaches P. The problem with the minimum $EST(n_j)$ criterion is that it is incapable of accounting for other nodes in the same virtual processor as n_j.

Another desirable property of the minimum $(PARTIME, EST(n_j))$ criterion is that it degenerates to traditional list scheduling with minimum $EST(n_j)$, when there is no communication overhead and the internalisation pre-pass simply assigns each node to a separate virtual processor. Let $(PARTIME_1, EST_1(n_j))$ and $(PARTIME_2, EST_2(n_j))$ be the values obtained by assigning node n_j to processors 1 and 2 respectively. If $PARTIME_1=PARTIME_2$, then the $(PARTIME, EST(n_j))$ and $EST(n_j)$ criteria will be equivalent. If $PARTIME_1 < PARTIME_2$ (say), then $EST_1(n_j) < EST_2(n_j)$ must be true if there is no communication overhead and each virtual processor contains a single node. In this degenerate case, an increase or decrease in PARTIME can only occur due to a corresponding increase or decrease in $EST(n_j)$. So again, the $(PARTIME, EST(n_j))$ and $EST(n_j)$ criteria will be equivalent.

Step 1 of procedure ScheduleGraph (Figure 5-15) initialises PA to the virtual processor assignment produced by the internalisation pre-pass. Step 2 calls procedure BuildPrimitiveGraph to construct the primitive graph. PRIORITYLIST is initialised to a total order (consistent with EDGES and PREC) of the primitive nodes. During the algorithm, LIST(*proc*) is maintained for each *proc* $\in \{1, ..., P\}$ as the sequence of nodes in $PA^{-1}(proc)$, according to their order in PRIORITYLIST. Each iteration of the

for loop in step 4 examines node n_j from PRIORITYLIST as a candidate for processor assignment. $PA(n_j) \in \{1, \ldots, P\}$ indicates that n_j has already been assigned to processor $PA(n_j)$ due to an earlier node in PRIORITYLIST. If $PA(n_j) \notin \{1, \ldots, P\}$ then Steps 4.a, 4.b and 4.c determine which processor n_j should be assigned to. 4.b considers all processors in $\{1, \ldots, P\}$ and stores the processor with the smallest value of $(PARTIME, EST(n_j))$ in p_{min}. Step 4.c updates LIST and PA to reflect the new processor assignment, which is actually a merge of virtual processor $PA(n_j)$ and real processor p_{min}. As in the internalisation pre-pass, the new sequence of the merged set is obtained by interleaving the two old sequences in order of increasing (LST, PRIORITYLIST).

Procedure ScheduleGraph takes $O(|PA^{\infty}(PN)| \times P \times (|PN| + |EDGES|))$ time, where $|PA^{\infty}(PN)| \leq |PN|$ is the number of virtual processors created by the internalisation pre-pass. Each execution of steps i to v in 4.b takes $O(|PN| + |EDGES|)$ time[18] and they are executed exactly $|PA^{\infty}(PN)| \times P$ times. This is the only algorithm in the dissertation which cannot exploit the hierarchical structure in GR to obtain a linear execution time for well-structured GR graphs. A divide-and-conquer approach cannot be used due to the interference which arises when different GR subgraphs share the same set of processors. If we assume that the primitive graph has a linear number of edges, $|EDGES| = O(|PN|)$, then the execution time of the processor assignment algorithm will be $O((\# \text{ virtual processors}) \times (\# \text{ real processors}) \times (\# \text{ primitive nodes}))$.

5.5. Performance Results

In this section, we present some performance results of our scheduling algorithms for the compile-time scheduling problem. As in section 4.4, the benchmark programs used are the ones described in Appendix A. The implementation of the scheduling and simulation systems is structured like Figure 4-11. Instead of the partitioner, we now have a compile-time scheduler, which is a complete implementation of the algorithms described in this chapter. The scheduler's output is the processor assignment and the node sequence for the function graph of the *main* function in the program. As in macro-dataflow, the multiprocessor simulation for compile-time scheduling consists of two steps:

---

[18]Note that $|PREC| < |PN|$, so that $|PREC| = O(|PN|)$.

1. A sequential execution of the extended IF1 interpreter, which produces dynamic trace files at the level of primitive nodes.

2. A second pass which reads in the trace files and builds the run-time primitive graph. The parallel execution time is then computed by following the processor assignments and node sequences produced by the scheduler.

It is relatively easy to augment this prototype implementation to build a compile-time scheduling system for SISAL on real multiprocessors. As before, we need a compiler for the target machine code as well as a mechanism to obtain execution profile information. However, scheduling at compile-time obviates the need for task scheduling at run-time. All inter-processor synchronisations and communications can be directly compiled into the target code. This prototype implementation of the compile-time scheduler will be used at Stanford to build SISAL and SAL compilers for multiprocessors in which compile-time scheduling is appropriate (e.g. NCUBE, MIPS-X-MP [Hennessy 86]).

The following parameters were used in the simulation experiments:

- The number of processors, P, was varied in the range 1 - 20.

- Communication overhead for compile-time scheduling was assumed to be entirely in the delay component, D_C, with no input and output components, R_C and W_C. This is exactly the opposite of the communication overhead values used in the macro-dataflow experiments. By using the same overhead value in different components, we observe if compile-time scheduling can exploit the potential overlap between communication and computation which is offered by the delay component. D_C is assumed to be linearly proportional to the size argument s. Thus

  - $R_C(i, j, s, l) = W_C(i, j, s, l) = 0$

  - $D_C(i, j, s, l) = 2 \times k \times s$

  where k is some constant. These experiments used $k = 0$, 0.125 and 1 cycles/byte. The factor of 2 is used to make the delay overhead, D_C, equal the sum of R_C and W_C used in macro-dataflow.

- Finally, the execution profile used to generate the partition was varied as SMALL, CORRECT and LARGE, with sequential execution times increasing by approximately a factor of 2, as the inputs were changed from SMALL to CORRECT and from CORRECT to LARGE.

Figures 5-17 to 5-20 contain speed-up plots for different simulation experiments. The speed-up is the ratio of the program's sequential execution time to the parallel execution time (including overhead) on P processors. Appendix B contains all the raw simulation data for these experiments and describes how the simulated speed-up value was computed.

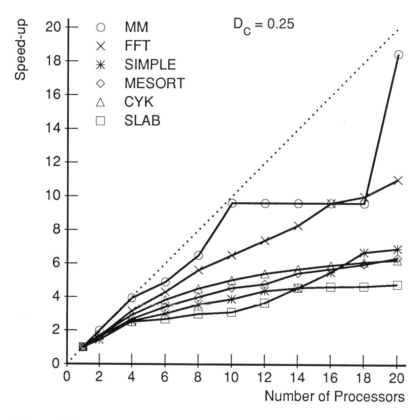

Figure 5-17: Compile-time Scheduling: Speed-up vs. Number of Processors

Figure 5-17 shows the variation in speed-up as the number of processors is increased from 1 to 20. The delay overhead was assumed to be 0.25 cycles/byte, corresponding to $k = 0.125$. As with macro-dataflow, all the speed-up curves are monotonically non-decreasing. The most striking difference with the speed-up curves of macro-dataflow is that the curves in Figure 5-17 are more jerky. MM shows this jerky behaviour to the largest extent. This is due to integer effects which occur when the number of iterations in a parallel node is comparable to the number of processors. The outer level Forall in MM has 20 iterations giving an ideal speed-up of $20/\lceil 20/P \rceil$ on P processors. Therefore, the ideal speed-up only equals 10 at P=18, and jumps to 20 at P=20.

How bad can this integer effect be? In general, a parallel node containing $N > 0$ iterations, with equal execution times, has a speed-up of $N/\lceil N/P \rceil$ on $P > 0$ processors. If $N \le P$ then $N/\lceil N/P \rceil = N$, which is the best speed-up we can expect. If $N \gg P$ then $N/\lceil N/P \rceil \rightarrow P$, which is again the best speed-up we can expect. The integer effect problem occurs when $N > P$ but N is still close to P. However

$$\lceil N/P \rceil < 1 + N/P \Rightarrow N/\lceil N/P \rceil > (1/N + 1/P)^{-1} \qquad (5.1)$$

and

$$N > P \Rightarrow (1/N + 1/P)^{-1} > P/2 \qquad (5.2)$$

Combining (5.1) and (5.2) gives

$$N > P \Rightarrow N/\lceil N/P \rceil > P/2 \qquad (5.3)$$

So, in the *worst* case, the integer effect gives a speed-up close to $P/2$, which is a factor of 2 away from what we would normally hope for.

Why was this integer effect not observed in the speed-up curves for macro-dataflow (Figure 4-13)? MM consists of 3 nested Forall's, each containing 20 iterations. The macro-dataflow partitioner expanded the outer Forall and partitioned the middle Forall into macro-actors with 4 iterations each. This partition yields 100 parallel macro-actors at run-time, which has a negligible integer effect when $P \le 20$. In compile-time scheduling, the node expansion algorithm (procedure ExpandNodes, Figure 5-6) replaced the outer Forall in MM by P sub-Forall nodes, assuming that all sub-Forall's take equal time. This assumption is violated when N is close to P and P is not a factor of N, leading to the integer effect described earlier. To try and avoid this integer effect in compile-time scheduling by using the same granularity as the macro-dataflow partition, it would be necessary to statically expand the outer Forall into 20 sub-Forall nodes, and then expand the middle Forall in each sub-Forall node into 5 sub-sub-Forall nodes! For simplicity and efficiency, procedure ExpandNodes (Figure 5-6) did not allow the possibility of expanding multiple levels of parallel nodes. The single level restriction is not a problem if $N \gg P$, but it is a simple job to extend the prototype implementation so as to expand multiple levels of parallel nodes, if necessary. However, there is a trade-off between the execution time of compile-time scheduling and the improved parallel execution time obtained from a finer granularity expansion.

For a tightly coupled, shared-memory multiprocessor, a hybrid solution would be to assign an entire Forall node to a set of processors at compile-time, and then have the processors execute the Forall iterations in a *self-scheduling* fashion at run-time. This approach is discussed as future work in section 6.2, along with other possible ways of combining compile-time and run-time scheduling.

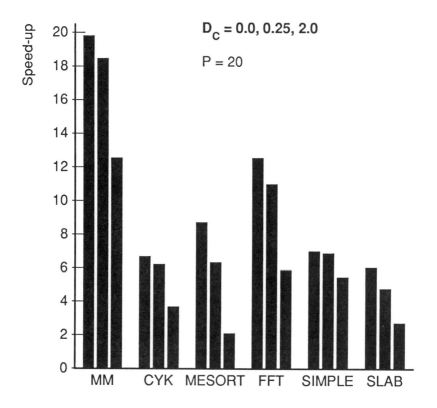

Figure 5-18: Compile-time Scheduling: Speed-up vs. Communication Overhead

Figure 5-18 shows the variation in speed-up as the delay component of communication overhead is increased through 0.0, 0.25 and 2.0 cycles/byte, for 20 processors. As in macro-dataflow, the speed-up falls as the communication overhead increases. However, the change is less drastic than macro-dataflow (Figure 4-15), showing that compile-time scheduling can indeed exploit the overlap between communication and computation, available in the delay component.

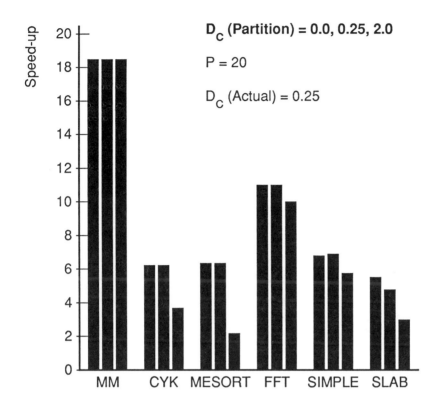

Figure 5-19: Compile-time Scheduling: Speed-up for different Multiprocessor Inputs

Figure 5-19 shows the variation in speed-up for 3 different partitions generated for $D_C = 0.0, 0.25, 2.0$ cycles/byte (LOW, MEDIUM and HIGH overhead respectively). Each partition was simulated on the MEDIUM overhead multiprocessor (with $P = 20$). The purpose of this experiment is to observe how the scheduler adapts to the input multiprocessor parameters. The LOW and MEDIUM overhead schedules had nearly identical speed-ups for all programs except SLAB, indicating that $D_C=0.0$ and $D_C=0.25$ were close enough to give nearly identical schedules. For SLAB, the LOW overhead schedule performed better than the MEDIUM overhead schedule, which is an anomaly. A close investigation of SLAB revealed that the problem was due to unbalanced iterations in a parallel node. In expanding a parallel node, compile-time scheduling assumes that all the new concurrent nodes (sub-Forall's) have the same execution time.

This was not true for SLAB, causing the LOW overhead partition to be better because of improved load balancing, despite the fact that the MEDIUM overhead partition was better tuned to the overhead of the target multiprocessor. Unlike macro-dataflow where the HIGH overhead partition was generally better than the LOW overhead partition, compile-time scheduling exhibits the opposite behaviour with the LOW overhead partition doing better than the HIGH overhead partition.

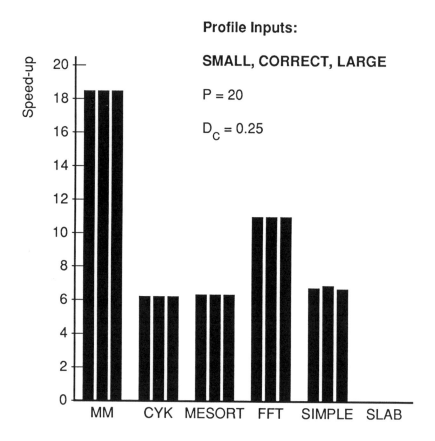

Figure 5-20: Compile-time Scheduling: Speed-up for different Profile Inputs

Figure 5-20 shows the variation in speed-up for 3 different partitions generated for SMALL, CORRECT and LARGE profile inputs, similar to Figure 4-17 in macro-dataflow. Each partition was simulated with the CORRECT input and $D_C = 0.25$

cycles/byte on 20 processors. The simulation results show virtually no variation for the three cases. At first glance, this is really surprising, because we would expect compile-time scheduling to be more sensitive to profile inputs than macro-dataflow. However, for these benchmark programs, varying the input basically amounted to changing the number of iterations in various loops, without essentially changing the computation paths during program execution. Programs with less predictable run-time behaviour would have shown a greater sensitivity to execution profile inputs.

6   Conclusions

In Chapter 2, we said that the goal of this dissertation is to automatically determine an efficient partition and schedule for a given parallel program and target multiprocessor.   The major contributions of this dissertation are two approaches to automatic partitioning and scheduling:

1. Macro-dataflow.

2. Compile-time scheduling.

In each case, the partitioning and scheduling problems were formalised as a compile-time optimisation problem with a single objective function. The use of a single objective function explicitly described the trade-off between parallelism and overhead, which is the central issue in partitioning and scheduling. The objective functions for macro-dataflow and compile-time scheduling were based on the program representation (GR) described in Section 3.2 and the multiprocessor model described in Section 3.5. The program representation and multiprocessor model were designed to support a wide range of parallel languages and multiprocessor architectures.

Now that all the details have been presented in Chapters 3, 4 and 5, it is time to wrap up. Section 6.1 presents a summary performance comparison between macro-dataflow and compile-time scheduling, and Section 6.2 suggests possible directions for future work.

6.1. Macro-Dataflow vs. Compile-time Scheduling

The shaded (not solid) bars in Figure 6-1 show the *ideal* speed-up obtained on 20 processors for the following 3 partitions and schedules generated for each benchmark:

1. The smallest granularity partition (with maximum parallelism) with run-time scheduling.

2. The partition generated for macro-dataflow (assuming $T_{sched} = 10$ cycles, $R_C = W_C = 0.125$ cycles/byte, $D_C = 0$) with run-time scheduling.

3. The partition and schedule generated for compile-time scheduling (assuming $D_C = 0.25$ cycles/byte, $R_C = W_C = 0$).

These speed-ups are *ideal* because they were obtained by simulating a multiprocessor

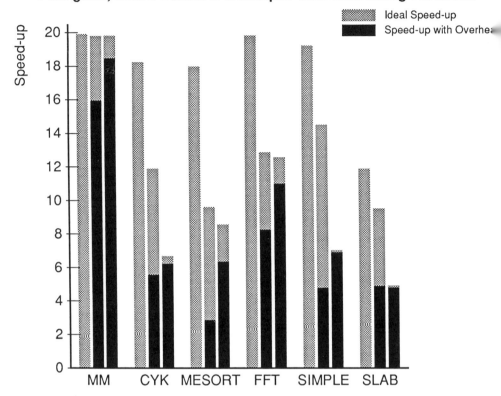

Figure 6-1: Comparison of Speed-ups

with zero overhead. For all programs, we see that the ideal speed-up decreases as the partition varies through 1, 2, 3 above. As expected, this shows that the partitions generated by macro-dataflow and compile-time scheduling contain less parallelism than the finest granularity partition. We also see that the partition generated for macro-dataflow has significantly more parallelism than the partition and schedule generated for compile-time scheduling.

The solid bars in Figure 6-1 summarise the actual speed-ups obtained for macro-dataflow and compile-time scheduling. These speed-up values were obtained by simulating a multiprocessor with the appropriate overhead, and are the same values as presented in sections 4.4 and 5.5. The amount by which the shaded bar rises above the solid bar is the amount of potential speed-up which was lost due to overhead. Macro-dataflow suffers much more from this loss than compile-time scheduling due to two main reasons:

1. Macro-dataflow incurs scheduling overhead, whereas compile-time scheduling does not.

2. Compile-time scheduling can better optimise communication overhead than macro-dataflow, by overlapping communication with computation.

The solid bars give a performance comparison between macro-dataflow and compile-time scheduling. SLAB was the only program in which macro-dataflow performed better than compile-time scheduling, and even that was practically a tie. This shows that compile-time scheduling does work well for predictable programs. It turned out that the benchmarks selected for this dissertation are mostly regular and predictable kinds of programs. However, compile-time scheduling would be unsuitable for programs in which the computation paths vary drastically for different inputs.

It would be useful to be able to predict at compile-time which approach would be better for a given program. A general solution is to extend the execution profile information and the cost assignment procedures, so as to obtain the *standard deviation* of execution times in GR, along with the average values. Programs with large standard deviations would generally be better suited to the macro-dataflow approach. Another way to choose between macro-dataflow and compile-time scheduling is to partition the program separately for each approach, and choose the one which has the best predicted speed-up.

Figure 6-2 compares the *predicted* and *actual* speed-up values obtained for macro-dataflow and compile-time scheduling, with the the same overhead values used for Figure 6-1. In macro-dataflow, the predicted speed-up is $P/F(\Pi)$, for P processors. In compile-time scheduling, it is simply T_{seq}/T_{par}, where T_{seq} and T_{par} are the estimated sequential and parallel execution times of the partitioned program. For all six benchmark programs, the predicted speed-up from compile-time scheduling was better than the predicted speed-up from macro-dataflow, by varying degrees. As mentioned earlier, the actual speed-up for compile-time scheduling was better than the actual speed-up for macro-dataflow, in five out of six programs. In the sixth program (SLAB), the actual speed-ups were nearly equal (4.8 and 4.9). Therefore, the predicted speed-up

Benchmark	Macro-Dataflow (Predicted)	(Actual)	Compile-time Scheduling (Predicted)	(Actual)
MM	15.4	16.0	18.0	18.5
CYK	8.1	5.6	14.7	6.2
MESORT	3.1	2.9	6.2	6.3
FFT	8.7	8.2	12.7	11.0
SIMPLE	8.8	4.8	9.8	6.9
SLAB	5.3	4.9	7.3	4.8

Figure 6-2: Comparison of Speed-ups (Predicted and Actual values)

is a reasonable criterion to use in choosing between macro-dataflow and compile-time scheduling.

Figure 6-2 also shows that there can sometimes be a large discrepancy between the predicted and actual speed-ups. The worst case was observed for compile-time scheduling of CYK, where the predicted and actual speed-ups were 14.7 and 6.2 respectively. This is due to the unbalanced load in the Forall expressions used in CYK (page 167).

Figure 6-3 shows the execution times taken by the macro-dataflow and compile-time scheduling implementations to generate the partitions and schedules used in Figure 6-1. The abscissa gives the total size (nodes + edges) of the input program graph and the ordinate gives the total CPU time (user + system) on the VAX-780 used for the prototype implementation. The prototype implementation was based on a simple, "correctness-first efficiency-later" approach with an extensive use of run-time checking of array bounds and *assert* statements. It may be possible to improve the execution times by a factor of 2 or so, in a more careful implementation. Figure 6-3 also includes the execution time of the SISAL front-end as a comparison.

Whereas both macro-dataflow and compile-time scheduling took under 1 CPU minute for MM, CYK, MESORT, the execution times became more significant for FFT and SLAB, ending with 45 and 50 CPU minutes respectively for SIMPLE. In comparison, the front-end just went up to 4 CPU minutes for SIMPLE. However, the

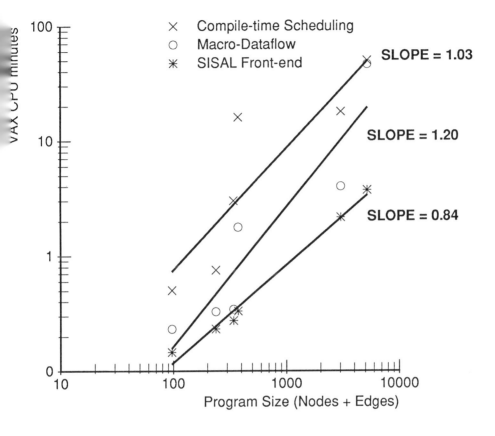

Figure 6-3: Comparison of Execution Times

factor of 12 or so by which macro-dataflow and compile-time scheduling are slower than the front-end for SIMPLE, is much less than the size of SIMPLE (5226 nodes and edges). The factor seems closer to log_2S rather than S, where S is the size of the program graph.

The straight lines plotted in Figure 6-3 are linear regressions of the data points. Since both axes are plotted on the same log scale, the slope of a line gives an estimate of the exponent of S, if the execution time function is approximated by a power of S. The slopes are 1.20 and 1.03 for macro-dataflow and compile-time scheduling, suggesting execution times which are close to linear. Of course, the data points show a large variance, so we really need more data points for a better estimate of the performance of the macro-dataflow and compile-time scheduling implementations.

The execution time for compile-time scheduling also depends on the threshold value, T_{min}, and on the number of processors, P. These parameters determine the size of the *primitive* graph (see Figure 5-6). The primitive graph usually grows larger with an increase in P, to expose more parallelism. The threshold value can then be increased to restrain the size of the primitive graph, if necessary. Unlike macro-dataflow, the execution time of compile-time scheduling is also linearly proportional to the number of processors, even if the size of the primitive graph remains constant. This is a property of the processor assignment algorithm (Figure 5-15) in compile-time scheduling.

As a final note on execution times, it should be mentioned that procedures PartitionGraph (Figure 4-6) and ScheduleGraph (Figure 5-15), which dominate the performance of macro-dataflow and compile-time scheduling respectively, are both algorithms which can be easily parallelised for execution on multiprocessors. This may be useful if the target multiprocessor ever has idle cycles for the compiler to use.

6.2. Future Work

This dissertation provides a starting point for further work in implementing parallel languages on multiprocessors, with automatic partitioning and scheduling. Some of the possible directions in future work are described in this section.

6.2.1. Implementing single-assignment languages on multiprocessors

The natural extension to the implementation work done for this dissertation is to add code generators to the partitioning system, so that the single-assignment language SISAL can be made to execute on real multiprocessors. These extensions for macro-dataflow and compile-time scheduling have already been discussed in Sections 4.4 and 5.5.

The first step is to develop uniprocessor compilers for SISAL. This is the subject of ongoing work at Stanford and Livermore. The most important problem in compiling single-assignment languages is the *copy avoidance* problem. Semantically, a *Replace* operation like *A[i: x]* returns a copy of array *A* with its ith element replaced by the value of x. The semantics of single-assignment languages does not allow for side-effects. However, it is important for the implementation to avoid copying the entire array whenever possible, and instead update the ith element of A *in situ*. This copy avoidance optimisation can reduce program execution times by orders of magnitude, e.g. it reduces the execution time of bubblesort from $O(N^3)$ to $O(N^2)$.

Possible solutions to the copy avoidance problem are:

1. Perform a compile-time analysis to detect when a replace operation can be safely performed in-place [Gopinath 87].

2. Maintain run-time reference counts for all structures during program execution. A replace operation can be performed in-place if the input structure has a reference count of 1 (i.e. the replace operation is the only remaining consumer of the value) [Gharachorloo 88].

3. Use a combination of 1 and 2, by optimising away at compile-time as much reference count code as possible [Hudak 86].

Copy avoidance is a hard problem to solve at compile-time, making 1 the most difficult approach. Approach 2 is simple to implement and can catch more replace operations than approach 1. The problem with approach 2 is the performance degradation due to the overhead of maintaining reference counts. Still, this degradation is usually a constant factor (like 2 or 3) which is much less than the order-of-magnitude overhead due to copying. [Gharachorloo 88] gives performance results obtained from a sequential implementation of SISAL developed at Stanford, using approach 2 with some local optimisations. Though this approach is the most general, it does not necessarily catch all replace operations, because the value of the reference count depends on the order in which operations are performed. In general, a compile-time reordering of operations may be needed to make approach 2 more effective. The idea in approach 3 is to combine the generality of run-time reference counts (approach 2) with the optimisations of compile-time analysis (approach 1). If successful, this approach can deliver the performance of approach 2 at the cost of approach 1. [Hudak 86] gives a theoretical basis for approach 3, but does not contain a real implementation.

6.2.2. Other languages

While automatic partitioning and scheduling is clearly well suited to single-assignment languages, it would be interesting to try this approach on other languages as well. All the partitioning and scheduling algorithms have been defined in terms of GR, so this approach should work for any language which can be reasonably translated to GR. The candidate languages may have implicit or explicit parallelism. If the parallelism is implicit, there should also be some mechanism to automatically detect parallelism in the programs.

Concurrent Prolog [Shapiro 86] is a promising candidate for automatic partitioning and scheduling. Like dataflow languages, the parallel execution model for Concurrent Prolog is defined at an idealised, fine level of granularity, namely at the granularity of *goals*. The macro-dataflow approach could be used to partition a Concurrent Prolog program into *macro-goals*, for execution on a multiprocessor. Compile-time scheduling would probably be less successful, because Prolog programs typically show a large dynamic variation in computation paths.

The same considerations mentioned above for Concurrent Prolog apply to *pure* Lisp as well, which offers parallelism in evaluating the arguments of a function call. Standard Lisp has side-effects, which makes the problem of identifying parallelism very difficult (like dusty decks of Fortran). Currently proposed parallel extensions to Lisp (e.g. QLisp [Gabriel 84], Multilisp [Halstead 86]) continue this trend of programmer-controlled side effects, at the loss of referential transparency.

Moving to procedural languages, a simple language like IBM's Parallel Fortran [IBM 88] with constructs equivalent to **cobegin-coend** and **doall**, is also well suited to automatic partitioning and scheduling. The PARALLEL CASES construct in Parallel Fortran is similar to **cobegin-coend** in that it creates a group of parallel tasks ("cases"). However, each task can optionally specify a set of tasks as its predecessors, allowing any arbitrary inter-task dependence graph to be expressed by the PARALLEL CASES construct[19]. It is commonly believed that structured parallel programs can only express *series-parallel* dependence graphs. This is not true for Parallel Fortran.

---

[19]Of course, the programmer could always introduce explicit synchronisation variables in a **cobegin-coend** construct to express arbitrary inter-task synchronisation. However, it is more convenient when the construct is directly available in the language, since it eliminates the possibility of synchronisation errors.

6.2.3. Combining macro-dataflow and compile-time scheduling

Throughout this dissertation, we have presented macro-dataflow and compile-time scheduling as two distinct approaches. *Macro-dataflow* is based on compile-time partitioning and run-time scheduling, whereas both partitioning and scheduling are performed at compile-time in *compile-time scheduling*. However, it may be possible to blur this distinction.

For instance, the internalisation pre-pass (Section 5.3) schedules the program on a number of *virtual* processors. These virtual processors can be thought of as *processes* to be scheduled on processors at run-time, just like any process-based language. The problem of finding the optimal partition in this case involves issues from both macro-dataflow (e.g. scheduling overhead) and compile-time scheduling (e.g. parallel execution time). This is a reasonable approach if the process scheduler in the target multiprocessor can do a good job of load balancing, without incurring excessive overhead due to context switching and process migration.

Macro-dataflow and compile-time scheduling can also be combined to match a two-level hierarchy in the target multiprocessor system. Consider a loosely-coupled collection of tightly-coupled multiprocessors. A parallel program can be partitioned for a very coarse grained macro-dataflow implementation at the outer level. Compile-time scheduling can then be used to partition and schedule the computation within each macro-actor for execution on a single tightly-coupled multiprocessor. Such two-level hierarchical systems are already becoming available as people use local area networks to connect small-scale multiprocessors. Whether a program will be able to execute efficiently at both levels depends mainly on the locality of communication in the partition, i.e. if the inter-multiprocessor communication traffic is much less than the intra-multiprocessor communication traffic.

An interesting extension to compile-time scheduling would be to allow *self-scheduling* [Polychronopoulos 87] of **doall** loops (i.e. parallel nodes in GR). This extension would only be feasible for tightly coupled shared-memory multiprocessors. In the current scheme, we statically expand a parallel node, n_p, into NC *concurrent* nodes ($1 \leq NC \leq P$), n_1, ..., n_{NC}, so that n_p's iterations are distributed evenly among n_1, ..., n_{NC}. Instead, we could use self-scheduling to let each concurrent node's processor repeatedly pick up an iteration (or a *chunk* of iterations) from n_p at run-time. This scheme should provide a superior load balancing of n_p's iterations, at the expense of the self-scheduling overhead which is quite reasonable in practise.

6.2.4. Relaxing the convexity constraint

An interesting extension to macro-dataflow would be to try and relax the convexity constraint, while still maintaining the desirable properties of good load balancing and low task management overhead. One approach would be to allow a macro-actor to spawn other macro-actors and suspend itself till they complete execution, as in the standard fork-join model. In this way, all *control dependences* (page 59) will be handled by task creation and completion, and all *data dependences* will be handled by the scheduler as before. There is no fundamental difference in the blocking mechanism needed to handle control and data dependences. Typically, a counter is used to reactivate a task in either scheme. For control dependence, the counter keeps track of the number of active children, and for data dependence, the counter keeps track of the number of active predecessors. Ideally, a run-time system for parallel execution should be able to efficiently support both control and data dependences. However, many multiprocessor operating systems provide a fork-join model for task management. It may be practical to use the task management routines provided by the operating system, so as to reduce the effort required to develop a run-time scheduler for macro-dataflow.

6.2.5. Improvements in the partitioning and scheduling algorithms

Since the optimisation problems for macro-dataflow and compile-time scheduling are NP-complete, we had to resort to the use of approximation algorithms. The algorithms presented in this dissertation work reasonably well in practise, but there is scope for improvement in the following areas:

1. Optimality and Efficiency
   Since we are dealing with approximation algorithms, we can informally call one algorithm "more optimal" than another, if it finds solutions with better values of the objective function. It would be desirable to design algorithms which are more optimal and more efficient in practise, than the approximation algorithms presented in this dissertation.

2. Performance Bounds
   For any combinatorial minimisation problem P and approximation algorithm A, let

- F(S) be the objective function to be minimised.

- S_{OPT} be an optimal solution of P, so that $F(S_{OPT}) \leq F(S)$ for all solutions S of problem P.

- S_A be the solution chosen by approximation algorithm A.

- $PR_A := F(S_A)/F(S_{OPT})$ be the *performance ratio* of algorithm A.

Even though it is intractable to find S_{OPT} (if P is NP-complete) and evaluate PR_A, it is possible in some cases [Garey 79] to prove that $PR_A \leq PB_A$, where PB_A is a worst-case *performance bound* of algorithm A. It would be desirable to design algorithms for the optimisation problems in this dissertation, which have provably low performance bounds.

3. Study of Simple Cases
   While the general optimisation problems are NP-complete, it is possible to design better algorithms for simplified, special cases of the optimisation problems. Some simple cases have already been discussed in Chapters 4 and 5. From our experience with SISAL programs, it appears that many traditional simplifications (e.g. unit execution times, tree-structured communications, etc.) are not valid assumptions for real programs. Nevertheless, a study of the simple cases may lend some insight to help design a better algorithm for the general case.

6.2.6. Symbolic costs

The graphical representation GR represents communication sizes, graph frequencies and execution times as floating-point numbers. One possible extension is to use symbolic expressions instead. This is a much more ambitious approach with potentially greater rewards due to the extra information contained in symbolic expressions. For example, consider the Fortran (an extended version with DOALL) program fragment shown below.

```
      DOALL 10 I = 1, N
         DO 20 J = 1, I
 20         . . .
 10      . . .
```

The execution time of each iteration of the DOALL 10 I loop depends on the value of I. However, execution profile data can only give average frequency values for the I and J loops, which implicitly (and incorrectly) assumes that each iteration of the I loop takes the same time. If we had symbolic expressions for the frequencies instead, then it would be possible to estimate the execution time of each DOALL iteration more accurately, thus leading to a better partition or schedule.

How can symbolic costs be incorporated in the partitioning and scheduling systems described in this dissertation? Let us assume that the programming language system can somehow provide symbolic expressions for all communication sizes, graph frequencies and simple node execution times in the GR program. Then, we could still do cost assignment as described in Section 3.4 by simply using addition and multiplication operators to combine symbolic expressions. The partitioning and scheduling algorithms mainly use costs for comparison. At each such decision point, the algorithm would now want to compare the values of two symbolic expressions. This can be hard if the expressions contain more than one variable. Even if all symbolic expressions use a single variable, some range information would be necessary to answer questions like *Is $100 \times N < N^2$?* or *Is $N > (log_2 N)^3$?*.

The use of symbolic expressions and symbolic analysis is likely to play an increasingly important role in compilers. It has already appeared in vectorising compilers for aliasing analysis of array subscript expressions. This dissertation offers another possible use of symbolic expressions.

6.2.7. Evaluation of different multiprocessor architectures

One of the biggest problems in architectural evaluation is the "compiler effect" – should an observed performance improvement be attributed to the architecture or the compiler? This problem will become more serious for multiprocessors, as architectural comparisons start to be based on widely different programs (and implementations) for the same problem. Automatic partitioning and scheduling provides a uniform compiler approach for all multiprocessors. The same program can be automatically targetted to a wide range of multiprocessors, allowing for a fair performance comparison. At Stanford, we intend to do such a comparison between shared-bus architectures (Encore Multimax, MIPS-X-MP), hypercube architectures (NCUBE) and distributed systems (SUN workstations connected by an Ethernet), when a complete parallel implementation for SISAL becomes available.

The multiprocessor simulator implemented for this dissertation is also an excellent tool for the evaluation of different multiprocessor architectures. The simulator can be used to simulate different numbers of processors, overhead values and interconnection networks (though the current version of the simulator ignores contention effects). The main problem with simulation is that it must be restricted to small input sizes for the sake of efficiency. While simulation is useful as a comparison tool, we definitely need to execute programs on real multiprocessors for a complete comparison.

6.2.8. Integration with an optimising compiler

A big challenge in automatic partitioning and scheduling systems is their integration with conventional code optimisations. Ideally, each sequential unit of computation in a partitioned program should be optimised to the same extent as a uniprocessor implementation of the entire program, so that large processor utilisation actually gives a large speed-up. This can get very tricky because some optimisations (e.g. copy avoidance in single-assignment languages) may be accompanied by a loss of parallelism. In general, there is a feedback path between the partitioning system and the optimising compiler. One efficient solution is to classify each optimisation as *pre-pass* or *post-pass*, so that it is decided *a priori* which optimisations should be performed before partitioning/scheduling and which optimisations should be performed after. This classification of optimisations can be a hard problem in general.

Appendix A: Benchmark Programs

The benchmark programs used to obtain the performance results presented in Sections 4.4 and 5.5 are described here. All these programs were written in the single-assignment language, SISAL [McGraw 85], and were executed on extended versions of DI, the Livermore IF1-level debugger and interpreter. The description of each benchmark program contains:

- **Static size:** This is intended to be a rough measure of the program's static size. It consists of the number of source lines in the SISAL program and the number of nodes and edges in the IF1 graphical representation.

- **Inputs:** The actual inputs used for a single execution of the program.

- **Parallelism profile:** A profile of the number of active processors over time during an idealistic fine-grained simulation which assumes that the multiprocessor has zero scheduling and communication overhead. Thus, the idealistic simulation is like an ideal dataflow machine operating at the granularity of IF1 nodes, with zero overhead for associative token matching! Two profiles are presented for each benchmark:

    1. For an unbounded number of processors ($P = \infty$).

    2. For 20 processors ($P = 20$).

  The parallelism profiles are provided solely as pictorial representations of the parallel behaviour of the benchmark programs. They do not directly represent performance on a realistic parallel machine.

- **Sequential execution time (T_{seq}):** The total number of hypothetical machine cycles executed by the program (over all processors). This measurement of execution time in machine cycles is discussed below.

- **Parallel execution time (T_{par}):** The parallel execution time of the program obtained from the idealistic simulation used to obtain the parallelism profile.

- **Ideal speed-up:** The ratio T_{seq} / T_{par}.

The execution time metric is an important parameter in describing these benchmark programs. The basic execution time unit used in the simulations is a single clock cycle of a hypothetical machine. Figure A-1 gives the values of cost parameters used by the simulator to determine execution times of simple nodes. The simulation experiments can just as easily be performed for a different set of values in Figure A-1. All the

```
AAddHcost              :=     1.0 ;        { Excludes copy cost}
AAddLcost              :=     1.0 ;        { Excludes copy cost}
AElementcost           :=     4.0 ;
AExtractcost           :=     1.0 ;
AGathercost            :=     1.0 ;        { Cost per element. }
AIsEmptycost           :=     1.0 ;
ALimHcost              :=     1.0 ;
ALimLcost              :=     1.0 ;
AScattercost           :=     1.0 ;        { Cost per element. }
ASetLcost              :=     1.0 ;
ASizecost              :=     1.0 ;
Abscost                :=     3.0 ;
IsErrorcost            :=     1.0 ;
Maxcost                :=     3.0 ;
Mincost                :=     3.0 ;
RangeGenerateCost      :=     1.0 ;
RElementscost          :=     1.0 ;
ARemHcost              :=     1.0 ;        { Excludes copy cost}
ARemLcost              :=     1.0 ;        { Excludes copy cost}

BRANCHcost             :=     1.0 ;
DBLDIVcost             :=     8.0 ;
DBLMULcost             :=     8.0 ;
DBLMODcost             :=     8.0 ;
DBLSUBcost             :=     8.0 ;
DBLADDcost             :=     8.0 ;
DBLEXPcost             :=     100.0 ;
DBLATANcost            :=     100.0 ;
DBLCOScost             :=     100.0 ;
DBLETOTHEcost          :=     100.0 ;
DBLLNcost              :=     100.0 ;
DBLSINcost             :=     100.0 ;
DBLSQRcost             :=     100.0 ;
DBLSQRTcost            :=     100.0 ;
FLOORcost              :=     3.0 ;
TRUNCcost              :=     3.0 ;
FLOATcost              :=     3.0 ;
ROUNDcost              :=     3.0 ;
INTADDcost             :=     1.0 ;
INTDIVcost             :=     1.0 ;
INTMODcost             :=     1.0 ;
INTEXPcost             :=     10.0 ;
INTMULcost             :=     1.0 ;
INTSUBcost             :=     1.0 ;
REALSUBcost            :=     8.0 ;
REALADDcost            :=     8.0 ;
REALDIVcost            :=     8.0 ;
REALMULcost            :=     8.0 ;
REALMODcost            :=     8.0 ;
REALEXPcost            :=     100.0 ;
NEGcost                :=     1.0 ;
NOTcost                :=     1.0 ;
ORcost                 :=     1.0 ;
ANDcost                :=     1.0 ;

BOOLsize               :=     1.0 ;
CHARsize               :=     1.0 ;
INTsize                :=     4.0 ;
REALsize               :=     4.0 ;
DBLsize                :=     8.0 ;
```

Figure A-1: Hypothetical execution times for simple operations

experiments reported in this dissertation used the values in Figure A-1. The parameters at the end of Figure A-1 are size parameters. These size parameters are typical for a byte-addressable architecture (like the VAX-780) with a byte as the basic data size unit. The size parameters are used to determine communication sizes of all values (scalars, arrays, records, etc.) when simulating communication overhead.

An important point to note about the input sizes used for the benchmark programs is that the corresponding sequential execution times are all less than 10^6 cycles. All the benchmark programs should execute in less than 1 CPU second on today's uniprocessors, for such small input sizes. The simulations were restricted to these input sizes because they took 10-20 CPU minutes to execute on the IF1 interpreter. These input sizes are too small to represent real execution times on multiprocessors, but the observed trends in speed-up values in the simulation experiments can be extrapolated to larger input sizes.

MM

A standard $O(N^3)$ implementation for multiplying two N×N matrices of real numbers.

- **Static size:** 2 functions, 20 lines, 32 nodes, 65 edges.

- **Inputs:** Two 20×20 matrices of real numbers.

Figure A-2 shows the ideal parallelism profile for MM on an unbounded number of processors. After the first 44 cycles, which were spent on initialisations, there are $N^2 = 400$ inner products which can be computed in parallel. The SISAL function used to compute each inner product is given below:

```
function InnerProduct(n:integer; a,b:realmatrix;
                         row,column:integer returns real)
    for i in 1, n
    returns value of sum a[row][i]*b[i][column]
    end for
end function
```

For input matrices of size 20×20, there are 8000 instances of the term a[row][i]*b[i][column], all of which be computed in parallel. The 16000 processors active during the time interval (44,48) compute 8000 a[row][i] values and 8000 b[i] addresses. The 20 a[row]'s were recognised as loop invariants, after in-line expansion of the call to function InnerProduct, and pre-computed during (40,44). Next, the 8000 processors active during (48,60) compute 8000 b[i][columns]'s followed by 8000 multiplications.

The time interval (60,100) is devoted to the additions required to reduce 8000 products to 400 inner products. Each sum is computed in a tree-like fashion, with a tree depth of $\lceil \log_2(N+1) \rceil = 5$, for N = 20. Each floating point addition takes 8 cycles (see REALADDcost in Figure A-1), so the time interval for 5 additions is 40 cycles. The final 10 cycles in (100,110) is wrap-up code used to check the value of the first inner product.

The profile in Figure A-2 contains a lot of white space, showing poor processor utilisation. The initialisation and wrap-up computations were basically sequential and took 44 + 10 = 54 cycles, which is nearly half the execution time of the entire program (110 cycles). The poor processor utilisation is also reflected in the fact that using upto 16000 processors gave a speed-up of 2037.7. The reason for the low utilisation, of course, is the fact that the program was allowed to use an unbounded number of processors. Figure A-3 shows the parallelism profile when the program was limited to 20 processors, and achieved approximately 100% processor utilisation.

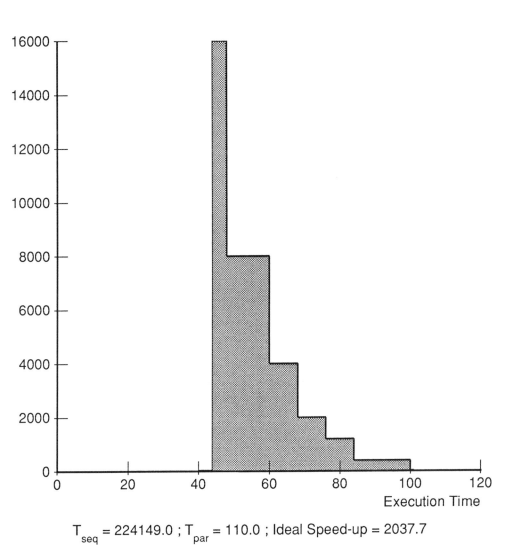

T_{seq} = 224149.0 ; T_{par} = 110.0 ; Ideal Speed-up = 2037.7

Figure A-2: MM – ideal parallelism profile for P = ∞

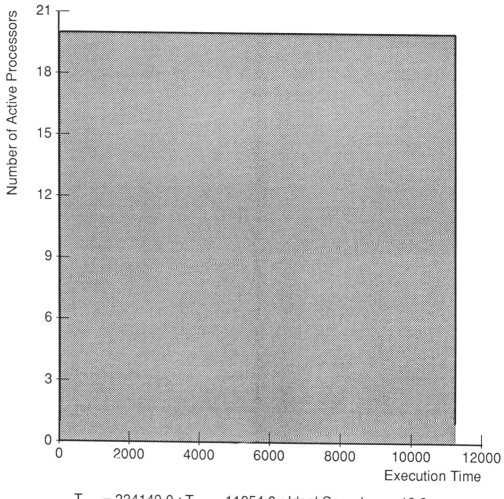

$T_{seq} = 224149.0$; $T_{par} = 11254.0$; Ideal Speed-up = 19.9

Figure A-3: MM – ideal parallelism profile for P = 20

CYK

The $O(N^3)$ Cocke-Younger-Kasami parsing algorithm based on dynamic programming [Hopcroft 79].

- **Static size:** 2 functions, 60 lines, 79 nodes, 160 edges.

- **Inputs:**

    1. A trivial but ambiguous grammar consisting of the productions,
       $A \rightarrow a$ and $A \rightarrow A A$.

    2. An input string consisting of 25 a's.

Figure A-4 shows the parallelism profile of CYK on an unbounded number of processors. This dynamic programming algorithm has the following loop structure:

```
for j := 1 to n-1         % Sequential for-loop expression
    forall i in 1, n-j      % Parallel forall-loop expression
        forall k in 1, j     % Parallel forall-loop expression
            . . .
        end forall
    end forall
end for
```

Since the outer j-loop is sequential, a new j iteration can only begin after all the computation in the previous j iteration has completed. Each j iteration basically contains (n-j)×j parallel units of work, since the inner i and k loops are Forall's. This structure is observed in Figure A-4, where there are n-1 = 24 peaks, with height proportional to (n-j)×j for $1 \leq j \leq 24$. The largest peaks were obtained for j = 12 & 13, since that is where (n-j)×j is maximised when n = 25.

Figure A-5 shows the parallelism profile for an idealistic simulation of CYK on 20 processors.

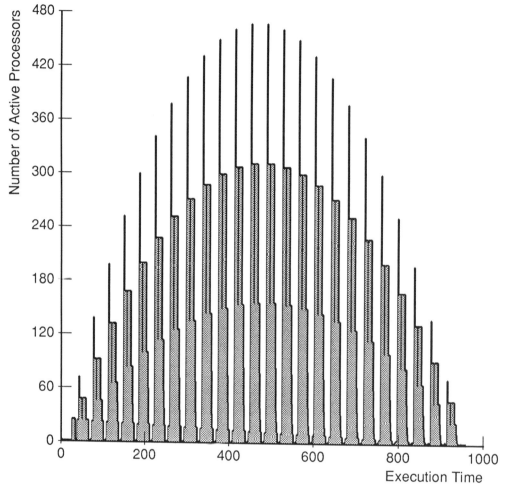

T_{seq} = 103384.0 ; T_{par} = 959.0 ; Ideal Speed-up = 107.8

Figure A-4: CYK – ideal parallelism profile for P = ∞

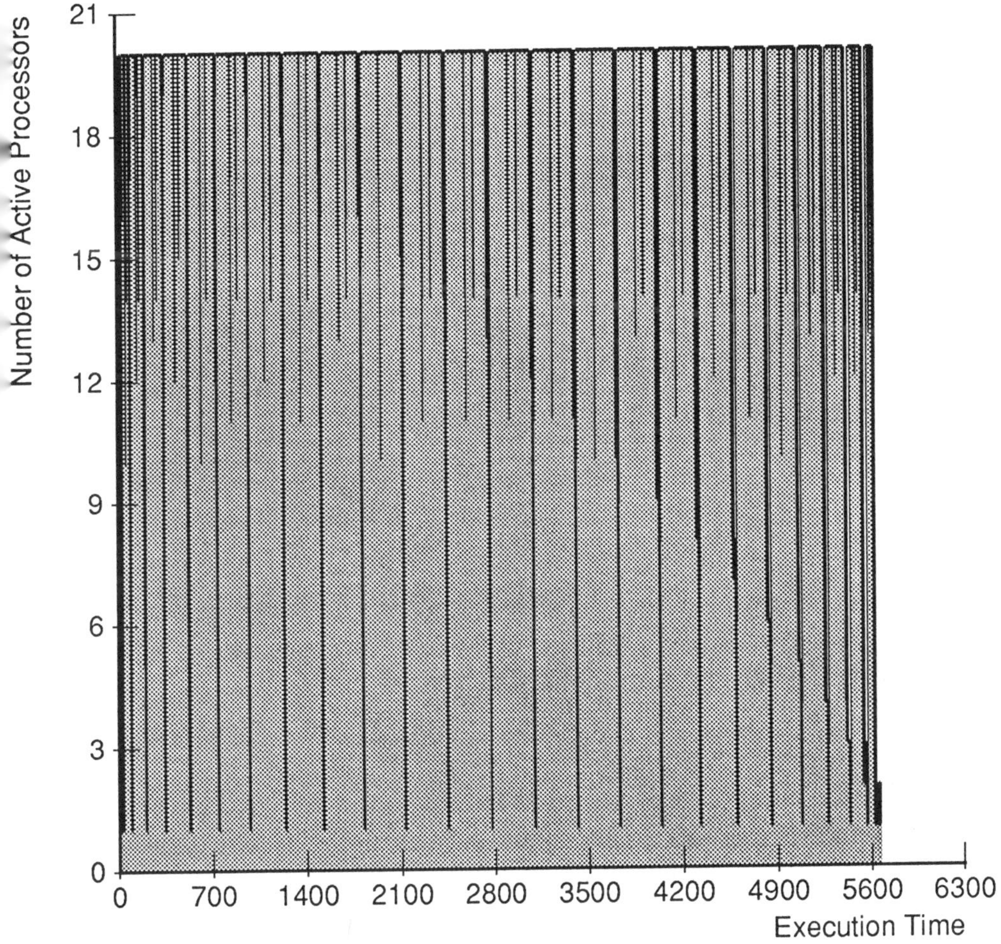

$T_{seq} = 103384.0$; $T_{par} = 5669.0$; Ideal Speed-up = 18.2

Figure A-5: CYK – ideal parallelism profile for P = 20

MESORT

An iterative (i.e. not recursive) version of Batcher's parallel merge-exchange sort algorithm [Batcher 68] [Knuth 73] on N integers. This algorithm has an $O(N (\log N)^2)$ sequential execution time, and an $O((\log N)^2)$ parallel execution time on N processors.

- **Static size:** 6 functions, 100 lines, 115 nodes, 227 edges.

- **Inputs:** An array of 100 integers.

Figure A-6 shows the parallelism profile of MESORT on an unbounded number of processors. The time interval (0,58) was spent on initialisations and the last peak during interval (660,678) was spent on a test to check the result array was really sorted. The main computation has the following loop structure:

```
for t := ⌈log₂n⌉ - 1 downto 0
    for u := ⌈log₂n⌉ - 1 downto t
    forall i in 0, n-1
        . . .
    end forall
    end for
end for
```

Since the outer t and u loops are sequential, we have $\lceil \log_2 n \rceil (\lceil \log_2 n \rceil + 1)/2 = 28$ peaks (for n = 100) in Figure A-6 corresponding to the 28 invocations of the innermost forall loop. The 28 peaks can be clearly divided into 7 groups with 1, 2, 3, 4, 5, 6 and 7 peaks. Each group corresponds to a single iteration of the outermost t loop.

Figure A-7 shows the parallelism profile for 20 processors.

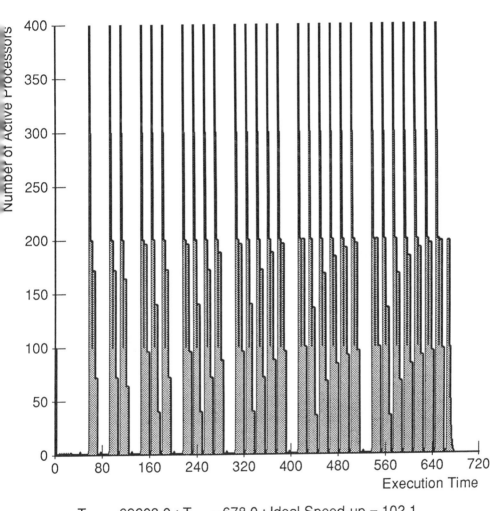

$T_{seq} = 69203.0$; $T_{par} = 678.0$; Ideal Speed-up = 102.1

Figure A-6: MESORT – ideal parallelism profile for $P = \infty$

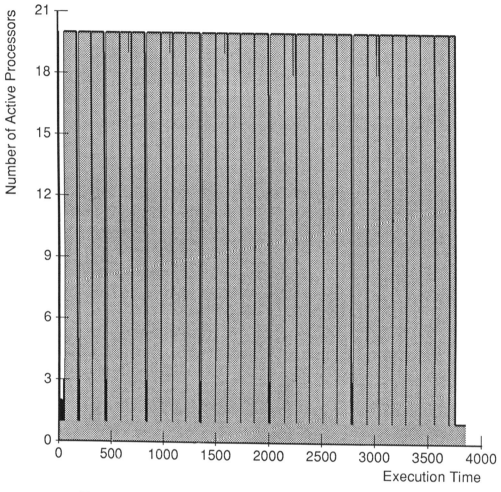

T_{seq} = 69203.0 ; T_{par} = 3853.0 ; Ideal Speed-up = 18.0

Figure A-7: MESORT – ideal parallelism profile for P = 20

FFT

A complex Fast Fourier Transform program which builds the result in a new array, distinct from the input array, thus requiring no *bit-reversal*.

- **Static size:** 10 functions, 111 lines, 117 nodes, 207 edges.

- **Inputs:** An array of 256 real numbers, representing a sinusoidal signal with wavelength = 16 time units.

Figure A-8 shows the parallelism profile of FFT on an unbounded number of processors. The interval (0,150) is used for initialisation, after which there are 8 similar sections for the $\log_2(256) = 8$ sequential iterations in the algorithm. The dominant costs in FFT are the evaluation of the trigonometric functions *sin* and *cos*, which are assumed to take 100 cycles each (see DBLSINcost and DBLCOScost in Figure A-1).

Figure A-9 shows the parallelism profile for 20 processors.

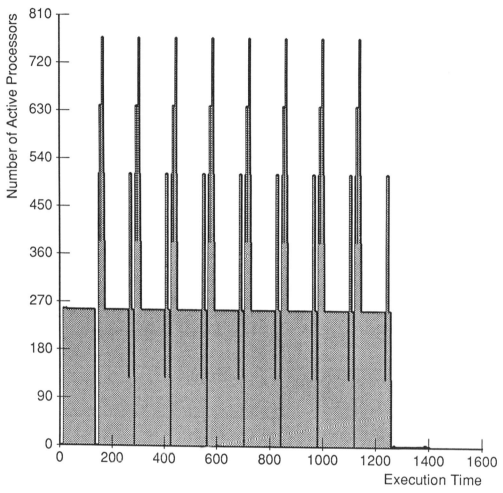

$T_{seq} = 382608.0$; $T_{par} = 1405.0$; Ideal Speed-up = 272.3

Figure A-8: FFT – ideal parallelism profile for P = ∞

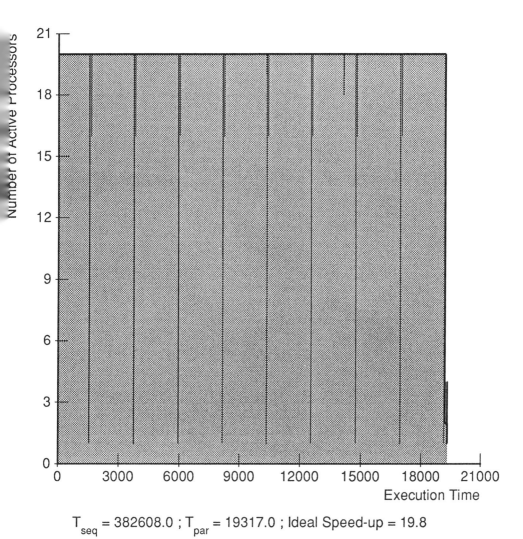

T_{seq} = 382608.0 ; T_{par} = 19317.0 ; Ideal Speed-up = 19.8

Figure A-9: FFT – ideal parallelism profile for P = 20

SIMPLE

SIMPLE is a benchmark program for computational fluid dynamics and heat flow [Gilbert 80].

- **Static size:** 25 functions, 1600 lines, 1601 nodes, 3625 edges.
- **Inputs:** The program was run on a 10×10 mesh for a single time step.

Figure A-10 shows the parallelism profile of SIMPLE on an unbounded number of processors and Figure A-11 shows the profile for 20 processors.

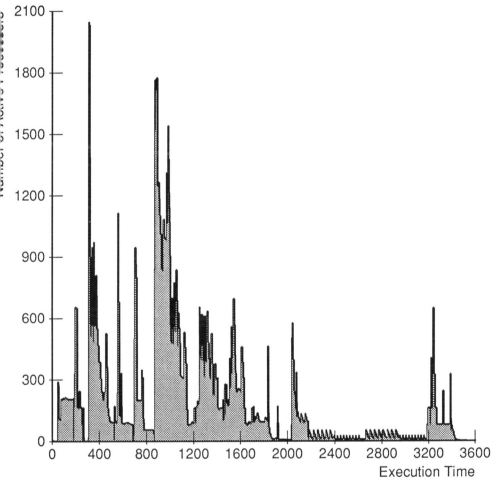

T_{seq} = 660507.0 ; T_{par} = 3529.0 ; Ideal Speed-up = 187.2

Figure A-10: SIMPLE – ideal parallelism profile for P = ∞

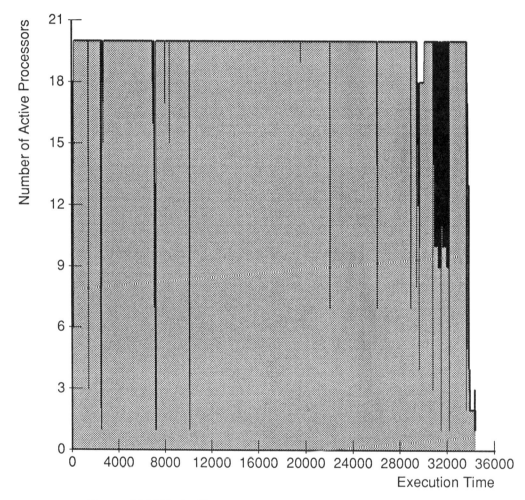

$T_{seq} = 660507.0$; $T_{par} = 34380.0$; Ideal Speed-up = 19.2

Figure A-11: SIMPLE – ideal parallelism profile for P = 20

SLAB

SLAB determines the radiation field on the faces of a slab, computed by the FN method using Hermite cubic splines. The output consists of:

1. μ, the direction cosines at which the splines are evaluated.

2. ψ_L, the outgoing radiation field on the left face of the slab.

3. ψ_R, the outgoing radiation field on the right face of the slab.

The input is the number of intervals to be used in the splines.

- **Static size:** 40 functions, 1200 lines, 1022 nodes, 2024 edges.

- **Inputs:** Number of intervals = 4.

Figure A-12 shows the parallelism profile of SLAB on an unbounded number of processors and figure A-13 shows the profile for 20 processors.

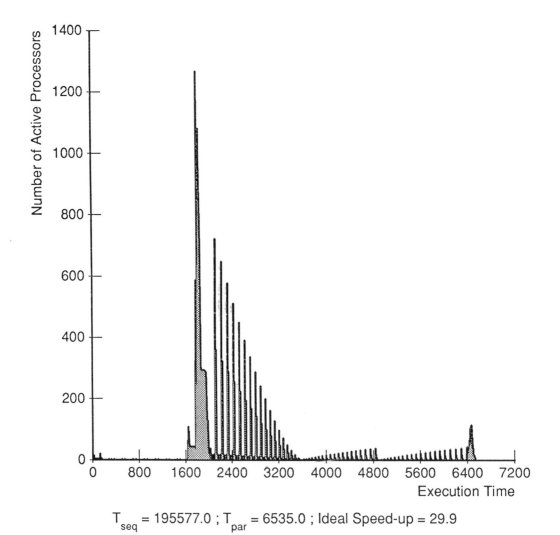

$T_{seq} = 195577.0$; $T_{par} = 6535.0$; Ideal Speed-up = 29.9

Figure A-12: SLAB – ideal parallelism profile for P = ∞

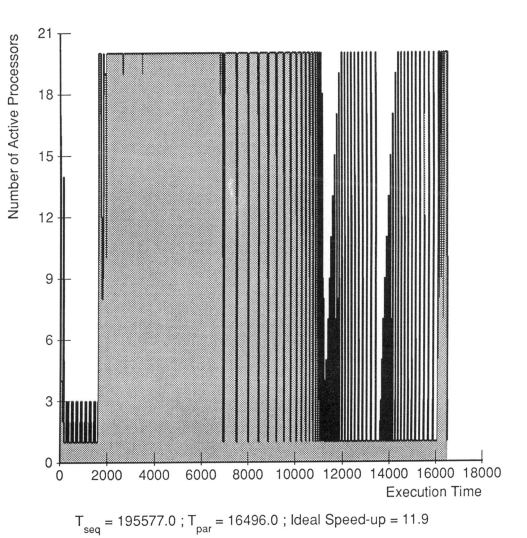

T_{seq} = 195577.0 ; T_{par} = 16496.0 ; Ideal Speed-up = 11.9

Figure A-13: SLAB – ideal parallelism profile for P = 20

Appendix B: Raw Simulation Data

The simulation data generated for this dissertation was stored in the INGRES (version 8.7) relational database system [Woodfill 79].   The simulation results presented earlier in the dissertation were in the form of speed-up plots.   For completeness, this appendix contains tables with all the raw simulation data from the database.   In these tables, columns represent simulation parameters and each row represents a different experiment.   Due to space limitations, each row had to be broken across two pages with a unique *id* entry to match the two halves.   The contents of each column are described below[20].

- *id* : unique identifier used to match up two halves of a tuple displayed on separate pages.

- *bench* : the name of the benchmark program.

- *method* : MD = macro-dataflow, CS = compile-time scheduling.

- *p* : number of processors.

- *_input, input* : program input used for the execution profile information and for the simulation respectively.

- *_rc, _wc, _dc, _ts, rc, wc, dc, ts* : overhead parameters (R_C, W_C, D_C, T_{sched}) used for the partition/schedule and the simulation respectively.

- *_s* : predicted speed-up for the generated partition/schedule.   This is the speed-up *estimated* by the macro-dataflow partitioner or the compile-time scheduler.

- *t_busy* : total busy processor time in the simulation, over all *p* processors. Busy time includes the processor component (see page 51) of overhead given by R_C, W_C and T_{sched}, but excludes the delay component given by D_C.

- *t_useful* : total useful processor time in the simulation, over all *p* processors.   Useful time is busy time without the overhead.

- *t_seq* : sequential execution time.   *t_useful* $\geq$ *t_seq* is always true and *t_useful* $\approx$ *t_seq* usually.   The difference between *t_useful* and *t_seq* is due to some small amount of extra computation in *t_useful* needed to split ranges of Forall iterations, which is not present in *t_seq*.

---

[20]For parameters which may have different values during partitioning and simulation, *_name* and *name* are used to denote the partitioning and simulation values respectively.

- *t_par* : the simulated parallel execution time.

- *s* : the ratio, *t_seq* / *t_par*. Note that *t_seq*, rather than *t_useful* or *t_busy*, is used as the numerator in the speed-up ratio so as to obtain the true speed-up rather than the total processor utilisation. The *s* column contains the speed-up values used in all the speed-up plots earlier in this dissertation.

id	bench	method	p	_input	_rc	_wc	_dc	_ts	_s	input
1	mm	MD	2	20x20	0.125	0.125	0.000	10	1.8	20x20
2	mm	MD	4	20x20	0.125	0.125	0.000	10	3.5	20x20
3	mm	MD	6	20x20	0.125	0.125	0.000	10	5.1	20x20
4	mm	MD	8	20x20	0.125	0.125	0.000	10	6.7	20x20
5	mm	MD	10	20x20	0.125	0.125	0.000	10	8.2	20x20
6	mm	MD	12	20x20	0.125	0.125	0.000	10	9.7	20x20
7	mm	MD	14	20x20	0.125	0.125	0.000	10	11.2	20x20
8	mm	MD	16	20x20	0.125	0.125	0.000	10	12.6	20x20
9	mm	MD	18	20x20	0.125	0.125	0.000	10	14.0	20x20
10	mm	MD	20	20x20	0.125	0.125	0.000	10	15.4	20x20
11	mm	MD	20	20x20	0.125	0.125	0.000	0	15.6	20x20
12	mm	MD	20	20x20	0.125	0.125	0.000	100	14.2	20x20
13	mm	MD	20	20x20	0.000	0.000	0.000	10	19.0	20x20
14	mm	MD	20	20x20	1.000	1.000	0.000	10	8.8	20x20
15	mm	MD	20	25x25	0.125	0.125	0.000	10	15.6	20x20
16	mm	MD	20	15x15	0.125	0.125	0.000	10	14.5	20x20
17	mm	MD	20	20x20	0.000	0.000	0.000	0	19.9	20x20
18	mm	MD	20	20x20	1.000	1.000	0.000	100	8.6	20x20
19	mm	MD	20	20x20	0.125	0.125	0.000	10	15.4	20x20
20	mm	CS	2	20x20	0.000	0.000	0.250	0	2.0	20x20
21	mm	CS	4	20x20	0.000	0.000	0.250	0	3.9	20x20
22	mm	CS	6	20x20	0.000	0.000	0.250	0	5.8	20x20
23	mm	CS	8	20x20	0.000	0.000	0.250	0	7.7	20x20
24	mm	CS	10	20x20	0.000	0.000	0.250	0	9.5	20x20
25	mm	CS	12	20x20	0.000	0.000	0.250	0	11.3	20x20
26	mm	CS	14	20x20	0.000	0.000	0.250	0	13.0	20x20
27	mm	CS	16	20x20	0.000	0.000	0.250	0	14.7	20x20
28	mm	CS	18	20x20	0.000	0.000	0.250	0	16.4	20x20
29	mm	CS	20	20x20	0.000	0.000	0.250	0	18.0	20x20
30	mm	CS	20	20x20	0.000	0.000	0.000	0	19.9	20x20
31	mm	CS	20	20x20	0.000	0.000	2.000	0	10.8	20x20
32	mm	CS	20	20x20	0.000	0.000	0.000	0	19.9	20x20
33	mm	CS	20	20x20	0.000	0.000	2.000	0	10.8	20x20
34	mm	CS	20	25x25	0.000	0.000	0.250	0	18.4	20x20
35	mm	CS	20	15x15	0.000	0.000	0.250	0	17.4	20x20
36	mm	CS	20	20x20	0.000	0.000	0.250	0	18.0	20x20
37	cyk	MD	2	25	0.125	0.125	0.000	10	1.5	25
38	cyk	MD	4	25	0.125	0.125	0.000	10	2.7	25
39	cyk	MD	6	25	0.125	0.125	0.000	10	3.8	25
40	cyk	MD	8	25	0.125	0.125	0.000	10	4.8	25
41	cyk	MD	10	25	0.125	0.125	0.000	10	5.3	25
42	cyk	MD	12	25	0.125	0.125	0.000	10	5.9	25
43	cyk	MD	14	25	0.125	0.125	0.000	10	6.6	25
44	cyk	MD	16	25	0.125	0.125	0.000	10	7.1	25
45	cyk	MD	18	25	0.125	0.125	0.000	10	7.7	25
46	cyk	MD	20	25	0.125	0.125	0.000	10	8.1	25
47	cyk	MD	20	25	0.125	0.125	0.000	0	10.8	25
48	cyk	MD	20	25	0.125	0.125	0.000	100	3.1	25
49	cyk	MD	20	25	0.000	0.000	0.000	10	11.2	25
50	cyk	MD	20	25	1.000	1.000	0.000	10	2.5	25
51	cyk	MD	20	30	0.125	0.125	0.000	10	8.7	25
52	cyk	MD	20	20	0.125	0.125	0.000	10	6.9	25
53	cyk	MD	20	25	0.000	0.000	0.000	0	17.6	25
54	cyk	MD	20	25	1.000	1.000	0.000	100	1.8	25
55	cyk	MD	20	25	0.125	0.125	0.000	10	8.1	25

id	rc	wc	dc	ts	t_busy	t_useful	t_seq	t_par	s
1	0.125	0.125	0.000	10	229889.0	224149.0	224149.0	115609.0	1.9
2	0.125	0.125	0.000	10	241529.0	225089.0	224149.0	61383.0	3.7
3	0.125	0.125	0.000	10	246209.0	225309.0	224149.0	44894.0	5.0
4	0.125	0.125	0.000	10	250829.0	225509.0	224149.0	33920.0	6.6
5	0.125	0.125	0.000	10	255469.0	225689.0	224149.0	26763.0	8.4
6	0.125	0.125	0.000	10	255469.0	225689.0	224149.0	24026.0	9.3
7	0.125	0.125	0.000	10	255469.0	225689.0	224149.0	21489.0	10.4
8	0.125	0.125	0.000	10	255469.0	225689.0	224149.0	18998.0	11.8
9	0.125	0.125	0.000	10	255469.0	225689.0	224149.0	16525.0	13.6
10	0.125	0.125	0.000	10	255469.0	225689.0	224149.0	14052.0	16.0
11	0.125	0.125	0.000	0	253399.0	225689.0	224149.0	13892.0	16.1
12	0.125	0.125	0.000	100	274099.0	225689.0	224149.0	15496.0	14.5
13	0.000	0.000	0.000	10	229019.0	224149.0	224149.0	11554.0	19.4
14	1.000	1.000	0.000	10	268099.0	224149.0	224149.0	22928.0	9.8
15	0.125	0.125	0.000	10	246209.0	225309.0	224149.0	15814.0	14.2
16	0.125	0.125	0.000	10	255469.0	225689.0	224149.0	14052.0	16.0
17	0.125	0.125	0.000	10	2463000.0	224149.0	224149.0	124016.0	1.8
18	0.125	0.125	0.000	10	229889.0	224149.0	224149.0	12775.0	17.5
19	0.000	0.000	0.000	0	225689.0	225689.0	224149.0	11328.0	19.8
20	0.000	0.000	0.250	0	224207.0	224207.0	224149.0	113139.0	2.0
21	0.000	0.000	0.250	0	224245.0	224245.0	224149.0	57016.0	3.9
22	0.000	0.000	0.250	0	224283.0	224283.0	224149.0	45793.0	4.9
23	0.000	0.000	0.250	0	224321.0	224321.0	224149.0	34570.0	6.5
24	0.000	0.000	0.250	0	224359.0	224359.0	224149.0	23347.0	9.6
25	0.000	0.000	0.250	0	224397.0	224397.0	224149.0	23349.0	9.6
26	0.000	0.000	0.250	0	224435.0	224435.0	224149.0	23351.0	9.6
27	0.000	0.000	0.250	0	224473.0	224473.0	224149.0	23353.0	9.6
28	0.000	0.000	0.250	0	224511.0	224511.0	224149.0	23355.0	9.6
29	0.000	0.000	0.250	0	224549.0	224549.0	224149.0	12132.0	18.5
30	0.000	0.000	0.000	0	224549.0	224549.0	224149.0	11312.0	19.8
31	0.000	0.000	2.000	0	224549.0	224549.0	224149.0	17872.0	12.5
32	0.000	0.000	0.250	0	224549.0	224549.0	224149.0	12132.0	18.5
33	0.000	0.000	0.250	0	224549.0	224549.0	224149.0	12132.0	18.5
34	0.000	0.000	0.250	0	224549.0	224549.0	224149.0	12132.0	18.5
35	0.000	0.000	0.250	0	224549.0	224549.0	224149.0	12132.0	18.5
36	0.000	0.000	0.000	0	224549.0	224549.0	224149.0	11312.0	19.8
37	0.125	0.125	0.000	10	128561.0	112434.0	103384.0	70382.0	1.5
38	0.125	0.125	0.000	10	128561.0	112434.0	103384.0	41752.0	2.5
39	0.125	0.125	0.000	10	128561.0	112434.0	103384.0	32330.0	3.2
40	0.125	0.125	0.000	10	128561.0	112434.0	103384.0	27706.0	3.7
41	0.125	0.125	0.000	10	128561.0	112434.0	103384.0	25029.0	4.1
42	0.125	0.125	0.000	10	183611.0	124008.0	103384.0	22941.0	4.5
43	0.125	0.125	0.000	10	183611.0	124008.0	103384.0	21069.0	4.9
44	0.125	0.125	0.000	10	216431.0	131226.0	103384.0	20918.0	4.9
45	0.125	0.125	0.000	10	216431.0	131226.0	103384.0	19765.0	5.2
46	0.125	0.125	0.000	10	216431.0	131226.0	103384.0	18602.0	5.6
47	0.125	0.125	0.000	0	178591.0	131226.0	103384.0	14190.0	7.3
48	0.125	0.125	0.000	100	183101.0	112434.0	103384.0	41193.0	2.5
49	0.000	0.000	0.000	10	169066.0	131226.0	103384.0	13112.0	7.9
50	1.000	1.000	0.000	10	373963.0	124008.0	103384.0	48257.0	2.1
51	0.125	0.125	0.000	10	183611.0	124008.0	103384.0	17706.0	5.8
52	0.125	0.125	0.000	10	244043.0	112434.0	103384.0	19531.0	5.3
53	0.125	0.125	0.000	10	760101.0	112434.0	103384.0	44536.0	2.3
54	0.125	0.125	0.000	10	128561.0	112434.0	103384.0	20043.0	5.2
55	0.000	0.000	0.000	0	131226.0	131226.0	103384.0	8696.0	11.9

id	bench	method	p	_input	_rc	_wc	_dc	_ts	_s	input
56	cyk	CS	2	25	0.000	0.000	0.250	0	1.9	25
57	cyk	CS	4	25	0.000	0.000	0.250	0	3.8	25
58	cyk	CS	6	25	0.000	0.000	0.250	0	5.5	25
59	cyk	CS	8	25	0.000	0.000	0.250	0	7.1	25
60	cyk	CS	10	25	0.000	0.000	0.250	0	8.6	25
61	cyk	CS	12	25	0.000	0.000	0.250	0	10.0	25
62	cyk	CS	14	25	0.000	0.000	0.250	0	11.3	25
63	cyk	CS	16	25	0.000	0.000	0.250	0	12.5	25
64	cyk	CS	18	25	0.000	0.000	0.250	0	13.6	25
65	cyk	CS	20	25	0.000	0.000	0.250	0	14.7	25
66	cyk	CS	20	25	0.000	0.000	0.000	0	17.6	25
67	cyk	CS	20	25	0.000	0.000	2.000	0	6.6	25
68	cyk	CS	20	25	0.000	0.000	0.000	0	17.6	25
69	cyk	CS	20	25	0.000	0.000	2.000	0	6.6	25
70	cyk	CS	20	30	0.000	0.000	0.250	0	15.0	25
71	cyk	CS	20	20	0.000	0.000	0.250	0	14.3	25
72	cyk	CS	20	25	0.000	0.000	0.250	0	14.7	25
73	mesort	MD	2	100	0.125	0.125	0.000	10	1.0	100
74	mesort	MD	4	100	0.125	0.125	0.000	10	1.6	100
75	mesort	MD	6	100	0.125	0.125	0.000	10	1.9	100
76	mesort	MD	8	100	0.125	0.125	0.000	10	2.2	100
77	mesort	MD	10	100	0.125	0.125	0.000	10	2.5	100
78	mesort	MD	12	100	0.125	0.125	0.000	10	2.6	100
79	mesort	MD	14	100	0.125	0.125	0.000	10	2.7	100
80	mesort	MD	16	100	0.125	0.125	0.000	10	2.8	100
81	mesort	MD	18	100	0.125	0.125	0.000	10	3.0	100
82	mesort	MD	20	100	0.125	0.125	0.000	10	3.1	100
83	mesort	MD	20	100	0.125	0.125	0.000	0	3.6	100
84	mesort	MD	20	100	0.125	0.125	0.000	100	1.4	100
85	mesort	MD	20	100	0.000	0.000	0.000	10	6.3	100
86	mesort	MD	20	100	1.000	1.000	0.000	10	1.0	100
87	mesort	MD	20	200	0.125	0.125	0.000	10	3.4	100
88	mesort	MD	20	50	0.125	0.125	0.000	10	2.5	100
89	mesort	MD	20	100	0.000	0.000	0.000	0	14.2	100
90	mesort	MD	20	100	1.000	1.000	0.000	100	1.0	100
91	mesort	MD	20	100	0.125	0.125	0.000	10	3.1	100
92	mesort	CS	2	100	0.000	0.000	0.250	0	1.7	100
93	mesort	CS	4	100	0.000	0.000	0.250	0	2.8	100
94	mesort	CS	6	100	0.000	0.000	0.250	0	3.6	100
95	mesort	CS	8	100	0.000	0.000	0.250	0	4.2	100
96	mesort	CS	10	100	0.000	0.000	0.250	0	4.7	100
97	mesort	CS	12	100	0.000	0.000	0.250	0	5.1	100
98	mesort	CS	14	100	0.000	0.000	0.250	0	5.4	100
99	mesort	CS	16	100	0.000	0.000	0.250	0	5.7	100
100	mesort	CS	18	100	0.000	0.000	0.250	0	6.0	100
101	mesort	CS	20	100	0.000	0.000	0.250	0	6.2	100
102	mesort	CS	20	100	0.000	0.000	0.000	0	11.0	100
103	mesort	CS	20	100	0.000	0.000	2.000	0	1.5	100
104	mesort	CS	20	100	0.000	0.000	0.000	0	11.0	100
105	mesort	CS	20	100	0.000	0.000	2.000	0	1.5	100
106	mesort	CS	20	200	0.000	0.000	0.250	0	6.1	100
107	mesort	CS	20	50	0.000	0.000	0.250	0	6.4	100
108	mesort	CS	20	100	0.000	0.000	0.250	0	6.2	100
109	fft	MD	2	256	0.125	0.125	0.000	10	1.3	256
110	fft	MD	4	256	0.125	0.125	0.000	10	2.5	256

id	rc	wc	dc	ts	t_busy	t_useful	t_seq	t_par	s
56	0.000	0.000	0.250	0	113694.0	113694.0	103384.0	61236.0	1.7
57	0.000	0.000	0.250	0	114654.0	114654.0	103384.0	35431.0	2.9
58	0.000	0.000	0.250	0	115614.0	115614.0	103384.0	27005.0	3.8
59	0.000	0.000	0.250	0	116574.0	116574.0	103384.0	22925.0	4.5
60	0.000	0.000	0.250	0	117534.0	117534.0	103384.0	20595.0	5.0
61	0.000	0.000	0.250	0	118494.0	118494.0	103384.0	19107.0	5.4
62	0.000	0.000	0.250	0	119454.0	119454.0	103384.0	18225.0	5.7
63	0.000	0.000	0.250	0	120414.0	120414.0	103384.0	17511.0	5.9
64	0.000	0.000	0.250	0	121374.0	121374.0	103384.0	16966.0	6.1
65	0.000	0.000	0.250	0	122334.0	122334.0	103384.0	16590.0	6.2
66	0.000	0.000	0.000	0	122334.0	122334.0	103384.0	15450.0	6.7
67	0.000	0.000	2.000	0	122334.0	122334.0	103384.0	28008.0	3.7
68	0.000	0.000	0.250	0	122334.0	122334.0	103384.0	16590.0	6.2
69	0.000	0.000	0.250	0	122334.0	122334.0	103384.0	28008.0	3.7
70	0.000	0.000	0.250	0	122334.0	122334.0	103384.0	16590.0	6.2
71	0.000	0.000	0.250	0	122334.0	122334.0	103384.0	16590.0	6.2
72	0.000	0.000	0.000	0	122334.0	122334.0	103384.0	15498.0	6.7
73	0.125	0.125	0.000	10	95057.0	72789.0	69203.0	55903.0	1.2
74	0.125	0.125	0.000	10	113803.0	73319.0	69203.0	41471.0	1.7
75	0.125	0.125	0.000	10	118003.0	73907.0	69203.0	34494.0	2.0
76	0.125	0.125	0.000	10	122175.0	74467.0	69203.0	30980.0	2.2
77	0.125	0.125	0.000	10	126179.0	74999.0	69203.0	28402.0	2.4
78	0.125	0.125	0.000	10	130519.0	75587.0	69203.0	27501.0	2.5
79	0.125	0.125	0.000	10	132451.0	75867.0	69203.0	26612.0	2.6
80	0.125	0.125	0.000	10	136791.0	76427.0	69203.0	25808.0	2.7
81	0.125	0.125	0.000	10	140739.0	76987.0	69203.0	25006.0	2.8
82	0.125	0.125	0.000	10	147179.0	77799.0	69203.0	24226.0	2.9
83	0.125	0.125	0.000	0	131479.0	77799.0	69203.0	20429.0	3.4
84	0.125	0.125	0.000	100	288479.0	77799.0	69203.0	58471.0	1.2
85	0.000	0.000	0.000	10	93499.0	77799.0	69203.0	10986.0	6.3
86	1.000	1.000	0.000	10	69213.0	69203.0	69203.0	69213.0	1.0
87	0.125	0.125	0.000	10	126179.0	74999.0	69203.0	27562.0	2.5
88	0.125	0.125	0.000	10	176411.0	81747.0	69203.0	27350.0	2.5
89	0.125	0.125	0.000	10	949665.0	69203.0	69203.0	63259.0	1.1
90	0.125	0.125	0.000	10	69213.0	69203.0	69203.0	69213.0	1.0
91	0.000	0.000	0.000	0	77799.0	77799.0	69203.0	7211.0	9.6
92	0.000	0.000	0.250	0	73067.0	73067.0	69203.0	42921.0	1.6
93	0.000	0.000	0.250	0	74131.0	74131.0	69203.0	25967.0	2.7
94	0.000	0.000	0.250	0	75195.0	75195.0	69203.0	20231.0	3.4
95	0.000	0.000	0.250	0	76259.0	76259.0	69203.0	17327.0	4.0
96	0.000	0.000	0.250	0	77323.0	77323.0	69203.0	15227.0	4.5
97	0.000	0.000	0.250	0	78387.0	78387.0	69203.0	14460.0	4.8
98	0.000	0.000	0.250	0	79716.0	79716.0	69203.0	12733.0	5.4
99	0.000	0.000	0.250	0	80818.0	80818.0	69203.0	12165.0	5.7
100	0.000	0.000	0.250	0	81920.0	81920.0	69203.0	11597.0	6.0
101	0.000	0.000	0.250	0	83022.0	83022.0	69203.0	10904.0	6.3
102	0.000	0.000	0.000	0	83022.0	83022.0	69203.0	7939.0	8.7
103	0.000	0.000	2.000	0	83022.0	83022.0	69203.0	32745.0	2.1
104	0.000	0.000	0.250	0	83022.0	83022.0	69203.0	10907.0	6.3
105	0.000	0.000	0.250	0	83022.0	83022.0	69203.0	31699.0	2.2
106	0.000	0.000	0.250	0	83022.0	83022.0	69203.0	10904.0	6.3
107	0.000	0.000	0.250	0	83022.0	83022.0	69203.0	10904.0	6.3
108	0.000	0.000	0.000	0	83022.0	83022.0	69203.0	8097.0	8.5
109	0.125	0.125	0.000	10	406002.0	385152.0	382608.0	227496.0	1.7
110	0.125	0.125	0.000	10	410526.0	385332.0	382608.0	131316.0	2.9

id	bench	method	p	_input	_rc	_wc	_dc	_ts	_s	input
111	fft	MD	6	256	0.125	0.125	0.000	10	3.5	256
112	fft	MD	8	256	0.125	0.125	0.000	10	4.6	256
113	fft	MD	10	256	0.125	0.125	0.000	10	5.4	256
114	fft	MD	12	256	0.125	0.125	0.000	10	6.1	256
115	fft	MD	14	256	0.125	0.125	0.000	10	6.8	256
116	fft	MD	16	256	0.125	0.125	0.000	10	7.6	256
117	fft	MD	18	256	0.125	0.125	0.000	10	8.0	256
118	fft	MD	20	256	0.125	0.125	0.000	10	8.7	256
119	fft	MD	20	256	0.125	0.125	0.000	0	8.9	256
120	fft	MD	20	256	0.125	0.125	0.000	100	7.1	256
121	fft	MD	20	256	0.000	0.000	0.000	10	13.1	256
122	fft	MD	20	256	1.000	1.000	0.000	10	2.6	256
123	fft	MD	20	512	0.125	0.125	0.000	10	8.7	256
124	fft	MD	20	128	0.125	0.125	0.000	10	8.2	256
125	fft	MD	20	256	0.000	0.000	0.000	0	18.5	256
126	fft	MD	20	256	1.000	1.000	0.000	100	2.5	256
127	fft	MD	20	256	0.125	0.125	0.000	10	8.7	256
128	fft	CS	2	256	0.000	0.000	0.250	0	1.9	256
129	fft	CS	4	256	0.000	0.000	0.250	0	3.6	256
130	fft	CS	6	256	0.000	0.000	0.250	0	5.1	256
131	fft	CS	8	256	0.000	0.000	0.250	0	6.5	256
132	fft	CS	10	256	0.000	0.000	0.250	0	7.8	256
133	fft	CS	12	256	0.000	0.000	0.250	0	9.0	256
134	fft	CS	14	256	0.000	0.000	0.250	0	10.0	256
135	fft	CS	16	256	0.000	0.000	0.250	0	11.0	256
136	fft	CS	18	256	0.000	0.000	0.250	0	11.9	256
137	fft	CS	20	256	0.000	0.000	0.250	0	12.7	256
138	fft	CS	20	256	0.000	0.000	0.000	0	17.8	256
139	fft	CS	20	256	0.000	0.000	2.000	0	4.2	256
140	fft	CS	20	256	0.000	0.000	0.000	0	17.8	256
141	fft	CS	20	256	0.000	0.000	2.000	0	4.2	256
142	fft	CS	20	512	0.000	0.000	0.250	0	12.7	256
143	fft	CS	20	128	0.000	0.000	0.250	0	12.7	256
144	fft	CS	20	256	0.000	0.000	0.250	0	12.7	256
145	simple	MD	2	10x10	0.125	0.125	0.000	10	1.4	10x10
146	simple	MD	4	10x10	0.125	0.125	0.000	10	2.5	10x10
147	simple	MD	6	10x10	0.125	0.125	0.000	10	3.5	10x10
148	simple	MD	8	10x10	0.125	0.125	0.000	10	4.2	10x10
149	simple	MD	10	10x10	0.125	0.125	0.000	10	5.1	10x10
150	simple	MD	12	10x10	0.125	0.125	0.000	10	5.9	10x10
151	simple	MD	14	10x10	0.125	0.125	0.000	10	6.7	10x10
152	simple	MD	16	10x10	0.125	0.125	0.000	10	7.4	10x10
153	simple	MD	18	10x10	0.125	0.125	0.000	10	8.1	10x10
154	simple	MD	20	10x10	0.125	0.125	0.000	10	8.8	10x10
155	simple	MD	20	10x10	0.125	0.125	0.000	0	9.0	10x10
156	simple	MD	20	10x10	0.125	0.125	0.000	100	6.4	10x10
157	simple	MD	20	10x10	0.000	0.000	0.000	10	14.7	10x10
158	simple	MD	20	10x10	1.000	1.000	0.000	10	2.2	10x10
159	simple	MD	20	13x13	0.125	0.125	0.000	10	8.3	10x10
160	simple	MD	20	7x7	0.125	0.125	0.000	10	7.9	10x10
161	simple	MD	20	10x10	0.000	0.000	0.000	0	18.7	10x10
162	simple	MD	20	10x10	0.125	0.125	0.000	10	8.8	10x10
163	simple	MD	20	10x10	1.000	1.000	0.000	100	1.9	10x10
164	simple	CS	2	10x10	0.000	0.000	0.250	0	1.7	10x10
165	simple	CS	4	10x10	0.000	0.000	0.250	0	3.3	10x10

id	rc	wc	dc	ts	t_busy	t_useful	t_seq	t_par	s
111	0.125	0.125	0.000	10	429989.0	385197.0	382608.0	101683.0	3.8
112	0.125	0.125	0.000	10	434461.0	385349.0	382608.0	80839.0	4.7
113	0.125	0.125	0.000	10	438949.0	385517.0	382608.0	70633.0	5.4
114	0.125	0.125	0.000	10	443429.0	385677.0	382608.0	63281.0	6.0
115	0.125	0.125	0.000	10	447909.0	385837.0	382608.0	57808.0	6.6
116	0.125	0.125	0.000	10	452381.0	385989.0	382608.0	51655.0	7.4
117	0.125	0.125	0.000	10	456869.0	386157.0	382608.0	49985.0	7.7
118	0.125	0.125	0.000	10	461349.0	386317.0	382608.0	46449.0	8.2
119	0.125	0.125	0.000	0	445949.0	386317.0	382608.0	45073.0	8.5
120	0.125	0.125	0.000	100	599949.0	386317.0	382608.0	58794.0	6.5
121	0.000	0.000	0.000	10	391477.0	386317.0	382608.0	30651.0	12.5
122	1.000	1.000	0.000	10	869093.0	386317.0	382608.0	153039.0	2.5
123	0.125	0.125	0.000	10	424107.0	385881.0	382608.0	69225.0	5.5
124	0.125	0.125	0.000	10	499437.0	387677.0	382608.0	45702.0	8.4
125	0.125	0.125	0.000	10	2021000.0	382605.0	382608.0	115866.0	3.3
126	0.125	0.125	0.000	10	461349.0	386317.0	382608.0	46449.0	8.2
127	0.000	0.000	0.000	0	386317.0	386317.0	382608.0	29769.0	12.9
128	0.000	0.000	0.250	0	385021.0	385021.0	382608.0	232447.0	1.6
129	0.000	0.000	0.250	0	385737.0	385737.0	382608.0	120797.0	3.2
130	0.000	0.000	0.250	0	386151.0	386151.0	382608.0	89084.0	4.3
131	0.000	0.000	0.250	0	386565.0	386565.0	382608.0	68209.0	5.6
132	0.000	0.000	0.250	0	386979.0	386979.0	382608.0	58894.0	6.5
133	0.000	0.000	0.250	0	387393.0	387393.0	382608.0	51800.0	7.4
134	0.000	0.000	0.250	0	387807.0	387807.0	382608.0	46217.0	8.3
135	0.000	0.000	0.250	0	388221.0	388221.0	382608.0	39833.0	9.6
136	0.000	0.000	0.250	0	388635.0	388635.0	382608.0	38340.0	10.0
137	0.000	0.000	0.250	0	389049.0	389049.0	382608.0	34802.0	11.0
138	0.000	0.000	0.000	0	389049.0	389049.0	382608.0	30485.0	12.6
139	0.000	0.000	2.000	0	389049.0	389049.0	382608.0	65128.0	5.9
140	0.000	0.000	0.250	0	389049.0	389049.0	382608.0	34802.0	11.0
141	0.000	0.000	0.250	0	389049.0	389049.0	382608.0	38252.0	10.0
142	0.000	0.000	0.250	0	389049.0	389049.0	382608.0	34802.0	11.0
143	0.000	0.000	0.250	0	389049.0	389049.0	382608.0	34802.0	11.0
144	0.000	0.000	0.000	0	389049.0	389049.0	382608.0	30485.0	12.6
145	0.125	0.125	0.000	10	796567.0	662552.0	660507.0	429800.0	1.5
146	0.125	0.125	0.000	10	825307.0	662958.0	660507.0	283020.0	2.3
147	0.125	0.125	0.000	10	897268.0	663596.0	660507.0	216544.0	3.0
148	0.125	0.125	0.000	10	1075000.0	662802.0	660507.0	208730.0	3.2
149	0.125	0.125	0.000	10	1084000.0	663076.0	660507.0	179142.0	3.7
150	0.125	0.125	0.000	10	1110000.0	664213.0	660507.0	168130.0	3.9
151	0.125	0.125	0.000	10	1114000.0	664171.0	660507.0	155503.0	4.2
152	0.125	0.125	0.000	10	1129000.0	664241.0	660507.0	150994.0	4.4
153	0.125	0.125	0.000	10	1135000.0	664767.0	660507.0	140310.0	4.7
154	0.125	0.125	0.000	10	1135000.0	664767.0	660507.0	138213.0	4.8
155	0.125	0.125	0.000	0	1182000.0	663230.0	660507.0	133270.0	5.0
156	0.125	0.125	0.000	100	1298000.0	665331.0	660507.0	152161.0	4.3
157	0.000	0.000	0.000	10	751037.0	664167.0	660507.0	44112.0	15.0
158	1.000	1.000	0.000	10	2913000.0	664708.0	660507.0	712314.0	0.9
159	0.125	0.125	0.000	10	1034000.0	665344.0	660507.0	152347.0	4.3
160	0.125	0.125	0.000	10	1412000.0	662404.0	660507.0	144218.0	4.6
161	0.125	0.125	0.000	10	2609000.0	660507.0	660507.0	195119.0	3.4
162	0.000	0.000	0.000	0	664767.0	664767.0	660507.0	45557.0	14.5
163	0.125	0.125	0.000	10	943398.0	663575.0	660507.0	157891.0	4.2
164	0.000	0.000	0.250	0	659839.0	659839.0	660507.0	459918.0	1.4
165	0.000	0.000	0.250	0	660607.0	660607.0	660507.0	259275.0	2.5

id	bench	method	p	_input	_rc	_wc	_dc	_ts	_s	input
166	simple	CS	6	10x10	0.000	0.000	0.250	0	4.3	10x10
167	simple	CS	8	10x10	0.000	0.000	0.250	0	5.1	10x10
168	simple	CS	10	10x10	0.000	0.000	0.250	0	6.1	10x10
169	simple	CS	12	10x10	0.000	0.000	0.250	0	6.7	10x10
170	simple	CS	14	10x10	0.000	0.000	0.250	0	7.3	10x10
171	simple	CS	16	10x10	0.000	0.000	0.250	0	8.5	10x10
172	simple	CS	18	10x10	0.000	0.000	0.250	0	9.9	10x10
173	simple	CS	20	10x10	0.000	0.000	0.250	0	9.8	10x10
174	simple	CS	20	10x10	0.000	0.000	0.000	0	11.0	10x10
175	simple	CS	20	10x10	0.000	0.000	2.000	0	5.7	10x10
176	simple	CS	20	10x10	0.000	0.000	0.000	0	11.0	10x10
177	simple	CS	20	10x10	0.000	0.000	2.000	0	5.7	10x10
178	simple	CS	20	13x13	0.000	0.000	0.250	0	11.7	10x10
179	simple	CS	20	7x7	0.000	0.000	0.250	0	8.3	10x10
180	simple	CS	20	10x10	0.000	0.000	0.250	0	9.8	10x10
181	slab	MD	2	4	0.125	0.125	0.000	10	1.4	4
182	slab	MD	4	4	0.125	0.125	0.000	10	2.5	4
183	slab	MD	6	4	0.125	0.125	0.000	10	3.4	4
184	slab	MD	8	4	0.125	0.125	0.000	10	3.9	4
185	slab	MD	10	4	0.125	0.125	0.000	10	4.5	4
186	slab	MD	12	4	0.125	0.125	0.000	10	4.8	4
187	slab	MD	14	4	0.125	0.125	0.000	10	4.9	4
188	slab	MD	16	4	0.125	0.125	0.000	10	5.1	4
189	slab	MD	18	4	0.125	0.125	0.000	10	5.2	4
190	slab	MD	20	4	0.125	0.125	0.000	10	5.3	4
191	slab	MD	20	4	0.125	0.125	0.000	0	6.8	4
192	slab	MD	20	4	0.125	0.125	0.000	100	3.5	4
193	slab	MD	20	4	0.000	0.000	0.000	10	10.1	4
194	slab	MD	20	4	1.000	1.000	0.000	10	2.0	4
195	slab	MD	20	4	0.000	0.000	0.000	0	16.1	4
196	slab	MD	20	4	1.000	1.000	0.000	100	1.7	4
197	slab	MD	20	4	0.125	0.125	0.000	10	5.3	4
198	slab	CS	2	4	0.000	0.000	0.250	0	1.8	4
199	slab	CS	4	4	0.000	0.000	0.250	0	2.8	4
200	slab	CS	6	4	0.000	0.000	0.250	0	3.0	4
201	slab	CS	8	4	0.000	0.000	0.250	0	3.8	4
202	slab	CS	10	4	0.000	0.000	0.250	0	4.3	4
203	slab	CS	12	4	0.000	0.000	0.250	0	5.2	4
204	slab	CS	14	4	0.000	0.000	0.250	0	6.4	4
205	slab	CS	16	4	0.000	0.000	0.250	0	6.7	4
206	slab	CS	18	4	0.000	0.000	0.250	0	7.1	4
207	slab	CS	20	4	0.000	0.000	0.250	0	7.3	4
208	slab	CS	20	4	0.000	0.000	0.000	0	10.6	4
209	slab	CS	20	4	0.000	0.000	2.000	0	3.0	4
210	slab	CS	20	4	0.000	0.000	0.000	0	10.6	4
211	slab	CS	20	4	0.000	0.000	2.000	0	3.0	4
212	slab	CS	20	4	0.000	0.000	0.250	0	7.3	4

id	rc	wc	dc	ts	t_busy	t_useful	t_seq	t_par	s
166	0.000	0.000	0.250	0	660773.0	660773.0	660507.0	219826.0	3.0
167	0.000	0.000	0.250	0	661293.0	661293.0	660507.0	185963.0	3.6
168	0.000	0.000	0.250	0	661499.0	661499.0	660507.0	170232.0	3.9
169	0.000	0.000	0.250	0	661860.0	661860.0	660507.0	150971.0	4.4
170	0.000	0.000	0.250	0	662221.0	662221.0	660507.0	144958.0	4.6
171	0.000	0.000	0.250	0	662551.0	662551.0	660507.0	120203.0	5.5
172	0.000	0.000	0.250	0	662931.0	662931.0	660507.0	98906.0	6.7
173	0.000	0.000	0.250	0	663203.0	663203.0	660507.0	95830.0	6.9
174	0.000	0.000	0.000	0	663203.0	663203.0	660507.0	94201.0	7.0
175	0.000	0.000	2.000	0	663156.0	663156.0	660507.0	120916.0	5.5
176	0.000	0.000	0.250	0	663203.0	663203.0	660507.0	97274.0	6.8
177	0.000	0.000	0.250	0	663156.0	663156.0	660507.0	114920.0	5.7
178	0.000	0.000	0.250	0	663285.0	663285.0	660507.0	98355.0	6.7
179	0.000	0.000	0.250	0	663015.0	663015.0	660507.0	97671.0	6.8
180	0.000	0.000	0.000	0	663203.0	663203.0	660507.0	94258.0	7.0
181	0.125	0.125	0.000	10	236493.0	197626.0	195577.0	135896.0	1.4
182	0.125	0.125	0.000	10	243950.0	197864.0	195577.0	84130.0	2.3
183	0.125	0.125	0.000	10	252545.0	198507.0	195577.0	66063.0	3.0
184	0.125	0.125	0.000	10	270670.0	195833.0	195577.0	56851.0	3.4
185	0.125	0.125	0.000	10	270682.0	195833.0	195577.0	50223.0	3.9
186	0.125	0.125	0.000	10	294995.0	195608.0	195577.0	48703.0	4.0
187	0.125	0.125	0.000	10	340281.0	206458.0	195577.0	45088.0	4.3
188	0.125	0.125	0.000	10	340281.0	206458.0	195577.0	42708.0	4.6
189	0.125	0.125	0.000	10	340281.0	206458.0	195577.0	40799.0	4.8
190	0.125	0.125	0.000	10	388696.0	195608.0	195577.0	40160.0	4.9
191	0.125	0.125	0.000	0	373098.0	195577.0	195577.0	34593.0	5.7
192	0.125	0.125	0.000	100	379250.0	195802.0	195577.0	55233.0	3.5
193	0.000	0.000	0.000	10	261428.0	212358.0	195577.0	26163.0	7.5
194	1.000	1.000	0.000	10	701200.0	195644.0	195577.0	111847.0	1.7
195	0.125	0.125	0.000	10	675078.0	195577.0	195577.0	55419.0	3.5
196	0.125	0.125	0.000	10	269108.0	195802.0	195577.0	38087.0	5.1
197	0.000	0.000	0.000	0	195608.0	195608.0	195577.0	20617.0	9.5
198	0.000	0.000	0.250	0	196470.0	196470.0	195577.0	115516.0	1.7
199	0.000	0.000	0.250	0	197288.0	197288.0	195577.0	78047.0	2.5
200	0.000	0.000	0.250	0	198010.0	198010.0	195577.0	73203.0	2.7
201	0.000	0.000	0.250	0	198770.0	198770.0	195577.0	65574.0	3.0
202	0.000	0.000	0.250	0	208365.0	208365.0	195577.0	63200.0	3.1
203	0.000	0.000	0.250	0	212640.0	212640.0	195577.0	53456.0	3.7
204	0.000	0.000	0.250	0	216044.0	216044.0	195577.0	42762.0	4.6
205	0.000	0.000	0.250	0	218305.0	218305.0	195577.0	42221.0	4.6
206	0.000	0.000	0.250	0	219711.0	219711.0	195577.0	41937.0	4.7
207	0.000	0.000	0.250	0	220509.0	220509.0	195577.0	40917.0	4.8
208	0.000	0.000	0.000	0	220509.0	220509.0	195577.0	32312.0	6.1
209	0.000	0.000	2.000	0	220509.0	220509.0	195577.0	71451.0	2.7
210	0.000	0.000	0.250	0	220509.0	220509.0	195577.0	35548.0	5.5
211	0.000	0.000	0.250	0	220509.0	220509.0	195577.0	65075.0	3.0
212	0.000	0.000	0.000	0	220509.0	220509.0	195577.0	40025.0	4.9

References

[Aho 74] Aho, A. V., Hopcroft, J. E., Ullman, J. D.
The Design and Analysis of Computer Algorithms.
Addison-Wesley, 1974.

[Aho 86] Aho, A. V., Sethi, R., Ullman, J.D.
Compilers Principles, Techniques, and Tools.
Addison-Wesley, 1986.

[Allen 82] Allen, J. R., Kennedy, K.
PFC: A Program to Convert Fortran to Parallel Form.
In *The Proceedings of the IBM Conference on Parallel Computers and Scientific Computations.* March, 1982.

[Allen 87] Allen, F.,Burke, M.,Charles P., Cytron, R. and Ferrante, J.
An Overview of the PTRAN Analyzer System for Multiprocessing.
In *Proceedings of the First Conference on Supercomputing.* 1987.
(To appear).

[Anderson 84] Anderson, R., Mayr, E.
Parallelism and Greedy Algorithms.
Technical Report STAN-CS-84-1003, Department of Computer Science, Stanford University, April, 1984.
(To appear in Advances in Computing Research).

[Archibald 86] Archibald, J., Baer, J.
Cache Coherence Protocols: Evaluation Using a Multiprocessor Simulation Model.
ACM Transactions on Computer Systems 4(4):273-298, November, 1986.

[Backus 78] Backus, J.
Can Programming Be Liberated from the von Neumann Style? A Functional Style and Its Algebra of Programs.
Communications of the ACM 21(8), August, 1978.

[Batcher 68] Batcher, K. E.
Sorting networks and their applications.
1968 Spring Joint Computer Conf., AFIPS Proc. 32:307-314, 1968.

[Brinch Hansen 75]
Brinch Hansen, P.
The programming language Concurrent Pascal.
IEEE Transactions on Software Engineering SE-1(2):199-206, June, 1975.

[Campbell 85] Campbell, M. L.
Static Allocation for a Dataflow Multiprocessor.
In *Proceedings of the 1985 International Conference on Parallel Processing*, pages 511-517. 1985.

[Cheriton 87] Cheriton, D. R. & Stumm, M.
The Multi-Satellite Star: Structuring parallel computations for a
Workstation Cluster.
Distributed Computing , 1987.
(To appear).

[Chow 83] Chow, F. C.
*A Portable Machine-Independent Global Optimizer - Design and
Measurements.*
PhD thesis, Stanford University, December, 1983.

[Cmelik 86] Cmelik, R. F., Gehani, N. H., Plotnick, M., Roome, W. D.
Concurrent C Project.
1986
(A collection of reports on Concurrent C).

[Cytron 86] Cytron, R.
Doacross: Beyond Vectorization for Multiprocessors.
In *Proceedings of the 1986 International Conference on Parallel
Processing.* August, 1986.

[Davis 82] Davis, A. L., Keller, R. M.
Data Flow Program Graphs.
IEEE Computer 15(2), February, 1982.

[Dekel 83] Dekel, E., Sahni, S.
Binary Trees and Parallel Scheduling Algorithms.
IEEE Transactions on Computers C-32(3):307-315, March, 1983.

[Ellis 85] Ellis, J. R.
Bulldog: A Compiler for VLIW Architectures.
PhD thesis, Yale University, February, 1985.
YALEU/DCS/RR-364.

[Encore 86] *Using the Encore Multimax*
Argonne National Laboratory, Mathematics and Computer Science
Division, ANL/MCS-TM-65, 1986.

[Finn 85] Finn, D. J.
Simulation of the Hughes Data Flow Multiprocessor Architecture.
In *First International Conference on Supercomputing Systems*, pages
330-340. December, 1985.

[Fisher 84] Fisher, J. A. *et al.*
Parallel Processing: A Smart Compiler and a Dumb Machine.
*Proceedings of the SIGPLAN '84 Symposium on Compiler
Construction* 19(6), June, 1984.

[Floyd 64] Floyd, R. W.
Algorithm 245: treesort 3.
Communications of the ACM 7(12):701, 1964.

[Flynn 72]   Flynn, M. J.
                Some Computer Organizations and Their Effectiveness.
                IEEE Transactions on Computers C-21(9):948-960, September,
                     1972.

[Fortune 78]   Fortune, S., Wyllie, J.
                Parallelism in random access machines.
                In *Proc. 10th ACM STOC*, pages 114-118. 1978.

[Gabriel 84]   Gabriel, R. J., McCarthy, J.
                Queue-based Multiprocessing Lisp.
                In *Proceedings of the ACM Conference on Lisp and Functional
                     Programming*. August, 1984.

[Gallivan 88]   Gallivan, K., Jalby, W., Gannon, D.
                On the Problem of Optimizing Data Transfers for Complex Memory
                     Systems.
                In *Proceedings of the 1988 ACM International Conference on
                     Supercomputing, St. Malo, France*, pages 238-253. July, 1988.

[Garey 79]   Garey, M. R., Johnson, D. S.
                *COMPUTERS AND INTRACTABILITY A Guide to the Theory of
                     NP-Completeness.*
                W. H. Freeman and Company, San Francisco, 1979.

[Gaudiot 84]   Gaudiot, J. J., Ercegovac, M. D.
                Performance Analysis of a Data-flow computer with Variable
                     Resolution Actors.
                In *Proceedings of the 4th International Conference on Distributed
                     Computer Systems*, pages 2-9. 1984.

[Gaudiot 86]   Gaudiot, J. L., Dubois, M., Lee, L. T., Tohme, N.
                The TX16: A Highly Programmable Multimicroprocessor
                     Architecture.
                IEEE Micro 6(10):18-31, October, 1986.

[Gharachorloo 88] Gharachorloo, K., Sarkar, V., Hennessy, J. L.
                A Simple and Efficient Implementation Approach for Single
                     Assignment Languages.
                In *Proceedings of the ACM Conference on Lisp and Functional
                     Programming*. July, 1988.

[Gilbert 80]   Gilbert, E. J.
                *An Investigation of the Partitioning of Algorithms Across an MIMD
                     Computing System.*
                Technical Report 176, Computer Systems Laboratory, Stanford
                     University, May, 1980.

[Goldberg 88]   Goldberg, B.
                Multiprocessor Execution of Functional Programs.
                PhD thesis, Yale University, 1988.

[Gopinath 87]   Gopinath, K., Hennessy, J.
                  Copy Elimination with Abstract Interpretation.
                  Technical Report Classic-87-17, Computer Science Department,
                        Stanford University, February, 1987.

[Graham 69]   Graham, R. L.
                  Bounds on Multiprocessing Timing Anomalies.
                  SIAM Journal on Applied Mathematics 17(2), March, 1969.

[Graham 79]   Graham, R. L., Lawler, E. L., Lenstra, J. K., Rinnooy Kan, A. H. G.
                  Optimization and Approximation in Deterministic Sequencing and
                        Scheduling: a survey.
                  In *Annals of Discrete Mathematics*, pages 287-326. North-Holland
                        Publishing Company, 1979.

[Graham 82]   Graham, S. L., Kessler, P. B., McKusick, M. K.
                  gprof: a Call Graph Execution Profiler.
                  In *Proceedings of the ACM SIGPLAN '82 Symposium on Compiler
                        Construction*, pages 120-126. June, 1982.

[Gurd 85]   Gurd, J. R., Kirkham, C. C., Watson, I.
                  The Manchester Prototype Dataflow Computer.
                  Communications of the ACM 28(1), January, 1985.

[Halstead 86]   Halstead, R. H.
                  Parallel Symbolic Computing.
                  IEEE Computer 19(8):35-43, August, 1986.

[Heart 73]   Heart, F. E. *et al.*
                  A New Minicomputer/Multiprocessor for the ARPA Network.
                  In *AFIPS Conference Proceedings*, pages 529-537. 1973.

[Hennessy 86]   Hennessy, J. L., Horowitz, M. A.
                  An Overview of the MIPS-X-MP Project.
                  Technical Report 86-300, Computer Systems Laboratory, Stanford
                        University, April, 1986.

[Hoare 78]   Hoare, C. A. R.
                  Communicating Sequential Processes.
                  Communications of the ACM 21(8), August, 1978.

[Hopcroft 79]   Hopcroft, J. E., Ullman, J. D.
                  Introduction to Automata Theory, Languages and Computation.
                  Addison-Wesley, 1979.

[Hornig 84]   Hornig, D. A.
                  *Automatic Partitioning and Scheduling on a Network of Personal
                        Computers.*
                  PhD thesis, Carnegie-Mellon University, November, 1984.

[Horowitz 76]   Horowitz, E., Sahni, S.
                  Fundamentals of Data Structures.
                  Computer Science Press, Inc., 1976.

[Hudak 85]   Hudak, P., Goldberg, B.
               Serial Combinators: "Optimal" Grains of Parallelism.
               In *Functional Programming Languages and Computer Architectures*,
                  pages 382-399. Springer-Verlag Publishing Company,
                  September, 1985.

[Hudak 86]   Hudak, P.
               A Semantic Model of Reference Counting and its Abstraction
                  (Detailed Summary).
               In *Proceedings of the 1986 ACM Conference on Lisp and Functional
                  Programming*, pages 351-363. August, 1986.

[Hunt 77]   Hunt, H. B., Szymanski, T. G., Ullman, J. D.
               Operations on Sparse Relations.
               Communications of the ACM 20(3), March, 1977.

[Hwang 84]   Hwang, K., Briggs, F. A.
               Computer Architecture and Parallel Processing.
               McGraw-Hill, New York, 1984.

[IBM 88]   *Parallel Fortran Language and Library Reference*
               International Business Machines, 1988.
               Pub. No. SC23-0431-0.

[Inmos 87]   Pountain, R., May, D.
               A tutorial introduction to Occam programming
               Inmos Corp., PO Box 16000, Colorado Springs, Colorado 80935,
                  1987.
               No. 72 OCC 046 00.

[Jackson 55]   Jackson, J. R.
               Scheduling a production line to minimize maximum tardiness.
               Technical Report Research Report 43, University of California, Los
                  Angeles, 1955.
               Management Science Research Project.

[Jones 80]   Jones, A. K., Gehringer, E. F.
               The Cm* Multiprocessor Project: A Research Review.
               Technical Report CMU-CS-80-131, Computer Science Department,
                  Carnegie-Mellon University, 1980.

[Kleinrock 75] Kleinrock, L.
               Queueing Systems, Volume 1: Theory.
               John Wiley & Sons, 1975.

[Knuth 71]   Knuth, D. E.
               An Empirical Study of FORTRAN Programs.
               Software -- Practice and Experience 1:105-133, 1971.

[Knuth 73]   Knuth, D. E.
                   *The Art of Computer Programming, Volume 3: Sorting and
                       Searching.*
                   Addison-Wesley, 1973.

[Kowalik 85]   Kowalik, J. S. (editor).
                   *Parallel MIMD Computation: HEP Supercomputer and Its
                       Applications.*
                   The MIT Press, 1985.

[Kuck 81]   Kuck, D. J. *et al.*
                   Dependence Graphs and Compiler Optimizations.
                   In *Proceedings of the 8th ACM Symposium on Principles of
                       Programming Languages*, pages 207-218. January, 1981.

[McFarling 86]   McFarling, S., Hennessy, J.
                   Reducing the Cost of Branches.
                   In *Proceedings of the International Symposium on Computer
                       Architecture Symposium.* June, 1986.

[McGraw 85]   McGraw, J. *et al.*
                   *SISAL: Streams and Iteration in a Single Assignment Language,
                       Language Reference Manual, Version 1.2.*
                   Technical Report M-146, LLNL, March, 1985.

[Mundie 86]   Mundie, D. A., Fisher, D. A.
                   Parallel Processing in Ada.
                   IEEE Computer 19(8):20-25, August, 1986.

[Padua 80]   Padua, D. A., Kuck, D. J., Lawrie, D. H.
                   High-Speed Multiprocessors and Compilation Techniques.
                   IEEE Transactions on Computers C-29(9), September, 1980.

[Pfaltz 77]   Pfaltz, J. L.
                   Computer Data Structures.
                   McGraw-Hill, Inc., 1977.

[Pfister 85]   Pfister, G. F. *et al..*
                   The IBM Research Parallel Processor Prototype (RP3): Introduction
                       and Architecture.
                   In *Proceedings of the 1985 International Conference on Parallel
                       Processing*, pages 764-771. August, 1985.

[Polychronopoulos 87]
                   Polychronopoulos, C. D., Kuck, D. J.
                   Guided Self-Scheduling: A Practical Scheduling Scheme for Parallel
                       Supercomputers.
                   IEEE Transactions on Computers C-36(12):1425-1439, December,
                       1987.

[Sarkar 86a]   Sarkar, V., Hennessy, J.
                  Partitioning Parallel Programs for Macro-Dataflow.
                  In *Proceedings of the 1986 ACM Conference on LISP and
                       Functional Programming*, pages 202-211. August, 1986.

[Sarkar 86b]   Sarkar, V., Hennessy, J.
                  Compile-time Partitioning and Scheduling of Parallel Programs.
                  In *Proceedings of the SIGPLAN '86 Symposium on Compiler
                       Construction*, pages 17-26. July, 1986.

[Sarkar 88]   Sarkar, V.
                  Synchronization Using Counting Semaphores.
                  In *Proceedings of the 1988 ACM International Conference on
                       Supercomputing, St. Malo, France*, pages 627-637. July, 1988.

[Scheifler 77]   Scheifler, R. W.
                  An Analysis of Inline Substitution for a Structured Programming
                       Language.
                  Communications of the ACM 20(9), September, 1977.

[Seitz 85]   Seitz, C. L.
                  The Cosmic Cube.
                  Communications of the ACM 28(1), January, 1985.

[Sequent 86]   *Using the Sequent Balance 8000*
                  Argonne National Laboratory, Mathematics and Computer Science
                       Division, ANL/MCS-TM-66, 1986.

[Shapiro 83]   Shapiro, E. Y.
                  A Subset of Concurrent Prolog and Its Interpreter.
                  Technical Report TR-003, The Weizmann Institute of Science, Israel,
                       February, 1983.

[Shapiro 86]   Shapiro, E.
                  Concurrent Prolog: A Progress Report.
                  IEEE Computer 19(8):44-59, August, 1986.

[Shaw 74]   Shaw, A. C.
                  The Logical Design of Operating Systems.
                  Prentice-Hall, Inc., Englewood Cliffs, N.J., 1974.

[Siegel 79]   Siegel, H. J.
                  A Model of SIMD Machines and a Comparison of Various
                       Interconnection Networks.
                  IEEE Transactions on Computers C-28(12):907-917, December,
                       1979.

[Skedzielewski 85a]
                  Skedzielewski, S., Glauert, J.
                  IF1 -- An Intermediate Form for Applicative Languages, Version 1.0.
                  Technical Report M-170, LLNL, July, 1985.

[Skedzielewski 85b]
Skedzielewski, S. K., Welcome, M. L.
Data flow graph optimization in IF1.
Functional Programming Languages and Computer Architecture
(Jean-Pierre Jouannaud, ed.).
Springer-Verlag Publishing Company, 1985, pages 17-34.

[Su 85]
Su, W., Faucette, R., Seitz, C.
C Programmer's Guide to the Cosmic Cube.
Technical Report 5203:TR:85, Computer Science Department,
California Institute of Technology, September, 1985.

[Tarjan 72]
Tarjan, R. E.
Depth first search and linear graph algorithms.
SIAM Journal on Compputing 1(2):146-160, 1972.

[Tjaden 70]
Tjaden, G. S., Flynn, M. J.
Detection and parallel execution of independent instructions.
IEEE Transactions on Computers C-19(10):889-895, October, 1970.

[Wall 86]
Wall, D. W.
Global Register Allocation at Link Time.
In *Proceedings of the SIGPLAN '86 Symposium on Compiler*
Construction, pages 264-275. July, 1986.

[Warshall 62]
Warshall, S.
A theorem on Boolean matrices.
Journal of the ACM 9(1), 1962.

[Widdoes 79]
Widdoes, L. C., Correll, S.
The S-1 project: Developing high-performance digital computers.
Energy and Technology Review , September, 1979.

[Woodfill 79]
Woodfill, J. *et al.*
INGRES Version 6.2 Reference Manual
1979.